Earthworms for Solid Waste Management

Satyendra M. Singh
Reader
Department of Animal Science
M.J.P. Rohilkhand University
BAREILLY - 243 006, Uttar Pradesh, India

IBDC
International Book Distributing Co.
(Publishing Division)

Published by

INTERNATIONAL BOOK DISTRIBUTING CO.
(Publishing Division)
Khushnuma Complex Basement
7, Meerabai Marg (Behind Jawahar Bhawan)
Lucknow 226 001 U.P. (INDIA)
Tel. : 91-522-2209542, 2209543, 2209544, 2209545
Fax : 0522-4045308
E-Mail : ibdco@airtelbroadband.in

First Edition 2007

ISBN 81-8189-202-X

Composed & Designed at :
Panacea Computers
3rd Floor, Agrawal Sabha Bhawan
Subhash Mohal, Sadar Cantt. Lucknow-226 002
Phone : 0522-2483312, 9335927082, 9452295008
E-mail : prasgupt@rediffmail.com

Printed at:
Salasar Imaging Systems
C-7/5, Lawrence Road, Industrial Area
Delhi - 110 035
Tel. : 011-27185653, 9810064311

Dr. Bhim Rao Ambedkar University
(Formerly Agra University)
Agra - 282 004
Tel.: Off. : 0562-2520051, 2852139
Tele Fax : 0562-2858670

Prof. Bhoomitra Dev
Former Vice-Chancellor

Foreword

Earthworms were called "the intestines of the earth" by Aristotle. Darwin said that "Long before man existed, the land was regularly ploughed and still continues to be thus ploughed by earthworms". Since the days of Aristotle and Darwin, considerable work has been done on the structure and physiology of a large number of species of earthworms. Consequently, earthworms are now not considered as mere burrowers, tillers and ploughers of soil. Many of the species of earthworms not only act as aerators while they burrow into soil, feed and move on, but also crush, grind, pulverize and recycle the soil containing vegetative debris; mix it with their intestinal and other secretions; stabilize the burrow-walls, making the soil more pervious to rains and plant-fibres; and augment water-holding capacity of soil, but also work as chemical degraders and biological stimulators for bacterial and fungal growth. Earth and earthworms have thus become lively partners in human agrarian revolutions. Lately, scientists have carefully interviewed a large number of species of earthworms; and recruited some of the most suitable ones for accelerating decomposition of different varieties of solid waste. In essence, Aristotle's so called intestines of earth have now acquired the role of co-managers and biodegradable solid waste; and foundations have been laid for a new scientific enquiry of vermicomposting. It is, therefore, need of the times to collect some of the most useful contributions in this area in the form of a book to accelerate relevant knowledge - flew fro all the concerned stake-holders. It is extremely heartening to note that Dr. Satyendra M. Singh, Reader in the Department of Animal Science at M.J.P. Rohilkhand University, Bareilly has taken the onerous responsibility of the publication of such a book on his able shoulders. I must sincerely congratulate him for such excellent academic endeavour. I am confident that the Book will further inspire the researchers on earthworms; eliminate any possibility of ecological or biochemical damage done by any of the species, especially the exotic ones; and ensure the ablest recruitment of worms for easy, quick, economic, appropriate, efficient and the best solid waste management of kitchen, municipal, agricultural, industrial and hospital wastes, which may, in addition, augment soil fertility and plant productivity.

Bhoomitra Dev

Preface

"One Earth and one Humanity" should be our motto as this planet is the only place in the Universe known to sustain life. Human activities are progressively reducing the planet's life-supporting capacities by adding million tons of 'ORGANIC WASTES' everyday into the environment. Uncontrolled dumping and improper handling of such wastes pose a great risk to human health and subsequent deterioration in the natural climatic conditions.

Prevention of environmental degradation has become a matter of serious concern. This is one of the many areas in which prevention is better, and much less costlier than the cure. In recent years, public attention has focused increasingly on environmental deterioration and its effect on man and other creatures. As such many ideas have been floated for the management of waste diposal, but a safer management for disposal of these organic wastes is a burning problem of modern society and great challenge to the scientific community. Amongst all the management methods tried in the world, vermicomposting has proved to be the best, cheapest and the most effective method for recycling of these wastes into organic manure.

All fourteen chapters of the book have been written by subject experts of the country. The first five chapters disclose the various devices of the technology and role of specific species of earthworms in solid waste management. The sixth to eleventh chapters with vermicomposting of different types of organic wastes. The last three chapters specifically deal with the impact of vermicompost on soil fertility and plant productivity.

I hope this book will be a remarkable asset for suggesting easy devices of technology for proper management of various types of solid organic wastes to the agrarians, agricultural scientists, earthworm ecologists, non-government organizations and policy-makers for upholding the law of nature and bringing about a clean, healthy environment.

I would, first of all like to thank all those who have contributed articles to make this book possible and most of all, to the publisher making this mission an esteemed success.

14 Jan, 2007 **Satyendra M. Singh**
Makarsankranti

Contents

Chapter 1

Vermitechnology : A Biological Device for Solid Waste Management

Radha D. Kale

Department of Entomology, University of Agricultural Sciences, G.K.V.K. Campus, Bangalore-560 065

The term 'waste' is a misnomer for the material that is mismanaged and underutilized. Its importance is lost for not having the proper methodology for recycling. Organic decomposable material is one of the resources derived from agriculture, animal husbandry and agro-industries. The quantum of waste generated from these sources will contribute to about 60 to 70% of the total rejects produced from various other activities. Unscientific way of disposal of these materials leads to air and water pollution. These wastes being from plant and animal resources have the necessary macro and micronutrients for plants growth and are the only source of organic carbon needed for microbial activity in soil. Composting of such material in a methodical manner will turn the organic waste into Bio-resources. There is need to make use of environmental resources for development instead of creating pollution by their mismanagement (Prapurna and Shashikanth, 2002). Macfadyen (1953) had referred to organism including earthworms as "decomposer industry" that can be considered for treating large quantities of decomposable waste. These organisms can be made to work on farmyard wastes and organic rich industrial wastes. (Lee, 1985).

Vermiculture

Vermiculture refers to the biomass production of earthworms in semi-natural conditions, providing suitable substrate and feed for them to remain active throughout the year. Culturing of earthworms started as entrepreneurship in the latter half of the 20th century to supply them to fishing enthusiasts. Darwin (1881) emphasized on the role of earthworms in fragmenting of organic debris and accelerating its decomposition but it could not catch the attention of scientists to extend the research in this direction. It was Hartenstein (1978); Appelhof (1981) associated vermiculture to disposal of large quantities of waste. Prince *et al.* (1981) had used vermiculturing for treating municipal solid waste and waste-water sludges.

Most commonly used earthworm for culturing is *Eisenia fetida* that has wide range of temperature tolerance, very high reproductive potential and less sensitive to density pressure (Watanabe and Tsukamoto, 1976; Tsukamoto and Watanabe, 1977; Hartenstein *et al,* 1979; Reinecke and Kriel, 1981). *Eudrilus eugeniae,* which is commonly called 'African night crawler' is also an efficient earthworm to maintain as culture. When compared to *Eisenia fetida,* this earthworm is more sensitive to physical and biotic stresses (Neuhauser *et al,* 1979). *Eudrilus eugeniae* is found to be a very efficient species for culture maintenance in India (Kale, 1994). Kale *et al.* (1982) have shown the feasibility of using *Perionyx excavatus* as culture using animal wastes. In recent times, *Eudrilus eugeniae, Eisenia fetida, Perionyx excavatus* and *P. sansibaricus* have been successfully used as mixed cultures for waste management in India. (Kale, 1994).

In contrast to the situation of culturing of earthworms, which started as entrepreneurship, before investigations in scientific laboratories in U.S.A. and Canada, in India earthworms were maintained as culture for different research activities. Khambata and Bhat (1974) had maintained the earthworm culture to assess the microbial population in the intestine of earthworms and their castings. Bhat (1974) has shown the influence of diet in the culture media of earthworms on microfloral population. He had stressed on the importance of cow dung in enhancing their feeding and also on colonization of N-fixers. Kale *et al* (1982), for the first time in Asia, reported the possibility of maintaining the culture of earthworm, *Perionyx excavatus* on animal dung.

In recent times, for a decade, farmers, agro-based industries and urban households are culturing earthworms as the biological material for organic waste management in India (Kale, 2003). Though many research laboratories are involved in carrying out research on this aspect, still there exists a lacuna in proper promotion of techniques for culturing of earthworms (Kale, 2003).

Recommendation of earthworm species for vermiculture

Earthworms are ecologically divided into three groups - epigeic, endogeic and anecic-based on their preference for soil horizons and food habits as described by Bouche (1977). Other tropical earthworms may come closer to this division in their distribution with slight variations (Lee, 1985). This classification is of importance as it provides information of their food habits, feeding and growth rate of population and life cycles.

There are certain controversies about the recommendation of earthworms for vermiculture in India. There are attempts to promote only indigenous earthworms for vermiculture. Species like *Eisenia fetida* and *Eudrilus eugeniae* being exotic species; the groups which want to promote indigenous earthworms discourage them. Persons who oppose the use of exotic species in India for vermicomposting lack the knowledge of ecology of earthworms and are unaware of the number of exotic species that are distributed in soils of the country (Stephensen, 1923). Though there are nearly 350 species of earthworms distributed in the country and nearly 3000 species at the global level, *Eisenia fetida* is the universally accepted species for the purpose.

Earthworms that can survive in captivity, under semi-natural conditions are tolerant to wide ranges of substrates and to other physical parameters like pH, temperature, moisture and physical disturbances can only be maintained as cultures. They should show good population growth for culture propagation. These characters are found in very few species of earthworms and hence, successful culturing is possible only with these earthworms irrespective of the place of their origin. A detailed study of biology of fifteen out of sixty species of earthworms collected from different places in Karnataka has shown the inability of majority of species to propagate in captivity (Kale, 1991).

In majority of the temperate regions, though large number of species are organic matter or litter feeders, *Eisenia fetida* for its ability to adapt to different organic decomposable wastes, short life cycle, high fecundity and tolerance to density pressure is the preferred earthworm for culturing (Edwards, 1995; Hartenstein and Bisesi, 1989; Hand and Hayes, 1983; Hartenstein *et al,* (1989). Epigeic earthworms are absent in agricultural lands subjected to disturbances. They are found in patches in places where the organic matter is stored above the ground throughout the year. They cannot survive below 5 pH to above 8 pH and above 3 millisiemens of electrolytic conductivity

(Hartenstein *et al,* 1989). It is very essential to identify the suitable earthworm and to create appropriate conditions for its survival in the organic material to be used as substrate.

Scientists, farmers, industrialists or entrepreneurs have to give a thought when it comes to the use of earthworm culture for treatment for different organic substances. Still there is scope for scientists to search for earthworms settling for long in compost heaps to find out their taxonomic position and make detail study of their biology in captivity. This may provide an opportunity to get more number of species of earthworms to use them for management of diversified bio-resources derived from agricultural and agro industrial sectors. In a country like India, where the geographical conditions show wide variations, it is better to identify appropriate species of earthworms to develop under varied situations.

Bird's eye-view on vermicomposting

Just as it is essential to use appropriate species of earthworms for culturing, it is essential to follow certain procedures for treatment of the material to be used as substrate and feed for earthworms. It is essential in the tropical countries to maintain the optimum temperature in the organic matter to be used for vermicomposting between 25° and 30°C and moisture level ranging from 40-60%. Any kind of agricultural residue along with cow-dung forms the major resource component for vermicomposting. In India, vermiculture is practised mainly for recycling of organic wastes. The awareness created among the farming community, regarding the imbalance created in the nutrient status of soil, has led them to adopt technologies to augment the breakdown of organic residues and return them to soil (Kale, 1994). In this process different kinds of organic residues like hedge trimmings, weeds, litter, hey, husk and animal excreta that are available in the farms are used for vermiculture.

The collected residues form activities along with cow dung is normally piled up on the ground surface and watered to maintain 40-60% moisture. This mix is turned two to three times in two weeks to provide aeration and for exposing the entire material to thermophillic phase. By the end of three to four weeks, material is ready for use as substrate and feed for epigeic earthworms.

Bright sunshine and unpredictable rains are the common features in India. During dry season, the lack of regular food in the vicinity forces rodents and other predatory mammals to find alternative and easily reachable food sources. It is advisable to practise vermicomposting in sheltered, protected conditions to avoid these problems. The tanks could be built depending on the availability of construction materials cement blocks, bricks, granite slabs or bamboo stems. The length of the tanks can vary based on the availability of raw materials in the farm. The breadth and height should be preferably 1.2 and 0.9 meters. A temporary thatched roof protects the tanks from inundation during heavy rains.

Earthworms that are identified or culturing are released on the surface layer. This enables them to feed on the organic material from surface to the base of the tank. As they start feeding they release the castings on the surface. It will be easy to collect the castings periodically without disturbing earthworms. This method of making earthworms to work from surface to downwards is more suitable in tropical conditions, where there may be chance for unexpected rise in temperature in the organic matter.

Vermicompost collected periodically will have cocoons and small earthworms. When small cow-dung balls of about 10 cm diameter are buried in the collected vermicompost at random and left for a period of ten to fifteen days, earthworms that hatch out of cocoons get attracted to these cow-dung balls. Thus, without much labour, earthworms can be separated from vermicompost.

Materials for vermicomposting

Vermicomposting is the means to bring down the level of organic pollution created by improper disposal of biodegradable materials from agricultural activity and by-products of agro-based industries. Agricultural residues require minimum of two to three weeks for earthworms to accept them as substrate and feed. Among them, sericultural waste requires minimum forty days for earthworms to accept this material as feed. This is because of chemicals used in the silkworm rearing beds and also due to uric acid and ammonia levels in excreta of silkworms. On increasing the time of primary decomposition, material can be used for vermicomposting. The recovered vermicompost will have high levels of plant organic matter (Gunathilagaraj *et al,* 1996). In this organic matter, heat generation will be high and persists for longer time. If this is mixed with other biomass and cow dung, the material becomes palatable for earthworms in forty days.

Agro industries like paper mills and breweries release effluents that will have high levels of nutrients required for plants. These effluents, when mixed with solid matter like coir pith and sawdust, can become the source of feed for earthworms to get vermicompost as final product. The coffee pulp, rejects from food processing units, press mud from sugar industries have been tried at different place to convert them into vermicompost. The same materials have become a matter of concern as air, water and soil pollutants when released into the environment, without proper treatment. The simple technology of using suitable earthworms and mixing these materials with other organic matter made them acceptable for earthworms to bring down the level of environmental pollution with minimum investment. Earthworms are biological tools in the industrial era and they are the work force to work continuously without any break or without asking for returns. What is essential to make them work successfully is to prepare heterogeneous mixture of organic materials in a way that is not deleterious to their survival. The factors like pH, temperature, moisture, EC, texture of the material and finally may be organic aromatic compounds determining their survival, growth and population increase in the given medium. When proper management of agricultural and agro-industrial residues of organic decomposable nature are practised, it leads to creating link between urban and rural areas to reach at a point of developmental progress. Vermicomposting accelerates the stabilization of composting process and thus reduction in period of composting reflects on the efficiency of the process (Frederickson, *et al*, 1997).

In city and town municipality areas more than 60% of waste generated is of organic decomposable matter. The lack of knowledge and commitment to segregate materials to be composted has led to loss of rich source of plant nutrients to landfill sites. There are evidences of successful attempts in some townships to segregate the garbage and use the decomposable material for vermicomposting. The Karnataka Compost Development Corporation is one of the examples for establishing vermicomposting unit in the country for handling of urban solid waste. A part of the city garbage is converted into vermicompost (150 to 200 tons/day) and the same amount is converted into enriched compost. The unit has good list of clients who are convinced with the quality of the compost. There are many units at the household levels who are practising vermicomposting of the organic residues produced at the source. This sort of interest that is gradually increasing has led to develop indigenous bins and other structures to promote vermicomposting for different levels of operations.

The question of non-availability of resources to produce good manure and problem of management of some of the by-products of agro-industries can be solved to greater extent by standardizing the methods for vermicompositing of these materials. The epigeic earthworms now identified for this purpose can convert many such materials into good quality soil additives (Arellano *et al*, 1994; Dominguez and Edwards, 1997, Gracia *et al*, 1994).

Importance of vermicompost production for sustainable agriculture

Bennett and Robinson (1967) have opined that chemical agriculture is not economically viable in tropical countries. According to them, for two-fold increase in yield, it requires ten fold increase in use of fertilizers, pesticides and other machinery. The water stress and high temperature make it expensive to maintain the crops in tropical zones (Best, 1962). The organic carbon content is very low in tropical soils. This is very essential for the activity of soil organisms. The soil microflora and fauna contribute to soil physical properties like aggregate stability, porosity, bulk density and water-holding capacity. They contribute to chemical processes like solubilization and mobilization of nutrients. Other meso and macro fauna stimulate the microbial activity by increasing the surface area for establishment of microorganisms or organic matter undergoing decomposition through their feeding and defecation. For these complex chemical processes to be operated in soil through complex web of decomposer organisms, it is essential to have sufficient humus component in soil. The organic amendment is essential to enhance the biological processes in soil. The organic manure applied to agricultural lands primarily contributes to the health of soil and secondarily acts as nutrient provider to crops.

Vermicompost can be prepared without much investment and effort for a small land holding to vast stretches of farmlands by following simple protocol of using appropriate species of earthworms, proper decomposition of organic matter collected from fields and protecting earthworms from predators. It is also true that research has to progress to understand the ability to earthworms to adapt to different organic materials under varied environmental conditions. This enables to use polyculture of earthworms for bioresource management rather than depending only on *Eisenia fetida*. It is true that extensive extension programmes like organizing meetings by government and non-government organizations, popular articles, exhibitions and demonstrations at fields has created awareness among farmers to adopt vermicompost production technology. The drawback lies in improper promotion and no set regulations to ascertain the quality of vermicompost produced either by farmers or commercial agencies. It is essential to identify the parameters to determine the maturity of vermicompost that will assure the safety measures for its use as good soil amendment. If this point is overlooked, then some of the products may even turn deleterious to soil and crops. Vermicompost produced in a proper manner must have certain physico-chemical, biological and biochemical characters and the same is provided below for reference (Radha Krishna, 2005, personal communication)

Physico-chemical characters of matured vermicompost

Parameters	Expected values
pH	6.8-7.5
Organic Carbon	25.4-27.5%
Nitrogen	1.2-1.6%
C/N ratio	15-18
NH_4-N	105-110 (mg/kg)
Phosphorus (Available)	0.3-0.5%
Potassium (Available)	0.6-0.7%
Calcium	4.2-6.7%
Magnesium	0.2-0.3.%
Sulphur	0.4-0.5%

Measured biochemical activities

Cellulase activity (μ g glucose g-1h-1)	3.0-3.4
Amylase activity (μ g glucose g-1 h-1)	57.6-113.1
Protease activity (mg tyrosine g-1 h-1)	33.8-140.0

Measured microbial biodiversity

Cellulose decomposers (CFU x 10^3)	1.3-1.7
Starch degraders (CFU x 10^3)	1.4-3.8
Protein degraders (CFU X 10^4)	3.6-3.7
N_2 fixers (CFU X 10^5)	15.5-29.0
P-solubilizers (CFU x 10^5)	15.6-25.0

How better is vermicompost over other organic manures?

Farmers to greater extent in the country use farmyard manure. The package of practices, released for various crops from agricultural universiteis of the country provide the recommendations for its application to different crops. Those who are in the practice of preparing and using this measure do not follow any strict regimes to restore good nutrient status in this manure. There will not be any specification for the pit size, care will not be taken to maintain the optimum moisture level needed for microbial activity and finally the conditions may turn anaerobic in the pits. Once the cow dung, soil and organic matter are added into pits at the end of the crop sesason, manure is collected only by next cropping season. This leads to loss of nutrients from the compost (FYM) and the decomposing process is not completed. This in course of time has led the farmers to consider FYM as not a required nutrient source for high-yielding varieties that depend on heavy energy input.

Vermicompost is prepared with utmost care using all available organic residues along with cowdung. Requirement of cow dung is also negligible and if other residues are of soft and easily degradable form, cowdung can be avoided. This compost preparation is in the reach of all farmers. The time required for vermicompost preparation is minimal. Once earthworms start working on decomposed material, vermicompost collection commences as and when their castings collect on the suface. It is a continuous process of compost production. Depending on earthworm population (400 to 500g / sq. m), vermicompost recovery in 1 m x 1 m x 0.3 m bin will be around 50 Kg in six to eight weeks.

Vermicompost will have more of available nutrients than regular FYM or compost. Secretions of earthworms that are in the vermicompost serve as plant growth stimulatory factors (Galli *et al*, 1990; Tomoti *et al*, 1990; Graff and Makeschin, 1980). In presence of vermicompost, plants show improved performance in uptake of added inorganic nutrients (Shi-Wei and Fu-Zhen, 1991). Spraying of extracted body fluid of earthworms (vermiwash) to tissue cultured *Anthurium andreanum* Lind, at regular intervals showed improved plant growth and flower bloom compared to spraying of urea (Karuna *et al*, 1990). Tomato and cucumber seedlings grown in the media containing humic acids extracted from vermicompost responded well to different levels of these substances, which ranged between 0 to 4000 mg. Humate/ Kg of soil free media (Atiye *et al*, 2002). Kulkarni *et al* (1996) in their studies have shown decrease in input of chemical fertilizers to 50% on application of vermicompost to mulberry crop. It is clear from these findings that vermicompost produced aerobically from varieties of organic residues has multifaceted advantages in improving the responses of different crops. Vermicompost can provide answer to the question of whether organic manure application can fulfil the requirements of high-yielding, sensitive crops that are promoted in recent years.

Other important features of vermiculture

Vermicompost extract as compost tea is gaining importance in USA and Canada. Microorganisms, present in vermicompost are considered to inactivate and suppress the growth of pathogens. The extract of vermicompost is used as foliar spray to crops. The extracted body fluid of earthworm that is called 'vermiwash' (Kale, 1997) has shown the formation of inhibitory zones for some plant pathogens in Petri plates at the point of applications of vermiwash (Das, 2005, personal communication). Vermiwash has also been tested as the component of nutrient media in tissue culture has resulted in good response of callus growth (Das, 2005, personal communication). Some more trials in this regard may help to develop organically developed tissue culture plants. Atlavinyte and Daciulyte (1969) has associated the improved germination, growth and yield of barley crop in pot cultures to the higher level of vitamin B_{12} in the medium due to activity of introduced earthworms. Graff and Makeschin (1980) has reported the stimulatory effect of earthworms exudates in enhancing growth and yield of crops. Ashwini (2004) has shown the stimulatory effect of vermicompost extract and vermiwash on rot induction in cuttings of two varieties of carnations (*Dianthus caryophyllus* L.).

Earthworm activity is always associated with the microflora in the organic material used for vermicompostingand in the final product 'vermicompost'. It is the interrelationship and interaction of primary and secondary decomposers in the decomposer chain. Modifications in the microfloral compostion will result in using certain materials as supplements in the organic matter at the time of decomposition. Neem cake (2%) when added to decomposing organic matter, vermicompost obtained had higher level of N-fixer population than in vermicompost from the same material without the addition of neem cake (Kale *et al*, 1986). Similary, for agricultural residues having 10% cowdung, incorporation of 12.5% rock phosphate and allowing the mateial to decompose for 45 to 60 days before introducing earthworms, resulted in increase of phosphate solubilising microorganisms by 90 days. When this vermicompost was applied to French bean at 7.5 to 10 tons/ha, the yield recovery was equivalent to the control receiving recommended dose of chemicals (Trimurthy, 2002).

Vermiculture has application in animal feed industry. Many scientists have reported high levels of nutrients in dried and powdered earthworms. (Schulz and Graff, 1997; Reinecke, 1990; Alberts *et al,* 1988; Edwards and Niederer, 1988). Earthworm meal has been tested as substitute for animal protein in feeds of poultry, fish and other animals (Edwards and Niederer, 1988; Nandeesh *et al,* 1987). Preliminary studies were carried out for possibilities of using vermiwash as supplement in the feed of mulberry silkworms. The results revealed the decline in incidence of diseases in silkworms, improved feeding efficiency and cocoon yield (Vijayakumar, 2005; personal communication). Vermiculture thus has good future in animal feed industry.

Vermitechnology when practised with proper perspective can become the tool for bringing down the levels of various organic pollutants entering water, soil and to some extent air. It is the field that remains open for research to be carried out at an interdisciplinary level. There are many questions that arise out of available research data that provide scope for further investigations in this field of study.

References

Alberts, J. N; Reinecke, A.J. and Venter J.M. 1988. The metabolizable energy value of earthworm meal (*Eisenia fetida,* Oligochaeta) as potential protein source for animal feeds. *S.A. Tydskrif vir Natuurwetenskap en tegonologie.* 7: 1-10

Arellano, R.P.; Barois, I and Arand, E. 1994. Earthworm carrying capacity for coffee pulp using *Eisenia andrei* and *Perionyx excavatus.* Paper presented at ISSE 5 held at Columbus, Ohio, USA.

Ashwini, S. 2004. Induction of rooting in terminal cuttings of Carnation (*Dianthus caryophyllus* L) by biological agents. Thesis submitted to UAS, Bangalore, India as partial fulfilment for the award of M.Sc. degree.

Atiye, R. M; Lee, S. Edwards, C. A; Aranquon, N. Q. and Metzger, J. D. 2002. The influence of humic acids derived from earthworm processed organic wastes on plant growth. *Bioresource Technology.* 84: 7-14

Atlavinyte, O. and Daciulite, O. 1969. The effects of earthworms on the accumulation of vitamin B_{12} in soil. *Pedobiologia* . 9: 165-170.

Atlavinyte, O. and Vanagas, J. 1982. The effect of earthworms on the quality of barley and rye grain, *Pedobiologia*, 23 : 256-262.

Bennett, I. L. and Robinson, H. L. 1967. The world food problem. A report of the President's Science Advisory Committee panel on the world food supply. Superintendent of Documents, Washington D.C. 3 vols.

Best, R. 1962. Production factors in the tropics. In : Fundamentals of dry matter production and distribution. *Netherland. J. Agri. Sci.* 10 (no. 5, Spl. Issue): 347-353.

Bhat, J. V. 1974. Suitability of Experimentation diets for earthworm culture. *Curr. Sci. 43*: 266-268.

Chan, P. L. S. and Griffiths, D. A. 1990. The vermicomposting of pretreated pig manure. *Biol. Wastes:* 24 : 57-69

Chaudhuri, P.S. Pal; T.K.; Bhattacharjee, G. and Dey, S.K. 2003. Rubber leaf litters (*Hevea brasiliensis*, var RRIM 600) as vermiculture substrate for epigeic earthworms, *Perionyx excavatus, Eudrilus eugeniae* and *Eisenia fetida. Pedobiologia.* 47: 796-800.

Dominguez, J. and Edwards, C. A. 1977. Effects of stocking rate and moisture content on the growth and maturation of *Eisenia fetida* (Oligochaeta) in pig manure, *Soil Biol. Bichem.* 29: 743-746.

Edwards, C.A. 1995. Commercial and environmental potential of vermicomposting: A historical overview. *Biocycle. June* 62-63.

Edwards, C.A. and Niederer, A. 1988. The production and processing of earthworm protein. In: Earthworms in waste and environmental management (eds. C.A. Edwards and E.F. Neuhauser). Publ. SPB Academic Publishing. The Hague. The Netherlands p. 169-179.

Elvira, C; Sampedro, L; Dominguez, J; Mato, S and Edwards, C.A. 1997. Vermicomposting of waste water sludge from paper pulp industry with nitrogen rich materials. *Soil Biol. Biochem* 759-762.

Frederickson, J; Butt. K. R; Morris, R.M; Daniel, C. and Edwards, C.A. 1997. Combining vermiculture with traditional green waste composting systems. *Soil Biol. Biochem.* 29: 725-730.

Galli, E; Tomati, V; Grappelli, A. and de Lena, G. 1990. Effect of earthworm cast on protein synthesis in *Agaricus bisporus.* Biol. and Fert. Soil 9: 1-2.

Graff, O. and Makeschin, F. 1980. Beeinflussung des Ertrags von Regenwurmern dreier verschiedener Arten *Pedobiologia.* 20: 176-180.

Gunadi, B; Edwards, C. A. and Arancon, N. Q. 2002. Changes in trophic structure of soil arthropods after the application of vermicomposts. *European J. Soil Biol.* 38: 161-165.

Gunathilagaraj, K. and Ravignanam, T. 1996. Vermicomposting of sericultural wastes. *Madras Agri. J.* 83: 455-457.

Hartenstein, R. 1981. Use of *Eisenia fetida* in organic recycling based on laboratory experiments. In: workshop on the role of earthworms in the stabilization of organic residues.

M. Appelhof-Compiler. Vol. I. Proc. Beech Leaf Press. Kalamazoo, USA p. 155-165.

Hartenstein, R; Neuhauser, E. F. and Kaplan, D.L. 1979. Reproductive potential of the earthworm *Eisenia fetida, Oecologia (Berl.)* 43 : 329-340.

Kale, R.D. 1991. Vermiculture: scope for new Biotechnology. In: Earthworms, resources and vermiculture. (ed. Director, ZSI, Calcutta, India). p. 105-108.

Kale, R.D. 1994. Promotion of vermicomposting for production of organic fertilizer. Report of the adhoc scheme sponsored by ICAR, New Delhi, Sanctioin no. ICAR No. F. No. 13 (3) 91-SW & DF dt. 26.3.1991.

Kale, R.D. 2002. Vermicomposting technology in India: An answer to shortages in nutrient supplies. In: Earthworms in the processing and utilization of organic wastes. (ed. C.A. Edwards). Publ. J.G. Press, PA. Chapter 22.

Kale, R. D; and Bano, K. 1994. Laboratory studies on age specific fecundity and mortality of earthworm *Eudrilus eugeniae. Mitteilungen aus dem Hamber gischen museum and Institut. Ferganzurgsband.* 89: 139-148.

Kale, R.D; Bano, K. and Krishnamoorthy, R. V. 1982. Potential of *Perionyx excavatus* for utilization of organic wastes. *Pedobiologia.* 23: 419-425.

Kale, R. D.; Vinayaka, K; Bagyaraj, D. J. 1986. Suitability of neem cake as an additive in earthworm feed and its influence on the establishment of microflora. *J. Soil Biol. Ecol.* 6: 98-103.

Karuna, K; Patil, C. R.; Narayanaswamy, P. and Kale, R.D. 1999. Stimulatory effect of earthworm body fluid (vermiwash) on Crinkle Red variety of *Anthurium andreanum* Lind. *Crop. Res.* 17: 253-257.

Kulkarni, B.S; Nalwadi, U.G. and Giraddi, R.S. 1996. Effect of vermicompost and vermiculture on growth and yield of China Aster (*Callistephus chinensis*) CV. Ostrich plume mixed. *South Ind. Hort.* 44 : 33-35.

Lee, K. E. 1985. Earthworms: Their ecology and relationship with soils and land use. Publ. Hartcourt Brace Jovanorich, Academic Press, Sydney, p. 411.

Macfayen, A. 1963. The contribution of the fauna to total soil metabolism. In: Soil organisms. (eds. J. Doekson and J. Van der Drift). North Holland Publ. Company . Amsterdam. p. 3-17.

Mahale, V. G; Ashok, T.H. and Kale, R. D. 2002. Vermicompost as rooting medium for Carnation (*Dianthus caryophyllus* L). *J. Plant Biol.* 29: 175-178.

Manna, M. C; Singh, M; Kundu, S; Tripathi, A. K. and Takkar, P. N. 1997. Growth and reproduction of the vermicomposting earthworm *Perionyx excavatus* as influenced by food materials. *Biol. Fer. Soils.* 24: 129-132.

Nandeesh, M. C; Srikant, G. K; Basavaraja, N; Keshavanath, P; Verghese, T.J; Bano, K. and Kale, R. D. 1987. Influence of earthworm meal on growth and flesh quality of common carp. *Biological Wastes.* 26: 188-198.

Neuhauser, F; Kaplan. D.L. and Hartenstein, R. 1979. Life history of the earthworm *Eudrilus eugeniae, Rev. Ecol. Biol. Sol.* 16: 525-534.

Nethra, N. N; Jayaprasaed, K. and Kale, R.D. 1999. China Aster (*Callistephus chinesis* L Ness) cultivation using vermicompost as organic amendment. *Crop. Res.* 17: 209-215.

Orazco, F. H; Cegarra, J; Trujillo, L. M. and Roig, A. 1996. Vermicomposting of coffee pulp using the earthworm *Eisenia fedida*: effects on C and N content and the availability of nutrients. *Biol Fert. Soils.* 22: 162-164.

Prapirna, N. and Shashikanth, K. 2002. Pollution level in Hussain Sagar lake of Hyderabad. A case study. *J. Poll. Res.* 21: 187-190.

Prince, A.R; Donovan, J.F. and Bates, J. E. 1981. Vermicomposting of municipal soild wastes and municipal waste water sludges. In: Workshop on the role of earthworm in the stabilization of organic residues. M. Appelhof-Compiler. Vol I. *Proc. Beech Leaf Press*, Kalamazoo, USA. p. 207-219.

Reinecke, A. J. and Kriel, J. R. 1981. Influence of temperature on the reproduction of the earthworm *Eisenia fetida* (Oligochaeta). *S. Afr. J. Zool.* 16: 96-100

Schulz, E and Graff. O. 1977. Zur Bewertung von Regenwurmmehl aus *Eisenia fetida* (Savigny, 1926) *Landbauforshung volkenrode*. 27: 216-218.

Stephensen, J. 1923. The Fauna of British India. Oligochaeta. Publ. Taylor and Francis, London, p. 508.

Tsukumoto, J. and Watanabe, H. 1977. Influence of temperature on hatching and growth of *Eisenia fetida* (Oligochaeta, Lumbricidae), *Pedobiologia.* 17: 338-342.

Watanabe, H. and Tsukamoto, J. 1976. Seasonal change in size and stage structure of Lumbricid *Eisenia foetida* population in a field compost and its practical application as the decomposer of organic waste matter. *Rev. Ecol. Biol. Sol.* 13: 141-146.

Zhao-Shi-wei and Huang Fu-Zhen. 1991. The nitrogen uptake efficiency from N^{15} labelled chemical fertilizer in the presence of earthworm manure (cast). In: Advances in Management and Conservation of Soil Fauna. (eds. G.K. Veeresh, D. Rajagopal and C.A. Viraktamath). Oxford & IBH Publ. Co. Pvt. Ltd. p. 539-542.

Chapter **2**

Vermiculture : A Technology to Manage Solid Wastes

R.K. Palta* and R.K. Bhatnagar**

** Division of Entomology, Indian Agricultural Research Institute, New Delhi. 110 012. ** 9/B Chibber Road, Arya Nagar, Dehradun-248 001.*

Waste production started from the day man came into existence on this planet. Waste is inevitable byproduct of human activities. It is defined as that material which is usually thrown away after utilization and do not have any other important use. It is an outcome of domestic, industrial, medical, agricultural and commercial activities. The terms like "trash" "refuse", 'garbage' are used to describe various types of waste. Waste production became a problem only when the production rate of waste increased more than the absorption or treatment capacity of the environment. Solid wastes can be grouped into different categories depending upon the source from which they are generated.

a. Municipal Solid Waste (WSW): it includes household waste, sanitation residue, waste from streets, construction and demolition debris

b. Industrial waste

c. Hospital waste

This subject of solid waste management includes various practices that tend to reduce the environmental, health and aesthetic consequences of solid wastes. In 1947, India generated an estimated 6 million tons of solid waste, which rose to 48 million tons by 1997 and by the year 2030 it will grow to 125 million tons (Gupta, 2001). During the last few years, the life style of people has been changing. People are now using more of disposable items like cans, plastic bottles, aluminum foils, plastics, polythene bags and many other non-biodegradable items whose disposal create lot of problems. The problem of solid waste management is also related to urban growth. More than 26 per cent of people of India live in urban cities and produce a variety of waste whose management is very complicated.

Amount of waste generated also depends on the average income. As economic condition improves, the amount of waste increases in weight and volume and larger share of the waste consist of luxury wastes such as plastics, cardboard, paper and organic matter. The same is true for developing and developed countries. Low-income countries have low percent of urban population with low spending capacity, so have low waste generation rate between 0.4 to 0.9 kg/capita/day. As GNP increases towards middle income, waste generation also increases from 0.5 to 1.1 kg/capita/day. For developed countries, with high per capita income waste generation varies between 1.1 to 5.07 kg/capita/day. In this way population, urbanization and average income affect amount of waste produced. Besides these, there are many other factors that affect the quantity of waste generated. These are social behavior, climate, source, industrial production and market for waste etc. Quality of waste produced also varies from place to place. The data collected by National Environmental Engineering Research Institute (NEERI), Nagpur from 43 cities is presented in Table 1. The data indicates that waste composition in India is highly organic and varies between 40-50 per cent (Vidhi and Maheshwari, 2000).

The quantity of generated waste is increasing day by day. But, municipalities have limited means to collect and dispose them. More than 25 per cent of municipal solid waste is not all collected. Seventy per cent of Indian cities have inadequate capability to transport them. For example, take our capital Delhi, where Municipal Corporation of Delhi (MCD) and New Delhi Municpal Corporation (NDMC), have capability to treat only 5000 tons of waste. The rest of 2000 to 3000 tons of waste remain untreated. A major portion of the collected waste is dumped into sanitary landfill sites (SLF). Uncontrolled garbage lying on one side rots and represents a very ugly sight and add to pollution and cause numerous health problems. The waste that is dumped in SLF releases many poisonous and greenhouse gases that pollute our environment. Leakage of substances from SLF releases toxic liquids that pollute ground water. Incineration (burning) of waste produces harmful gases, which affect endocrine system and may cause cancer.

Thus, management of solid waste (MSW) is not an easy task. The problem is taking a serious turn day-by-day and deserves very careful attention to avert its serious consequences. The topic has been considered seriously by many workers and organizations to find its safe and economical solution (Bhatnagar, 1994; Kalia *et al.*, 2000; Gupta, 2001; Palta, 2002; Upadhyay and Soni, 2002)

HAZARDS AND IMPACTS ASSOCIATED WITH MISMANAGEMENT OF WASTES

Mismangement of waste may lead to many problems. Some of them are as follows:

(i) **Pollution:** Increasing population, changed life style and industrialization are leading to increased waste production which in turn results in water, soil, and air pollution. Open burning of wastes produce dioxins, which are very hazardous to health.

(ii) **Health problems:** Waste materials dumped here and there, act as favorable medium for the growth and multiplication of rats, flies and diseases causing organisms. Some of the important diseases spread by them are cholera, typhoid, jaundice, plague etc. Hundreds of people lost their lives in Surat city due to garbage and prevailing unhygienic conditions, which led to spread of plague. Even waste collection workers face occupational hazards. Collection and sorting of dangerous items like explosives, needles, glass, razor blades; healthcare wastes, aerosol cans; explosive containers and harmful chemicals may cause injury or poisoning. Landfill gas like methane (produced by the decomposition of wastes) can be explosive and may cause warming due to its greenhoiuse effect. The polluted water (leachate) flowing from waste dumps can cause water pollution and may pose very serious health hazards.

(iii) **Aesthetic/Social problems:** Mismanaged waste cause aesthetic nuisance in terms of smell and appearance. It is a general belief that the environment in which one lives shapes the way of thinking. A man living in dirty and polluted environment may tend to be pessimistic and may develop culprit attitude. Children brought up in such environment may develop negative thinking and in future may lead to polluted and distorted society. Thus, the progress of the whole nation may get hampered due to pollution.

(iv) **Economic problems:** A large share of the annual budget is spent for disposal of wastes. During the year 2000, Municipal Corporation of Delhi spent 361 crores of rupees for disposal of wastes. The urban areas of Asia spend about US$ 25 billion for waste management per year and it is expected to increase to US$ 47 billion in 2025. Thus, the management of waste is also an economic problem.

TYPE OF WASTES

Wastes can be grouped into different categories like:

1. **Based on physical state:** Waste can be classified as solid, liquid or gaseous waste. Solid wastes include agricultural residues, cattle dung, paper etc. Animal urine, sewage, biogas slurry etc. are included in liquid wastes. Gaseous wastes comprise of gases and smoke emitted from industries, kitchen and automobiles.
2. **Moisture content:** Wastes with low moisture content or dry wastes include polythene, rubber, thermocoal, plastics etc. These wastes are usually non-biodegradable. Agricultural residues, animal dung, urine, litter etc. are grouped as moist or biodegradable wastes.
3. **Source of origin:** Based on the source of origin, wastes can be classified as 'domestic waste' that includes rotten residues of fruits, vegetables, kitchen waste, wood, cloth, paper, cotton etc. Wastes can also be classifed as industrial and hospital wastes. Agricultural wastes include straw, husk, rotten cereals, vegetables, fruits etc. Wastes generated from farmyard *viz.*, animal dung, urine and their bedding as well as their wash out are included as farmyard wastes.

MAIN SOLID WASTE DISPOSAL METHODS

For the disposal of wastes various methods are available (Palta, 2002). Each method has its own advantages and can be used for specific categories of wastes. Some of their methods are as follows:

1. **Landfills:** Wastes are collected and transported to low-lying areas on the outskirts of cities are dumped there. It is very costly affair. The decomposition of garbage disposed in an unorganized way, produces some poisonous gases as methane, sulphurs disoxide, carbon dioxide, hydrogen sulfide etc. that results to environmental pollution. Leakage of toxic substances from these wastes pollute ground water and run off from these landfills can even pollute water in ponds, rivers and streams. The resulting pollution increases health-related problems. Because of rapid increase in population and industrialization,

land is getting costly and its availability is being reduced. So landfill sites must be shifted from the inhabited areas. Thus, transportation charges will also increase. Effulents discharged from industries may contain heavy metals like arsenic, lead, cadmium etc. These heavy metals may cause many health-related problems like joint pain, weakness, anorexia, heart, skin, kidney and mental problems.

2. **Incineration:** Burning is a traditional method for disposal of wastes. However, the method is linked with many disadvantages (Kalia *et al.*,2000). By burning of dry waste toxic dry ash, dioxins, furans and many other toxic gases are produced. These toxic pollutants affect various physiological processes of mammals, fish and birds. Besides these pollutants, some green house gases like CO_2, SO_2 are also produced which cause global warming. In terms of energy recovery output is 43 per cent of its operating cost. Thus, this method is not very effective and safe for disposal of Indian waste because of its low calorific value.

3. **Biogas production:** Biodegradable substances present in wastes can be utilized in 'biogas plants' for production of very precious fuel; biogas and the spent slurry can be used in agricultural fields as manure for nourishing soil. These methods alleviate pollution but also produce neat and clean fuel as well as manure at very low cost. Thus, cutting of forests and burning of cattle dung cakes for supply of energy can be avoided.

4. **Hydrogen gas production:** Many anaerobic microbes produce H_2 by decomposing organic molecules like glucose, xylose, fatty acids etc. Bio wastes including corn, potato, rotten cereal grains and other fruits, vegetables can also be fermented to produce H_2 gas. Hydrogen gas is an important source of energy. It has high calorific value, does not leave any residue after burning and is safer for environment. The energy contained in hydrogen gas can be transformed into steam (heat energy) and electricity. The generated energy can be used for running scooters, buses, cars, aeroplanes etc. From 1 kg of biodegradable waste, 40 to 100 litres of H_2 can be produced (Kalia, *et al,* 2000). In future, this method may prove to be very effective and safe for disposal of wastes.

5. **Briquetting:** With this process, highly voluminous and troublesome wastes can be converted to pollution free, neat and clean fuels. The process is completed by pyrolysis of the wastes in controlled anaerobic conditions. Obtained fuel is compact, thus, the storage and transportation cost is reduced. This method is ideal for disposal of ligno-cellulosic wastes.
6. **Composting:** Composting is ecofriendly and every effective method to recycle biodegradable wastes. Under MSW Rules, 2000, all municipal bodies of the country are required to compost city wastes. The Rule states, "Biological wastes shall be processed by composting vermicomposting, anaerobic digestion or any other appropriate biological process for stabilization of wastes". Process of composting will not only solves waste problem but also provide nutrients to farmers at very reasonable rate and will alleviate unemployment. Use of compost in fields reduces need for fertilizers and pesticides.

VERMITECHNOLOGY FOR RECYCLING OF SOLID WASTE

Earthworms in soil play an important role in maintaining its fertility by various biological, chemical and physical activities. Earthworm abundant soils are rich in nutrients, more resistant to erosion, show stable pH, improved pest resistant, and water retention and biological activity. Such beneficial activities of earthworms are utilized for conversion of organic rich biodegradable wastes to compost and the latter is used in agricultural fields to get desired results. Use of vermitechnology for waste recycling is gaining more and more importance day-by-day. According to a survey conducted in 43 Indian cities by National Environmental Engineering Research Institute (NEERI), Nagpur indicates that garbage in India is highly organic (40 to 50 per cent) (Table 1). Use of vermitechnology is the easiest and most appropriate technology in India to recycle majority of wastes. In our country, over a million people are earning their livelihood from waste collection and recycling. Such people after acquiring some easy training can do vermicomposting and may supplement to their income. So technology of vermicomposting for recycling organic biodegradable wastes is economically viable option available that will not only help in employment generation but also will reduce consequences related with mismanagement of wastes.

Table 1. Physical characteristics of municipal solid waste in Indian cities (all values are in percent calculated in wet weight basis)

Population range (million)	Number of cities suveyed	Paper	Rubber, leather and synthetics	Glass	Metal	Compo-stable material	Inert Materials
0.1 to 0.5	12	2.91	0.78	0.56	0.33	44.57	43.59
0.5 to 1.0	15	2.95	0.73	0.56	0.32	40.04	43.38
1.0 to 2.0	09	4.71	0.71	0.46	0.49	38.95	44.73
2.0 to 5.0	03	0.48	0.48	0.48	0.59	56.67	40.07
5.0 and above	04	0.28	0.28	0.94	0.80	30.84	53.09

Source: Vidhi & Maheshwari, 2000

To meet the food requirements for increasing population, use of chemical fertilizers is increasing in our country. Indiscriminate use of excessive fertilizers is doing a lot of harm to agriculture. Use of excessive fertilizers is causing the soil to deteriorate and is making it more and more fertilizer dependent and renderening it barr. Excess fertilizers used in field are carried to aquatic bodies and not only cause aquatic pollution but also by eutrophication cause mortality of aquatic life. Crops become more sensitive to pests by excessive use of fertilizers. In paddy fields, excessive use of fertilizers causes release of nitrous oxide, which depletes ozone layer (necessary to save our planet from harmful radiations). It is now general belief that food products grown on chemical fertilizers are inferior in quality and taste in comparison to those grown on compost. Such products are being sold in market as 'Organic Food' and fetch more price than the ordinary ones. Use of synthetic fertilizers cannot be totally checked by careful practice of integrated plant nutrient management (IPNM), use of synthetic fertilizers can be reduced considerably. Today there is gap of 6 million tons a year in production and requirement of nutrients. India's 35 largest cities can supply 5.7 million tons a year of organic manure by composting their biodegradable wastes (Gupta, 2001). In our country, 300 million tons of crop residue is produced annually. Besides this, 200 million tons of cow dung are produced. These crop residues and dung is usually burnt. Their proper composting have potential of generating 14.92 million tons of nutrients (Table 2).

Table 2. Availability of nutrients from cattle dung and crop residues (million tons)

Item	Quantity	Nitrogen	Phosphorus	Potash	Total nutrient
Cattle dung	200	3.44	1.31	2.21	6.96
Crop residue	300	6.04	0.32	1.59	7.96
Total	500	9.49	1.63	3.80	14.92

Source: Singh and Sharma, 2001.

VERMICOMPOSTING OF WASTE MATERIALS

Recycling of biodegradable waste by vermicomposting is gaining worldwide attentions, as it is very convenient, effective and eco-friendly way to reduce and recycle waste materials. It is ideal technology for developing countries like India where wastes are dominated by organic biodegradable portion. Earthworms feed on such substrates and pass them though their intestine. During the passage they are acted upon by certain enzymes and microbes, which convert complex organic compounds to simpler fragments. This excreted material by earthworms is termed as vermicasts. The casts forms a suitable medium for the growth and multiplication of many beneficial microbes, which further act on the substrate and continue decomposition of organic molecules into simple fractions. Thus, earthworms along with certain microbes form a very powerful and effective system, which decompose the organic waste in very short time and supplement it with some other useful components.

A study of Soil Ecology laboratory, Ohio State University in vermicoposting of pig manure slurry and agro-forestry byproducts indicates that presence of earthworms reduces organic nitrogen content and increases rate of nitrification.Carbon from fulvic acids is reduced and an increase in percentage of carbon from humic acids was reported during vermicomposting process. By vermicoposting process humic substances increase by 40 to 60 per cent. During the process of mineralization carbon loss is there and the total amount of heavy metals increases (between 25 to 30 per cent) but the amount of bioavailable heavy metals decrease. A decrease of 35 to 55 per cent of bioavailable metals in two months was also reported. The study further indicated that after a period of 60 days of vermicomposting, fecal coliform bacteria in biosolids decreased from 39,000 MPN/g to 0 MPN/g. During the same period *Salmonella* sp.decreased from < 3MPN/g to 1MPN/ (Dominguez, 1997).

Vermicompost is a stable nontoxic material, which is a very good soil conditioner for plant growth. Vermicompost is a fine material with excellent texture, porosity, aeration, drainage and water holding capacity. Final composition of the earthworm castings depends upon feedstock fed to earthworms (Table 3).

Table 3. *Chemical composition of earthworm castings fed with different feedstock

(as per cent of fresh weight)

Feed	N	P	K	C	Mg	Organic matter
Cow manure	1.70	0.62	1.22	10.0	1.53	44.5
Pig manure	1.89	1.50	0.34	10.8	1.46	44.0
Sheep manure	1.51	0.64	0.78	4.40	1.37	37.5
Coffee pulp	2.01	0.27	2.14	1.96	0.37	53.8
Sugarcane pulp	2.67	2.11	0.40	4.08	1.89	68.5
Banana	2.50	0.56	3.74	2.36	1.50	65.5
Ruminal Contents	1.68	0.62	1.21	9.80	1.58	45.5
Urban/domestic waste	0.90	0.44	3.60	3.60	3.10	26.5

* Werner and Cuevas, 1996

The vermicomposting technology for conversion of solid organic wastes to useful product has been ranked higher than composting in certain aspects (Dominguez *et al,* 1997). Composting is defined as an accelerated bio-oxidation of organic matter passing through a thermophilic stage(45 to 65°C) where microorganisms like bacteria, fungi and actinomycetes liberate heat, carbon dioxide and water. While, vermicomposting is also bio-oxidation and stabilization process by joint action of earthworms and microbes and does not involve thermophilic stage. Earthworms act as agent for turning, aeration and does decomposition of organic matter. It is also reported that nitrogen mineralization and humification is faster during vermicomposting. The vermictechnology brings about a greater decrease of bioavailable heavy metals than the composting process. There are also evidences to support the fact that vermicompost contain hormone- like substances that accelerate plant growth.

It is a general belief about vermicomposing that it is a natural process and needs little management. Successful vermicomposting requires careful management and research. To start vermicomposting on a new substrate, first step is to start purely as a test experiment on a small scale (Bhatnagar and Palta, 1996a). Vermiculturist should record every detail of steps followed and their responses on earthworms like how these fair in particular medium with increase or decrease in their numbers, waste matters conversion, casts production and composting etc.

a) Planning Vermicomposting

For planning vermicomposting the following points should be considered carefully:

1. Selection of site
2. Availability of decomposable organic waste, its daily quantity, chemical composition alternate organic material, transportation to the site, stocking availability of manpower etc.
3. Marketable outlets and requirements with future scope.
4. Considering the quality of waste, collection and study of know how on earthworms to be cultured.
5. Collection or procurement of suitable species
6. Testing suitability of species on performance in available organic waste in terms of their survival, multiplication and bio-conversion of waste
7. Maintenance of seed culture which can eventually be used in vermicomposting beds

Besides these other important points, which should be considered, are availability of funds, availability of labor, quality of wastes, packaging etc. All these points comprise essential steps in any project formulation.

For wider utilization of vermicomposting and convenience, the vermitechnology may be represented by flowchart given in Fig.1.

b) Selection of suitable species

In India there are more than 500 species of earthworms. Based on ecological parameters earthworms can be grouped into three categories:

1. Epigeics: There are surface dwellers and mainly feed on litter and organic matters. Most of the species are good biodegradators and are good nutrient releasers but do not redistribute nutrients. They are not good for use in field

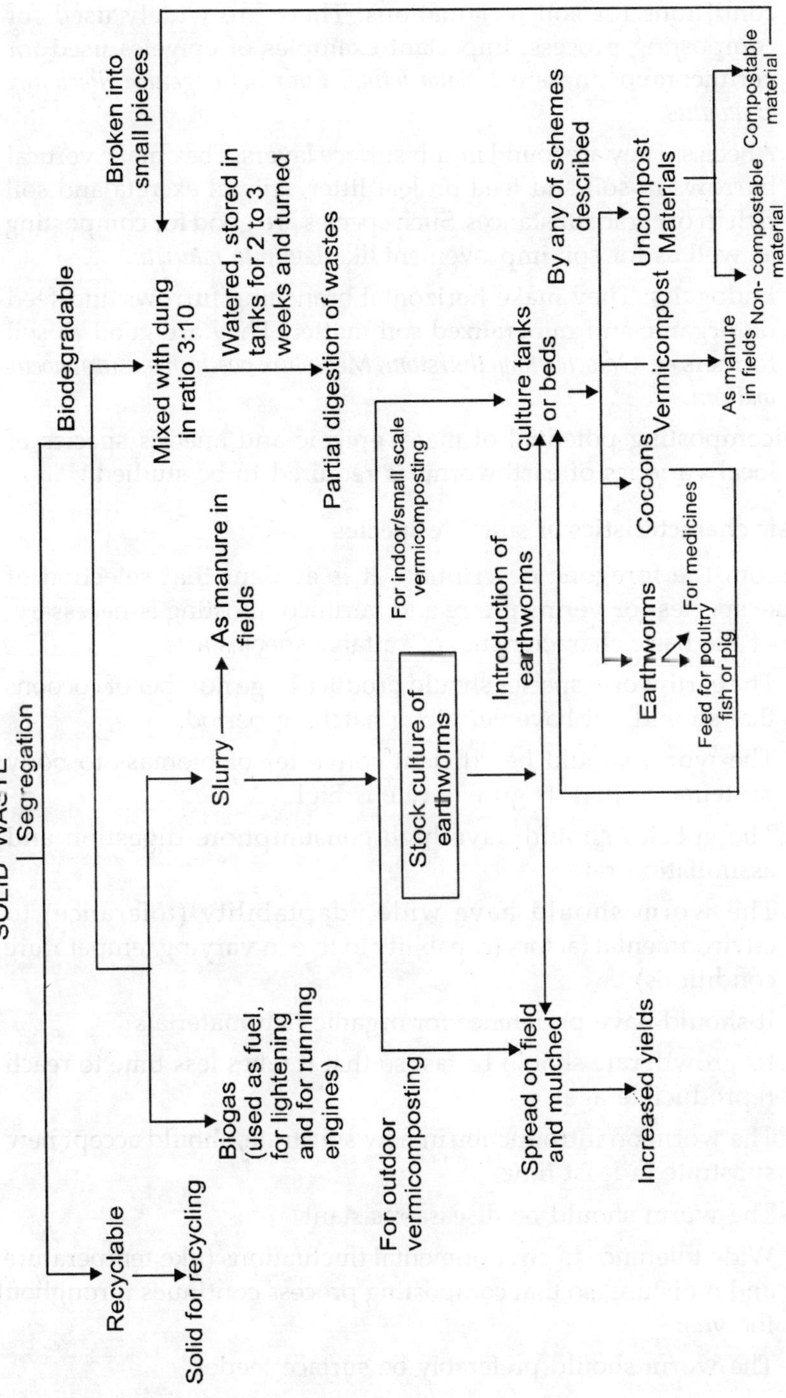

Fig. 1. Flowchart for vermitechnology

conditions for soil reclamations. There are widely used for composting process. Important examples of epigeics used for vermicomposting are *Eisenia fetida, Eudrilus eugeniae, Perionyx excavatus.*

2. Anecics: They are found in sub-surface layers. They make vertical burrows in soil and feed on leaf litter, animal excreta and soil rich in organic substances. Such species are good for composting as well as for soil improvement like *Lampito mauritii.*

3. Endogeics: They make horizontal branching furrows and feed on organic and mineralized soil matter. They are good as soil formers *eg. Octochaetona thurstoni, Metaphire posthuma, Eutyphoeus waltoni.*

Vermicomposting potential of many epigeic and anecics species of local varieties of earthworms is required to be studied.

c) Basic characteristics of suitable species

From the foregone description, it is evident that selection of suitable species for vermiculture and vermicomposting is necessary. Some of the basic characteristics of suitable species are:

i) The earthworm species should produce large number of cocoons that should not have very long hatching period.

ii) The worm should be efficient converter of biomass to body proteins, so that its growth rate is high.

iii) The species should have high consumption, digestion and assimilation rate

iv) The worm should have wide adaptability (tolerance) to environmental factors (capability to live in varying temperature conditions)

v) It should have preference for organic rich materials

vi) Its growth rate should be fast so that it takes less time to reach reproducible age

vii) The worm on introduction in new substrate, should accept new substrate in least time

viii) The worm should be disease-resistant

ix) Wide tolerance to environmental fluctuations (like temperature and moisture) so that composting process continues throughout the year

x) The worm should preferably be surface feeder

The Indian subcontinent is rich in biodiversity of earthworms. Two or three species are widely used in India for vermicomposting. Potential, however, exists for utilization of several other indigenous species and deserve attention. This is on several reasons like inbuilt adaptability to climatic conditions per existing distribution range, local availabilty and in view of needs for better wastes conversion rates.

d) Species which are being used widely in India for vermicomposting:

Eisenia fetida

Eudrilus euginiae

Lampito mauritii

Perionyx excavatus

e) Collection and segregation of waste

Collection and segregation of wastes constitue very important step of waste management. First step of recycling and composting is waste separation. The materials to be recycled can be separated as the generator, known as source separation or from the general waste stream at a mixed waste recovery facility.Different techniques are available for separation. Different sized wastes can be separated by a screening method. The magnetic and Eddy current separation can be used to separate ferrous and non-ferrous materials. Air classification, ballistic separation and wet separation may be used to separate heavy and light, organic and non-organic materials. Most popular used method is manual separation, which is still widely used in developing countries, where manpower is not a problem (Vidhi and Maheshwari, 2000).

In 1997, India generated 48 million tons of waste. Out of this, more than 25 per cent of MSW is not at all collected. Even 70 per cent of the cities in our country lack sufficient capability to transport the waste and there are no SLF for the disposal of wastes. The existing SLF are neither well built nor properly managed to protect against contamination of soil or ground water. Maintenance of modern engineered SLF is very costly affair. It is claimed that garbage going to SLF sites could be reduced by 40 per cent if recyclable materials are separated from the waste (The Hindu, 24 June, 2003). This will not only increase life of SLF but also will boost recylcing industry. It is possible to separate cloth, paper, cardboard, leather, plastics, metals, glass, batteries and bottles and can be sold to factories for recylcing.In our country over a million people find their livelihood in field of waste collection (known as ragpickers), segregation and recycling. In future,this sector linked with waste, may play a vital role for its management. So, there is urgent need to strengthen the existing system instead of replacing it blindly with some other method from other developed countries. Depending upon situation and source of generation, garbage may be segregated at the source or at Dhalao or at some other place. At some places very right practice of separating garbage at source into recyclable and biodegradable wastes in blue and green containers is being adopted. In this direction educating the people for making separation of their house waste, before throwing, would be the best solution. By organizing the sector of waste collection, segregation or recycling and composting, not only pollution is reduced but also the waste is managed effectively and safely besides providing jobs to millions of people. In this context government authorities and NGOs have to play a vital role.

f) Other Compostable materials

Almost all types of biodegradable and decomposable organic wastes can be made use for vermiculture and vermicomposting. Commonly used composting materials are listed below:

1. Agricultural wastes including stems, leaves, husk, peels, vegetable waste, orchard leaf litter, processed food waste, baggase and processing wastes.
2. Animal dung like cattle dung, sheep dung, horse dung, goat dung and poultry dropping etc.
3. Forestry wastes like wood shavings, peels, sawdust and pulp and leaves etc.
4. City leaf litter
5. Waste paper and cotton cloth
6. Biogas slurry
7. Industrial wastes *viz.*, wastes from food processing, distillery, leather cuttings etc.

The authors conducted experiment to assess suitability of leather cutting wastes(cut into pieces < 2m) for vermicomposting (Table 4). The experiment was conducted in glass jars in replicated sets. Ten earthworm, *E. fetida* were used in each treatment. The best combination for composting was leather cutting + cattle dung (1:3).

Table 4. Different amendments for vermicomposting of leather cuttings

Amendments	Number of surviving earthworms	Young ones produced	Condition of composting
Leather cuttings (100g) + cattle dung (250g) + Field soil (50g)	10	Nil	Partial
Leather cuttings (100g) + Cattle dung (300 g)	10	6	Complete
Leather cuttings (100g) + Cattle dung (250g) + Crushed leaves of Jamun Tree (50g).	10	3	Partial

Care should be taken that hazardous wastes (from industries and hospitals) and biomedical wastes (like swabs, disposable syringes, body fluids, bandages and other infectious materials) do not get mixed with other decomposable materials for vermicomposting as their mixing may cause serious health hazards.

g) Testing the suitability of waste for vermicomposting

Response of various organic wastes differs according to their chemical and biological composition. Poultry waste should be handled carefully when it is fresh because it contains toxic components. It is always advisable to test suitability of a waste before putting it for vermicomposting.

The procedure is very simple (modified from Werner and Cuevas,1996). Take boxes (30 x 15 x 7 cm) and fill them with waste/ wastes to be tested. Pour water to keep moisture level up to 40 per cent. Take same species of earthworms, which are going to be used for vermicomposting. Wash them and transfer 50 earthworms to each box containing waste. Cover them or tie muslin cloth at top to prevent their escape and to provide darkness. In this way make four replicate for each waste material. After 24 hours, the contents are poured on a glass sheet and the worms are counted. The substrate that gives minimum 96 per cent of survival of earthworms will be considered suitable for vermicomposting.

Vermicomposting systems

Many vermicomposting systems are available. Adoption of a particular system depends upon many factors like availability of waste quantity, its site of production, site where vermicompost is to be used, type of land and associated infrastructures available, rain fall, sun shine, temperature, availability of shaded area, raw material facilities for transportation of vermicompost, primary objective-earthworm or compost production etc. Broadly, two types of system of vermicomposting are in practice (Dominguez *et al*,1997). The first is open system and the second is in-vessel vermicomposting system.

1. **Open system of composting:** includes traditioanl methods of composting on beds or windrows. Windrows composting consist of placing the raw materials in long narrow piles. These methods require little capital investment. These methods have several drawbacks such as they require large area and are labor intensive, even after using machinery. With such system rate of composting is slow.
2. **In-vessel composting system:** includes those methods in which vermicomposting materials are confined to a vessel, container, pit or box. The vessel can be simply a locally available used earthen pot, washbasin, garden pot, and wooden or metallic box with provision of a hole in the bottom for exit of water. Holes can also be drilled along the sides of the container for aeration.

Even a small barrel or drum with holes at bottom and sides can be used for this purpose. Now a days even three-chambered bins are also in practice.These work on an assembly line idea. They process three batches of compost in varying stages of decompostion.The raw material along with worms is put in the first bin for 3 to 5 days. Then the contents are shifted into the second bin for 4 to 7 days; while a new batch is started in the first bin. Finally, contents of the second bin are shifted to third, first to second and first are restarted again. This method allows good aeration of the substrate. There are advanced in-vessel methods available with different combination of vessels, aeration devices and turning mechanisms. In some system bins or large containers are stacked in racks. These methods when used on large scale require lot of handling and lifting machinery. They also face the problem of adding water and additional layers of feeds. **'Batch Reactors'** have been developed and tested at National Institute of Agriculture Engineering in Silsoe, England and currently used in several places in the U.S. In this technique the containers are raised on legs above the ground. The feed is added from the top and is removed mechanically from the bottom through mesh floors using breaker bars. Another recent technique of vermicomposting is **'continuous flow reactor'**. This system is completely automatic and hydraulically driven. By use of this technology 3 feet deep layers of organic wastes can be vermicomposted in less than 30 days. These methods are capital intensive and require skilled management.

Cuba has introduced a "Sanitary Box System" of vermicomposting for home use(Werner and Cuevas, 1996). The system consits of two boxes, which can be stacked on top of one another. Kitchen waste is added in the first box and moistened. When feedstock reaches 15 cm height then 20 to 40 per cent by volume, waste paper is added. The composting worms are added @ 1 kg per m^2 andvermicomposting is allowed to progress. After the completion of composting, the second box is kept on top of the first and is provided with fresh food.The earthworms from first box move to the second box through slats. In this way, earthworms are easily separated from vermicomposted material. To prevent excessive population, about one-fourth of the earthworms are removed from the box at each harvest.

(i) Pre-treatment of wastes

Waste material offered to earthworms after certain preliminary treatments decompose faster. After proper collection and segregation of wastes into decomposable and recyclable materials, the decomposable organic material is tested for their suitability for vermicomposting. Such tested organic material is spread on the ground upto to 1 foot layer. Large lumps are broken. The contents are exposed to the sun for the day or so. It will kill unwanted organisms and will remove foul smell. The wastes may also be mixed with 10 to 40 per cent of the leaf litter.

Pre-treatment of leaf litter and agricultural waste involve cutting them into small pieces upto 2 or 3 cm. Beating with bamboo sticks can crush large pieces. Even vegetable and fruit wastes can be cut into small pieces. Sometimes vegetable waste are infected with insects. In this case, chop the waste into small pieces and spray 4 per cent aqueous solution of some Neem insecticide formulation. This will kill the insect pests and their young ones and will make the waste fit for composting (Bhatnagar and Palta, 1996b).

(j) Feedstock for earthworms

Earthworms can feed on almost all types of decomposable materials and convert them to vermicompost. Care should be taken that earthworms are not fed with toxic chemicals, agricultural wastes sprayed with pesticides, metals, foils, glass, plastics, oil, soap, paint etc. Avoid citrus products, onion, garlic, acid and spicy food. Meat products, diary products and fecal matter of pets should also be avoided. Even poultry dropping are not recommended as they may contain contamination of pathogens and toxic substances.

Prof. R.D. Kale has given standard diet for earthworms which include cowdung or mixed dung + gram bran+wheat bran + vegetable waste (10:1:1:1) + some powdered eggshell.

Palta and Bhatnagar(2002) reported that mixture of 1 kg field soil + 500 g cattle dung + 25 g crushed Jamun leaves (*Syzygium* sp.) as ideal substrate for culture of *Metaphire posthuma.*

In an experiment conducted in punctured plastic bags it was found that bag containing mixture of cattle dung and rice bean (3:1) attracted the maximum number of *E. fetida* adults and produced the maximum cocoons. Addition of mulberry leaves to the said substrate reduced cocoon production and attracted less numbers of earthworm adults. Thus, indicating that mixture of cattle dung and rice bean as ideal substrate for culture of *E. fetida* (Palta and Srivastava, 2001).

Mixture of cattledung, dried crushed leaves and waste vegetable(cattledung 42.3 kg + dried jamun leaves 9.8 kg + cut okra fruits 3.0 kg) was found suitable for culture of *E. fetida.* The substrate was composted in 90 days and during this period number of earthworms was incrased by four times (Palta, 2002).

Palta (2001) tested a number of diets for culture of *E. fetida.* Most promising was found mixture of FYM (FarmYard Manure), 500 g + 5g oral rehydration powder followed by diet containing mixture of 500 g FYM and 1 capsule of multivitamins. In the former treatment, per cent incrases in adults over control was 266.67, young ones produced were 209.3 and cocoons produced were 61.7; while in later treatment, figures were 150.0, 3.0 and 46.0 respectively.

Here are given few more combinations of diet which are good for most of the species of earthworms used for vermiculture and vermicomposting. (Bhatnagar and Palta,1996a). However, exact proportions may have to be adjusted after considering the food and feeding habits and the ecology of worm under consideration.

- Mature cattle dung (minimum 7 days old)
- Cowdung + sheep dung + horse dung mixed in equal proportion
- Cowdung or mixed dung + rice polish/wheat bran/gram bran/vegetable waste/agricultural waste/sewage/sledge/kitchen waste/municipal waste/crushed leaf litter in ratio of 10:3
- Cowdung + sawdust in ratio of 10:3
- Biogas slurry with leaf litter in ratio of 10:3
- Cowdung + bagasse in ratio 10:3

Waste paper can also be composted and may be added to any of the above combinations but its volume should not exceed 20 to 40 per cent. It is reported that amendment of cowdung sawdust promote numbers and with paper promote biomass of earthworms (Ismail, 1997). Mushroom spent or deoiled neem cake can also be composted.

In all the above-mentioned diet combinations, cattle dung or mixed dung is main ingredient because it is rich in nitrogen. Nitrogen is essential for microbial decomposition of organic wastes. For vermicomposting of any substrate C:N (carbon and nitrogen) ratio plays important role. The ratio should not exceed 40:1 otherwise decomposition rate will be very slow. For composting of materials rich in carbon (like sawdust, straw etc.) in the absence of cattle dung 1% actual nitrogen (urea) or nitrogenous supplements like drumistick (*Moringa olefera*) and subabul (*Leucaena leucocephala*) may be added. Even such trees may be planted along the vermicomposting beds so that their falling leaves contribute to composting stuff (Ismail, 1997). Feed layers added should not exceed 5-10 cm, as deeper layers generate heat so earthworms will move away and so speed of vermicomposting would slowdown.

In addition to the above mentioned combinations several other combinations can be tried with care. Simple procedure for testing any new substrate has already been described in the above columns under heading "Testing the suitability of waste for vermicomposting". The best substrate for vermicomposting is that which is easily and locally available. For example, entrepreneurs staying near a vegetable market or a farmer growing vegetables may use vegetable waste, farmhouse owner may use agricultural waste and a housewife can use kitchen waste for vermicomposting. Table-5 gives details of some experiments conducted by the authors that indicate potential of some agricultural wastes for vermicomposting.

Table 5. Effect of substrate amendments and technique on composting period

Composting system and dimensions	Substrate amendments	MEAN Earthworm counts per 20 cm x 20 cm x 10 cm		Composting time (Days)
Cemented tank 94 cm x 55 cm x 50 cm (freshly laid bed)	BANANA LEAVES	intial	Final	
	32 kg cattle dung (basal layer)+ 1.2 kg chopped leaves + 16 kg cattle dung on top	12	102.67	83
	32 kg cattle dung (basal layer) + 1.8 kg chopped leaves + 16 kg cattle dung on top	12	123.33	71
Cemented tank 94 cm x 55 cm x 50 cm (freshly laid bed)	CABBAGE			
	32 kg cattle dung + 10 kg chopped cabbage	102.67	110.00	28
	32 kg cattle dung + 10 g chopped cabbage partially decomposed for 15 days	123.33	143.67	15
Cemented tank 94 cm x 55 cm x 50 cm (freshly laidbed)	OKRA			
	Chopped 5 kg okra + 15 kg cattle dung on top	124.0	155.0	16
	Chopped 5 kg okra + 15 kg cattle dung periodically turned	146.0	171.0	11

Composting system and dimensions	Substrate amendments	MEAN Earthworm counts per 20 cm x 20 cm x 10 cm		Composting time (Days)
	Chopped 5 kg okra + 15 kg cattle dung partially decomposed for 15 days	135.0	168.0	9
	Chopped 7.5 kg okra + 15 kg cattle dung on top	181.33	178.0	12
	Chopped 7.5 kg okra + 15 kg cattle dung periodically turned	141.33	178.0	9
	Chopped 7.5 kg okra + 15 kg cattle dung partially decomposed for 9 days	117.50	136.0	7
	Chopped 7.5 kg okra + 7.5 kg cattle dung on top	178.0	176.0	17
	Chopped 7.5 kg okra + 7.5 kg cattle dung periodically turned	147.0	181.0	15
	Chopped 7.5 kg okra + 7.5 kg cattle dung partially decomposed for15 days	121.33	169.0	10
	Vermibeds on ground 745 cm x 52 cm x 25 cm (freshly laid bed)	POTATO	-	-

Composting system and dimensions	Substrate amendments	MEAN Earthworm counts per 20 cm x 20 cm x 10 cm		Composting time (Days)
-	45 kg chopped potato + 150 kg cattle dung partially decomposed for 20 days	55.5	41.0	41
Vermibeds on ground 745 cm x 50 cm x 25 cm	CABBAGE			
	20 kg cabbage chopped + 65 kg cattle dung	59.5	106.25	43
Vermibeds on ground 745cm x 50 cm x 25 cm	BRINJAL			
	42 kg chopped brinjal covered with gunny bag	57.25	87.75	17
	42 kg chopped brinjal uncovered	85.5	96.75	Incomplete composting after 17 days

(k) Partial decomposition of waste/feedstock

For vermiculture or vermicomposting any of the above combinations may be used. The ingredients are thoroughly mixed and arranged into heaps. Large pieces of waste are beaten or cut into small pieces. It is watered as and when required to keep the stuff moist. The heaps are kept for partial decomposition for 2 to 3 weeks depending upon the nature of waste. During this period heaps are turned twice or thrice a week. Such partially decomposed wastes are put to earthworm beds for vemicomposting. The process of partial decompostion makes the process of vermicomposting faster and removes unpleasant odor or kills pathogens.

The authors conducted a series of experiments (Table 5) on vermicomposting of vegetable wastes. It is evident that vermicomposting took minimum time when the substrate is partially decomposed followed by the amendment in which substrate was periodically turned twice a week. The maximum time for decomposition was taken when cattle dung was put on top of the waste.

(l) Maintenance of base culture

Base culture can be maintained in concrete nursery tanks or in boxes or in windrows. Base culture may be maintained on cattle dung or any of the above-mentioned feedstocks. Earthworms are reared in nursery beds and then they are seeded into new windrows or beds.

(m) Setting up of vermicomposting bed and container

Various types of containers, which can be used for vermicomposting, have already been discussed in section "vermicomposting systems". Best container or box is that which is easily available or is not in any other important use or can be made from locally available materials. Wash it thoroughly so that it does not contain any toxic substance or chemical. At the bottom put a layer of fine sand (3 cm thick). Over this a 5-7 cm thick layer of sawdust is laid which is covered with equally thick layer of garden soil. The layers are watered. The soil or sand is added to provide grit for the better digestion of worms. Garden soil also provides starting culture of decomposing bacterial or as a variation straight way put some bedding materials as first layer. Bedding material that is rich in cellulose help to aerate bin so that worms may breathe easily. Even the bedding material can be made from locally available biodegradable materials like hay, straw, shaded leaves, sawdust, peat moss, mushroom 'spent', coconut and other leaves and cattle dung. On this lay a 10-15 cm high layer of one of combinations of feed or waste. Release earthworms @ 1000 per m^2. Cover with gunny bag or leaves. After completion of composting add another layer of waste and keep on repeating this.

For setting up a vermibed or windrow, it is important to select the site very carefully. The site should be under shade and on an elevated area. It may also be set in similar way as discussed above. If sawdust is not available make layers of sand and soil or a layer of any biodegradable material. Moist the layer and introduce earthworms. Put 10-15 cm high waste layer and keep on adding layers as explained above. Keep on watering it as and when required to provide necessary level of moisture. Vermibed may also be started with first layer of waste that is 10-15 cm thick and keep on adding similar layers on completion of composting. Such similar variations for forming vermibeds have been shown in Fig. 3 (Bhatnagar and Palta, 1996a).

Ismail (1997) describes another method for setting up a vermibed. First place basal layer of broken bricks or pebbles followed by a layer of sand (6-7.5 cm). On top of it put 15 cm high layer of loamy soil, moist it. Into this release about hundred epigeic and anecic

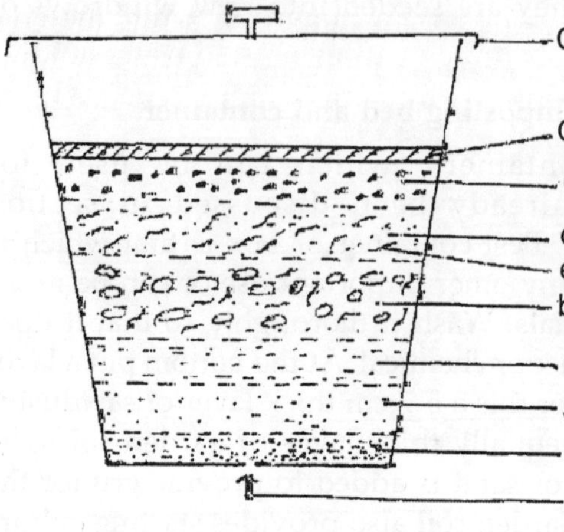

Fig. 2 Layers of composting container

earthworms. Make small lumps of cattle dung at many places on top of soil. Cover it with 10 cm thick layer of dried leaves or hay. Water is sprinkled to keep the bed moist. Bed is covered. Maintain proper moisture level till 30 days. On thirty-first day spread 5 cm thick layer of locally available organic waste. Keep on adding subsequent layers of waste after completion of composting. Repeat the process until the whole pit is filled or height of bed goes upto 65-75 cm, cover it and continue irrigation to maintain moisture level. Overturn the waste once in a week. (Fig. 4)

Alternatively, for making a vermibed or pit, lay first layer of biodegradable material followed by a layer of waste (5 to 8 cm), on top of it cattle dung layer(3 to 5 cm) thick cover and water it. On completion of vermicomposting repeat addition of waste and cattle dung layers. In case the feedstock is pre-decomposed with cattle dung, addition of dung layer may be deleted.

Time taken for composting of wastes depends upon many factors, like species of earthworm used; their populatioin density; quality and quantity of waste; chemical composition of waste; temperature; moisture content; maintenance of beds, technology used etc. Table 5 shows results of some of the experiments conducted by the authors. The results indicate how various feedstock amendments and technique affect the composting time.

Depending upon the availability of land and manpower each composting unit may have two or three beds. When the labor is free

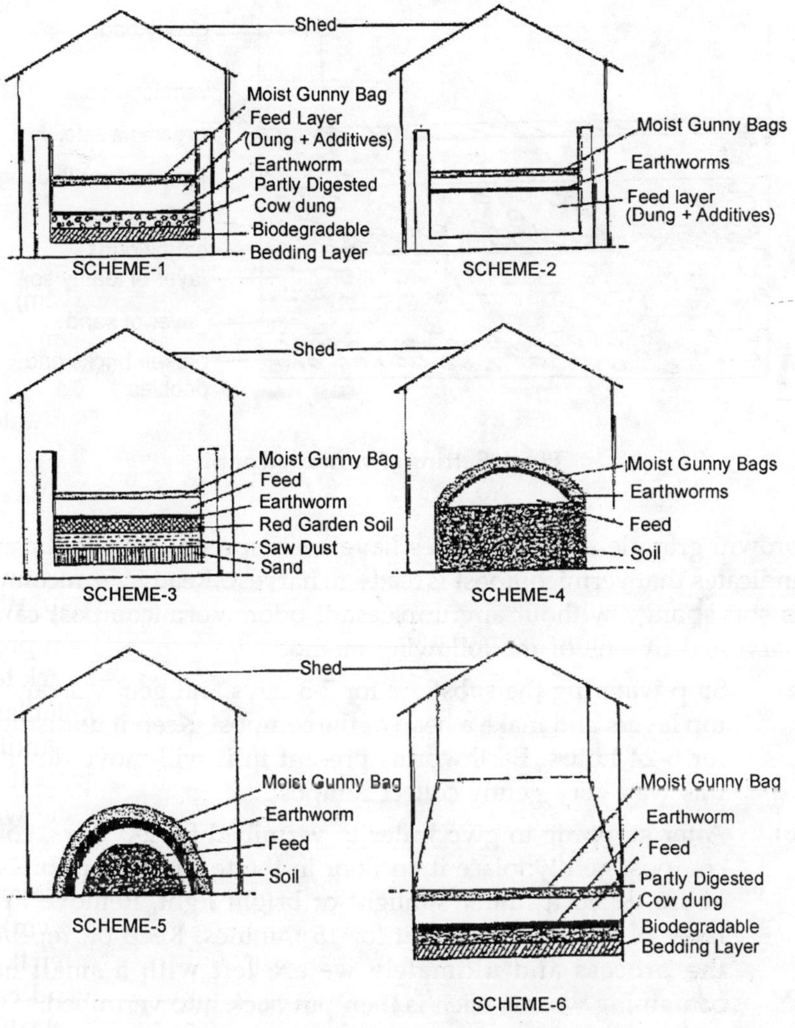

Figure -3. Setting of vermicomposting beds

from one bed, another bed many be started in such a way optimum utilization of labor is there. Due to economic reasons such units are recommended.

(n) Harvesting and packing of vermicompost

When the top layer of vermicomposting substrate becomes dark

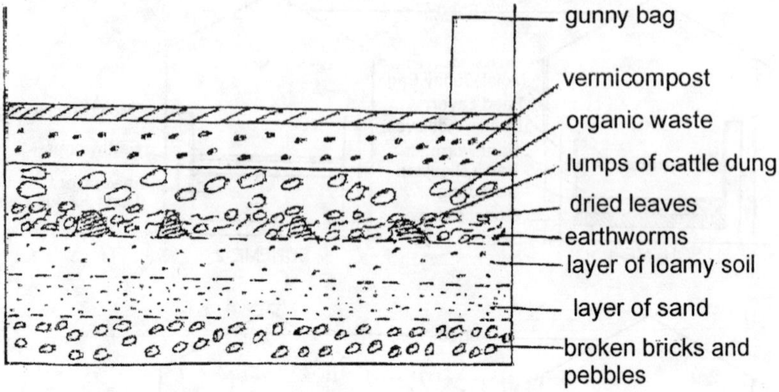

Fig. 4. Setting of vermibed or pit

brown, granule as if tea leaves have been spread over the layer, it indicates that vermicompost is ready to harvest. Ready vermicompost is soft spongy without any unpleasant odor. Vermicompost can be harvested by one of the following methods.

a) Stop watering the substrate for 2-3 days and gently scrape the top layers and make a heap of the compost. Keep it undisturbed for 6-24 hours. Earthworms present in it will move down. In this way very gently collect compost.

b) After stopping to give water to vermibed for 2-3 days, collect compost gently; place it on floor in the form of heap for 24-36 hours. Keep it under sunlight or bright light. Remove upper layer of compost and wait for 15 minutes. Keep on repeating the process and ultimately we are left with a small mass containing worms wich is then put back into vermibed.

c) After discontinuing irrigation for 2-3 days, add a fresh layer of feed on the surface and irrigate to moist the fresh layer. After 5-7 days skim the top 10 cm layer. This method ensures 80 percent of the removal of worms. A second feeding can bring out of 90 to 92 of harvesting of worms.

d) Another very convenient and effective method of separating worms from compost is that when the vermibeds are being set up leave a gap of 1 m between two successive beds. After the completion of composting in between two beds put a fresh feedstock. Earthworms will move from mature beds to newly constructed bed. After 5-7 days, remove the mature bed containing vermicompost.

e) Earthworms can also be separated from compost by sieving through a mesh of size 2-2.5 mm. Undecomposed and larger pieces can be returned to vermibeds for their complete composting.

In other countries mechanical harvesters are being used for separation of earthworm from compost. For example in Cuba mechanical harvester called 'Circular Cilindrica" (cylindrical, circulars chute) is used for this purpose. Collected vermicompost can be stocked on ground under shade. After passing it through mesh of size 2-2.5 mm, pack them in plastic bags and put a label. It should retain moisture contents of 20-25 per cent. Do not let it dry otherwise activity of many beneficial enzymes, hormones and microbes will be reduced.

(o) Transportation of earthworms and cocoons

As vermicomposting proceeds, a stage is attained when surplus number of earthworms is present. These can be sold to other vermiculturists for various other usages. In such a situation transport of earthworms arises. As cocoons occupy less space and are economical to transport so sometimes they are also in demand. Cocoons are handpicked with brush. But it is very laborious and time consuming. In order to produce a large number of earthworms and cocoons in reduced volume, here is presented an ideal technique (Werner and Cuevas,1996). On a vermibed keep layer of papers on top of it. Put a layer of cattle dung. Earthworm lay cocoons in between paper layers. The cocoons can be easily collected and transported. If large population of earthworm is required, the cocoons may be allowed to hatch and after 30 days a large population of earthworms is available.

Collected cocoons are packed in some container in same substrate from which they are collected. The medium is moistened a bit. Feed material should be ½ g per cocoon for 24 hours of transportation journey. Pack cocoons gently in any clean perforated container. *viz.,* softly put a muslin bag which is put in any other plastic jar having perforeated lid for aeration. Final postal packing or Air Freight Packing should also be perforated.

Similarly, pack earthworms with moist fed substrate in a plastic container with perforated lid. Container space should be ½ $inch^3$ per individual. During transportation journey, each individual is given 1.5 g feed for 24 hours. One litre capacity jar can hold 200-500 earthworms. For short journeys, earthworms can also be packed in plastic buckets with perforated lid.

(p) Frecautions

1. Vermicomposting site should be under shade and preferably on some elevated land to prevent stagnation of water.
2. Length and breadth of bed and pit can be selected according to availability of space.
3. Protect vermibed against direct sunlight and rain.
4. In areas of plentiful rainfall, avoid pit formation.
5. Moisture content during vermicomposting should be maintained between 30-40 per cent.
6. The pH of substrate should be between 6.8-7.5. If large quantities of pine leaves or fruits are to be composted, add some lime.
7. Once or twice a week keep on turning the medium. The process ensures aeration of the medium so that composting activity of aerobes and earthworms is faster.
8. Intruduce earthworm @ 1000 worms per m^2 surface area.
9. Keep on covering the beds with coconut or palmyrah fronds or other broad leaves or jute bags. Do not cover with plastic sheets as it will trap heat and gases and will harm earthworms. Experiment conducted (Table -5) by the authors on waste brinjal fruits reveals that vermicomposting is faster when beds are covered.
10. For increasing efficiency of vermicomposting it is preferable to use predecomposed feed for earthworms.
11. Each feed layer should not excced 10-15 cm. after completion of vermicomposting second layer of same depth may be added and so on. In this way make ultimate height of bed upto 60-70 cm.

(q) Use of vermicompost for crop production

Vermicompost is rich in nutrients, which are present in readily available form for plants. Besides nutrients, compost also contains plant growth hormones, promoters and number of microbes, which are essential for plant and soil health. Vermicompost added to soil act as an ideal soil conditioner.

Several reports are available that indicate the beneficial effect of vermicompost on various crops. Tomar *et al,* (1999) reported brinjal and carrot production per pot treated with vermicompost as 97.0 g and 44.94 g against 65.0 g and 29.90 g, respectively in untreated control. Palta (2003) also reported increase in yield of brinjal plants. In case of tomato plants 157.45 and 78.33 per cent increase in number of flower and fruits over untreated control after treatment with vermicompost were reported. (Singh and Palta, 2003). Production of grass, wheat and clover increases many times in the presence of earthworms (Rhee, 1965). Growth of maize (Spain *et al,* 1992) and ornamental plants(Kale *et al,*1987) has also been reported.

With the increasing awareness of organic food and organic farming, importance of vermicompost in agriculture is increasing. Vermicompost can be added at the time of field preparation. The dose of vermicompost for cereal crop is 5 tons/ha and for vegetable crops is 10-12 tons/ha. In case of fruit trees, make a ring around the tree that is ½ to 1 foot deep and 1 to 2 feet wide. Fill it with vermicompostand water it after mulching. Alternatively, several small pits are made around the tree and are filled with compost then mulching and watering should be done. For preparing garden pots, mix 10 to 40 parts of vermicompost with garden soil and fill the pots, Next dose may be repeated after 30-45 days according to requirements. In garden pots use vermicompost @ 100 g per pot (Lal *et al.,* 2001; Palta, 2002). After applying vermicompost, it is finally covered with some organic matter comprising dry leaves, weeds, husk, coir or even old hesian. This process is called mulching and then watering should be done. The process of mulching keeps the system of microbes and growth promoters in active and dynamic form for a longer duration and finally adds beneficial effect on plants.

Conclusion

Due to explosion of urban population, industrialization and changed style of living, waste production is likely to increase by tremendous amount and the problem will become more serious than the present day. So it is important to find its solution presently before it goes too late. The root causes of the problems are: lack of awareness, knowledge, skills, and unconcerned attitude of general public and absence of real and practical policies on waste management. Insufficient management and disposal of water is leading to degradation of environment and is causing health hazards. Some of the suggesations to tackle the problems are as follows:

The general public should be made aware about the environmental and health consequences of throwing wastes here and there in an unorganized way.

Those units or technologies producing excess and problematic wastes should be discouraged.

Use of disposable substances or 'use and throw' technologies should be discouraged.

For effective management of solid waste, public awareness and supportive response is necessary. The people should be ready to use shared waste containers, their willingness to segregate the wastes, readiness to pay for waste management services and should not oppose setting up of waste treatment units in their area provided it is highly objectionable.

Decrease production of waste by practising **three Rs**:- Reduce, Reuse and Recycle.

Reduce means source reduction and wasting less. It prevents generation of waste in the first place. It includes purchase of long lasting products. It discourages use of disposable products. **Reuse** means reusing the product to same purpose or for some other purpose. For example, use of refilling bottles, use of refillable pens, empty jars can be used as domestic containers, reusing boxes etc. **Recycling** turns a waste into resource. It has environmental, financial and social benefits. It is important that waste should be segregated at the source itself into recyclable and biodegradable wastes. Recyclable waste like paper, metal, glass, plastics etc. can be recycled and generate revenue for the collector and will increase employment potential in recycling sector. We should buy recycled product to encourage recycling industry. Recycling also includes composting of biodegradable wastes by conventional composting and vermicomposting. Recycling has many benefits like it suppplies valuable raw resources for our children's future. By reducing, recycling and reusing,the quantity of garbage going to SLF can be reduced by 40 per cent. This would automatically increase life of SLF and prevent release of several greenhouse gases and wastes pollutants. It is worth mentioning that Municipal Corporation of Delhi (MCD) has decided to opt for 'Zero Waste Management' strategy for long-term solid waste management. Projected waste production in Delhi is going to increase from its present 6000-7000 tons to 17,000 to 20,000 tons by the year 2020. Under 'Zero Waste Management'strategy household would have to adopt the twin bin system blue for recyclable waste and the green one for biodegradable wastes. In this context major mass awareness is required for which NGOs and resident welfare association will play major role.

For managing solid wastes effectively, a multi-pronged approach is required instead of depending on one tecnology. In this contenxt a good example is being set-up by MCD. MCD is in the process of preparing a Master Plan for next 20 years for waste management. The plan suggests provision of engineered sanitary landfill sites, besides composting; refuse developed fuel, construction material for development and methanization. A study has estimated that MCD would require an investment of more than Rs. 37000 crores till 2024 for SWM. If the plan were properly executed, the solid waste would genrate an income of over Rs. 2,850 crores. It means an investment of Rs. 850 crores is required in the next 20 years on waste management (The Hindu, June, 13, 2004).

There is need to change the attitude towards waste. So the wastes should not be considered as waste rather it is a resource for generating income and employment. The Tata Energy Research Institute has set up two plants, including the one in NOIDA, UP where organic wastes are treated effectively for generation of energy. So waste, that is creating so many problems, can be wealth.

The issue of waste is inextricably linked with urban poverty. In our country, over a million people are linked with collection, segregation and recycling of waste. An NGO, Srishti conducted a recycling reserach and identified many types of new materials that can be recycled by some appropriate technology. In the interest of such people there is need to integrate existing system instead of replacing them blindly with new technology from other developed countries (Gupta, 2001).

The MSW Rules, 2000 requires that 'biodegradable wastes shall be processed by composting. So authorities should have provision for providing easy subsidiary for composting unit and should develop markets for compost so that more and more people can adopt vermicomposting.

Important factors which should be considered before framing waste policies are: waste composition, social and religious customs, climate and seasonal differences, budget, standard of living, management and technical resources. Such factors may vary from one region to other so will vary their management practices. Here is an example in support of given point. Incinerators are very successful in developed countries. An incineration plant based on Dutch technology was set up in Delhi to generate power at a cost of Rs. 220 million. It ran for just one week in 1984 as the calorific value of the waste was far less than required to run it. In such cases adding wheat, paddy, sorghum and other agricultural wastes may increase calorific value of the waste. So multidisciplinary researches with support from government is required on the issue.

Management of hazardous and hospital wastes is also difficult. The best way to handle such waste is to reduce their generation at source. The generator of the waste should be given responsibility to manage it. After the notification of the Biomedical Waste Rules, 1998, the establishments have to carry the process of waste segregation, collection, treatment and disposal. Many large hospitals have made such waste treatment facilities. For units producing electronic wastes, MCD is on way to introduce producer-end responsibility for disposal of e-waste.

For better management of solid waste, cost benefit analysis of existing solid waste management system is required.

Various NGOs may play a vital role in managing solid wastes. They should be given judicial powers by slapping fines on litterbugs. Awareness should be developed against littering. Enforcement of laws should be strict. The Delhi high court has recently directed MCD to slap fines on those throwing plastic waste and garbage at in appropriate places.Such measures are very effective and will make the differences provided they are properly implemented.

Our earth is a beautiful planet to live. For bright future of man we have to keep it neat and clean otherwise our survival on this planet will be in danger. We must remember that by mismanaging waste we are depriving our people of precious fuel (biogas) and our land by valuable nutrients. It is right time to wake and manage waste appropriately.

References

Anonymous, 2003. New strategy to tackle garbage disposal. *The Hindu*, June 24th, 2003.

Anonymous, 2004. Master plan for waste management on the anvil. *The Hindu*, June 13th, 2004

Bhatnagar, R.K. and Palta, R.K. 1996a. *Earthworm: Vermiculture and Vermicomposting*, Kalyani Publishers. p. 106.

Bhatnagar, R.K. and Palta, R.K. 1996b. Insect pest control in vermiculture, substrates. *Shashpa,* **3** (1) : 79-80.

Dominguez, J. 1997. Testing the impact of vermicomposting. *Biocycle,* April 1997, p. 58.

Dominguez, J., Edwards, C.A. and Subler, S. 1997. A comparison of vermicomposting and composting, *Biocycle.* April, p. 57-59.

Gupta, S.K. 2001. Rethinking waste management in India. *Humanscape,* April 20th, 2001.

Ismail, S.A. 1997. *Vermicomposting: The Biology of Earthworms,* Orient Longman, p. 92.

Kale, R. D., Bano, K., Sreenivasa, M.N. and Bagyaraj, D.J. 1987. Influence of wormcast (Vee. Comp. E. UAS'83) on the growth and mycorrhizal colonization of two ornamental plants. *South Indian Horticulture,* **35** : 433-437

Kalia, V.C., Raizada, N. and Somokya, V. 2000. The possible approaches for the management of wastes and their potential to generate electricity. *National Vigyan Conference on Swadeshi Vigyan.* IARI, New Delhi.

Lal, O.P., Palta, R.K. and Srivastava, Y.N.2001. Vermicomposting (Hindi). p.63-65. **In:** *Krishi Adharit Vyavasaya Takniki.* Subhash Chandra (ed.). Extension Bulletin No. 4. Agriculture Training and Information Centre, IARI, New Delhi.

Palta, R.K. 2001. Evaluation of some media for centre of sewage worm, *Eisenia fetida. National symposium on plant protection strategies for sustainable agrihorticulture,* 12-13 October, Jammu, p. 53-54.

Palta, R.K. 2002. Role of vermicomposting in safe management of wastes. *Vigyan Bharti Pradeepika,* **8** (1):39-44.

Palta, R.K. 2003. Response of vermicompost on brinjal plants. 2nd *International Congress of Plant Physiology on Sustainable Plant Productivity under changing Environment.* 8-12 January, 2003.I.A.R.I., New Delhi, p. 403.

Palta, R.K. and Bhatnagar, R.K. 2002. Tests on culture substrate for Indian species of earthworm, *Metaphire posthuma* (Valliant) 4th Indian Agricultural Scientist and Farmers'Congress. 16-17 February, CCS University, Meerut, p. 20-21.

Palta, R.K.and Srivastava, C.2001. Feed substrate preference by earthworms, *Eisenia fetida, National Symposium on Ancient Indian Science and Technology Interfaced with Modern Knowledge.* 14-15 December, IARI, New Delhi, p. 110-111.

Rhee, J.A.van.1965. Earthworm activity and plant growth in artificial cultures. *Plant Soil,* **22**: 45-48.

Singh, J.P. and Sharma, C.V.2001. Karbonic Kheti, p. 48-55. **In**:*Krishi Adharit Vyawasaya Techniki*. Subhash Chander (ed.). Extension Bulletin No. 4. Agriculture Training and Extension Centre.IARI, New Delhi.

Singh, V.S. and Palta, R.K. 2003. Effect of vermicompost on flowering and fruiting of tomato. *National symposium on integrated pest management in horticultural crops for protection of environment and biodiversity*. 10-12 February, Chhindwara, M.P.

Spain, A.V., Lavelle, P. and Mariotti, A.1992. Stimulation of plant growth by tropical earthworms. *Soil Biology and Biochemistry*, **24**: 1629-1633.

Tomar, V.K., Bhatnagar, R.K. and Palta, R.K.1998. Kenchuye dwara nirmit compost ka bangan aur gajar utpadan par prabhav. (Hindi). *Bhartiya Krishi Anusandhan Patrika*, **13**: 3/4 :153-156.

Upadhyay, D.K. and Soni, S. 2002. Kachra Prabandhan (Hindi). *Vasundhara Institute of Bio-agricultural Research and Development*. Champa. p.1-19.

Vidhi, Yves Loerincik and Maheshwari, R.C. 2000.Availability and disposal of waste in Developing Countries. *J. Bio Energy*. **1** (2): 85-90.

Werner, M. and Cuevas, J.R.1996. Vermiculture in Cuba. *Biocycle*. June, p. 57-61.

Chapter **3**

Organic Matter Decomposition and Vermicompost Enrichment Technology

D. Radhakrishna

Department of Agricultural Microbiology, University of Agricultural Sciences, G.K.V.K. Campus, Bangalore-560 065.

Organic matter decomposition is the process of biological conversion of complex organic substances to simple readily available substances by the combined action of a mixed microbial population. This process is called composting and the product obtained is the compost. The quality of the organic manure depends on the organic product. Composting of organic wastes is one of the important parts in nutrient cycling. This is governed by the biotic as well as abiotic factors. The composting process has two limitations (1) the process is prolonged over a period, often depending on the chemical constituents of organic matter and (2) the low nutrient quality. Therefore the strategy of the process is to manipulate for rapid biotransformations of organic materials and to enrich the wastes for enhanced nutrient value. The composting ecology is best understood by studying the biotic and abiotic factors that are specifically influencing the microbial community activity within the composting ecosystem (Bagyaraj and Radhakrishna, 2000).

Compost Process

Compost is an aerobic process involving the microbiological decomposition of organic constituents in waste under controlled conditions. Composting process can be basically divided into four phases, namely,

(a) An initial stage or low active phase during which the readily available constituents are used up leading to rise in temperature.

(b) Thermophilic or elevated temperature phase, the period normally lasting for 45 to 60 days, based mainly on the chemical nature of the substrates used (if woody components more, the cellulolytic activity will be predominant at this phase),

(c) Curing or cooling stage, a period of decline in temperature, along with the recolonization and establishment of the mesophilic populations, the activity tending towards stabilization of the process,

(d) Maturity or the stabilization phase, wherein the decompostion rates decrease, mesophilic population density becomes predominant, leading to the formation of humus.

With the advancement in processing technology and the concepts, the decomposition of the organic wastes is at the crossroads of an important position in balancing the ecosystem and also the sustenance of soil productivity. Organic substrates such as crop residues, food processing wastes etc. with adequate moisture and proper aeration in presence of a mixed population of microorganisms, results in the bioconversion, along with the increase in microbial biomass, metabolite production and CO_2 evolution. From this basic process of decompostion different end products could be obtained by various amendments either to improve the nutrient status of the finished product or provide nutrients to sitmulate the growth of a specific group of microorganism which under high population density express the biological activities that may lead to the enhancement of plant growth, control the incidence of soil-borne plant pathogens or enrigh low grade nutrients or the production of value based product. The composts thus prepared when applied to soil, influence the soil fertility, biocontrol of pathogens or help in bioremediation of the toxic soils, Even though decomposition can take place both under aerobic and anaerobic situations, aerobic process of decomposition of waste is preferred for faster degradation and for quicker rise in temperature (>60°C) of the composting bulk. In several studies the chemical composition of plant residues and nature of microbial flora have been identified as factors in the decomposition process and nutrient release (Berendse *et al.*, 1987). The rate of decomposition is also influenced by moisture, temperature, pH and oxygen with secondary influences including the age of plant material. By proper management of these wastes either individually or collectively in combination become the process production for quality end product, the compost (Radhakrishna and Bagyaraj, 1998).

The chemical composition of a substrate is a selective factor for the determination of the microbial activity, resulting in the formation of metabolic products influencing the composting ecosystem. Composting means piling up crop residues and other farm wastes in layers to make them decompose quickly. Composting is done to produce an organic fertilizer that is balanced in plant nutrients. This organic fertilizer, improves soil fertility, moisture retention and soil aeration. Compost can be used in all soils with low fertility. It is especially good in areas that have low rainfall; it is also useful in sandy soils, which have poor water-holding capacity. Compost improves the structure and drainage of all soils. Maintaining soil fertility is one of the most important things farmers can do.

Compost Processing Strategies

The processing strategy can be better developed, based on certain specific conditions, more particularly, the nature of the substrate, temperature of decomposition and aeration, along with the activity of microorganisms. Even though much research has been done on the qualitative nature of microorganisms in composts, very little information exists on the activity of diverse groups of microorganisms present during composting.

Compost is an aerobic process involving the microbiological decomposition of organic constituents in wastes under controlled conditions. The microbial population that take part in the process belongs to both thermophilic as well as mesophilic organisms (De Bertoldi *et al.*, 1987). Composting process can be basically divided into four phases, namely, (a) an initial stage or low active phase during which the readily available constituents are used up leading to rise in temperature, (b) thermophilic or elevated temperature phase, the period normally lasting for 45 to 60 days, based mainly on the chemical nature of the substrates used (if woody component is more, the cellulolytic activity will be predominant at this phase), (c) curing or cooling stage, a period of decline in temperature, along with the recolonization and establishment of the mesophilic population, the activity tending towards stabilization of the process, (d) maturity or the stabilization phase, wherein decomposition rates decrease, mesophilic population density become predominant, leading to the formation of humus.

With the advancement in processing technology and the concepts,the decomposition of the organic wastes is at the crossroads of an important position in balancing the ecosystem and also the sustenance of soil productivity. The available resource materials for composting are varied. Any organic rich substrate can be utilized for, the process. Organic substrates such as crop residues, food processing wastes and effluents, animal wastes, sewage sludge etc., with adequate moisture and proper aeration in presence of a mixed population of microorganisms, result in the bioconversion, along with the increase in microbial biomass metabolite production and CO_2 evolution. From this basic process of decomposition different end products could be obtained by various amendments through microbial inoculants either to improve the nutrient status of the finished product or provide nutrients to stimulate the growth of a specific group of microorganism which under high population density express the biological activities that may lead to the enhancement of plant growth, control the incidence of soil-borne plant pathogens or enrich low grade nutrients for the production of value-based product. The compost thus prepared when applied to soil will influence the soil fertility, biocontrol of pathogens or help in bioremediation of the toxic soils (Balakrishna *et al.*, 1991)., Even though decomposition can take place both under aerobic and anaerobic situations, aerobic process of decomposition of waste is preferred for faster degradation and for quicker rise in temperature of the composting bulk. Various sources and types of organic substances that are susceptible for microbial attack can be used for composting. Although the thermophilic fungi play a major role in degrading cellulose and other major polymers in composts, the activities of bacteria also are important. Microorganisms are associated with earthworms that are adopted for specific functions facilitating the earthworm activity (Patil *et. al.*, 1998).

Method of composting

The main source of organic materials is the agricultural wastes consisting mainly of crop residues; green leaves, cover crops and all other farm residues including cattle shed wastes. Select organic material of different plant types (crop residues, green leaves, cover crops, etc) from different places (on-farm or off-farm). Production of vermicompost is in two stages. The first phase is the partial decomposition of the organic matter during which process suitable conditions are created for ready acceptability of the substrate by earthworms. The period is for 20 to 30 days depending on the raw materials used. The second phase consists of release of earthworms to the partially degraded organic matter. Earthworms feed such a material very fast and castings appears in 5 to 7 days, which is a indicative of the acceptance of the feed stock.

i. First Phase: Mix different types of organic material, cereal and leguminous crop residues and green leaf. The mixing of residues are important to adjust the C:N ratio to around 60:1 for rapid decompostion by the microorganisms. Mix eight parts of non-legume residues with two parts of legume crop residue (8:1). There are different techniques for the enhancement of initial phase of decomposition. Some of the common methods are:

a. Nutrient additives: Addition of nutrient elements basically depend on the chemical composition the raw materials used in the process. Generally nitrogen rich plant materials are recommended for narrowing the C/N ratio of the organic wastes, so as to increase the microbial activity. These inputs also bring about nutrient enrichment of the finished compost.

b. Microbial inoculants: The manipulations of the factors of composting are done mainly to enhance the microbial activity, where the rate of decomposition of the organic wastes is enhanced. Organic wastes contain natural microflora to bring about the decomposition under suitable environmental conditions. The microbial inoculant is for selective degradation (Patil *et. al.*, 1999), posphate solubilization and nitrogen fixation. The inoculants found to promote the composting process are the fungi such as *Aspergillus, Trichurus, Trichoderma, Phanerochaete,* etc., these biodegrading fungi reduce the composting period by about three weeks. The enriched compost through microbial inoculants has been reported to have higher nutrient content and there by enhancing the crop yields.

c. Method of preparation: Choose a sheltered site for the compsot pile. Chop up long stems and big leaves for quick action by decomposing microbes. Organic materials are piled layer by layer. Sprinkle adequate water on every layer, and ensure that the compost is moist all the time (moisture maintained at 70%). The compost heap usually heats up in 24-48 hours. Heat should be maintained at 60°C or higher. The compost activator, consisting of a cellulolytic fungus, is broadcast onto the substrates during piling. The amount of activator used is usually 0.5% of the total weight of the substrates (i.e. about 5 kg compost activator per 1000 kg substrate). Decomposition is faster if the activator is mixed thoroughly with the substrate. A greater amount of activator can be used if faster decomposition is desired. Turn the pile every 3-4 weeks for providing better aeration. Protect that finished compost from sun,wind and rain. Don't use materials the might contaminate the soil. Don't step on the pile and compact the layers. Don't use waxy leaves (such as eucalyptus leaves). Avoid over-watering the compost pile and use of materials that do not decompose.

ii. Second Phase: Vermicomposting: Partial decomposed organic matter used for vermicompost preparation. Initial decomposition of compost critically affects the successful production of vermicompost and its further application in agriculture, especially as an organic manure and soil conditioner. Immature composts with high C/N ratio when applied to soil results in the immobilization of mineral nitrogen causing nitrogen deficiency to the plants. But vermicomposts with optimum C/N ratio makes ready available the nutrients to the plant uptake. Low C:N ratio composts cause ammonium toxicity and interfere with plant growth.

The compost with a C:N ratio of 20:1 is ideal. Earthworms are introduced into the composting system to hasten the process of decomposition. Earthworms are released into the decomposing wastes after a period of 15 to 20 days of preliminary decomposition. They act as good pulverisers of organic matter and promote microbial activity. Higher mineralizing properties of the microorganisms during decomposition resulted in increased urease activity in vermicompost when agricultural wastes amended with cattle dung and RP (Fig. 1). The organic matter passes through the gut and is release as castings that are rich in nutrients. Because of burrowing nature of earthworms, compactness is losened and better aeration is provided. This process is known as vermicomposting. The common species of earthworms used are *Eisenia fetida, Eudrilus eugeniae* and *Perionyx excavatus* which have increasing effectivenss of composting organic wastes. After partial decomposition for a period of 30 days the decomposed materials are rich in nitrogen. At this stage introducing earthworms results in higher worm activity, hence formation of worm castings will be faster.

Vermicompost as organic fertilizer:

One of the main limiting factors of the vermicomposting system to be used as an organic fertilizer is low nutrient quality. Enrichment of vermicompost is by blending with nutrient rich organic materials with desired nutrient elements and inoculation of efficient microorganisms to bio-inoculants (Patil *et al.,* 1999). Such an enriched product is required for intensive crop production, (Gowda *et. al.,* 1991). The manurial value of different types of organic manures on

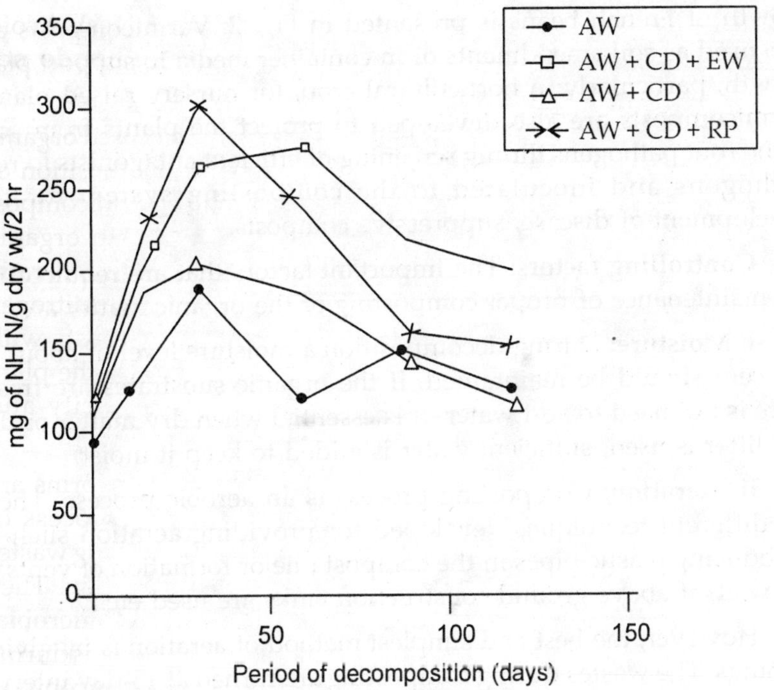

Fig. 1. Changes in urease activity during decomposition process

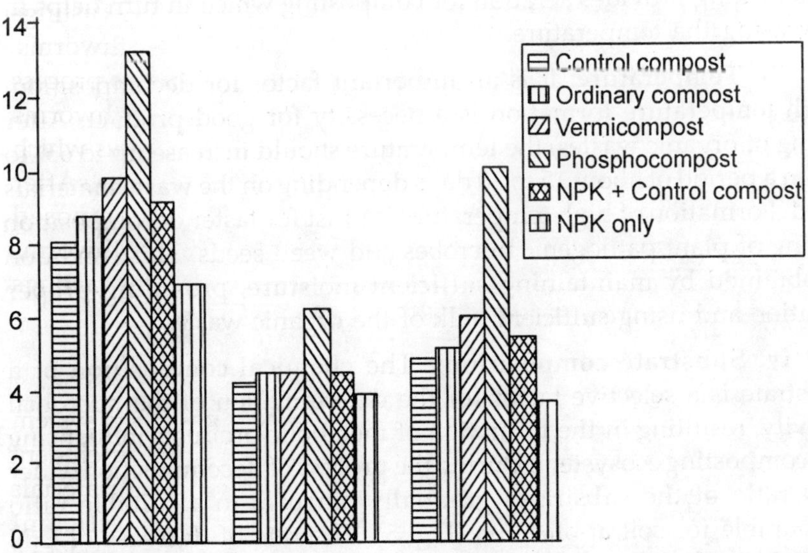

Fig. 2. Manurial evauation of different composts

growth of French beans is presented in Fig. 2. Vermicomposts are also used as soil amendments or in container media to support plant growth, particularly in horticultural crop, for nursery raised plants. Vermicomposts are also developed to protect the plants from soil-borne root pathogens throug screening of efficient antagonists to root pathogens and inoculated to the composting system for the development of disease, suppressive composts.

Controlling factors: The important factors that are required for the maintenance of proper composting of the organic matter are:

i. Moisture: During decomposition a moisture level of about 70 per cent should be maintained. If the organic substrates are fresh, there is not need to add water. It is essential when dry matter or dry leaf litter is used, sufficient water is added to keep it moist.

ii. Aeration: Composting process is an aerobic process. There are different techniques developed for providing aeration such as introducing plastic pipes in the compost pile or formation of vents in the walls if above ground construction tanks are used etc.

However, the best and simplest method of aeration is by giving turnings. The wastes during composting are turned at 15-day interval or monthly interval depending on the nature of the organic wastes. This turning provides aeration for composting which in turn helps in increasing the temperature.

iii. Temperature: It is an important factor for decomposition. High temperature formation is a necessity for good product. After piling of organic wastes, the temperature should increase up to 65° to 72° in a period of about 15 to 20 days depending on the waste materials used. Formation of high temperature is must for faster decomposition killing of plant pathogenic microbes and weed seeds. This condition is obtained by maintaining sufficient moisture, providing proper aeration and using sufficient bulk of the organic wastes.

iv. Substrate composition: The chemical composition of a substrate is a selective factor for the determination of the microbial activity, resulting in the formation of metabolic products influencing the composting ecosystem. During the process of decomposition wider C:N ratio of the substrates gradually narrows to a suitable ratio favourable for soil application (Fig. 3). The rate of decrease of C:N ratio depends on the nature of amendments. The available substrate per unit volume generally provides the requirement for aeration as well as heat transfer. The earthworm's activity increased in

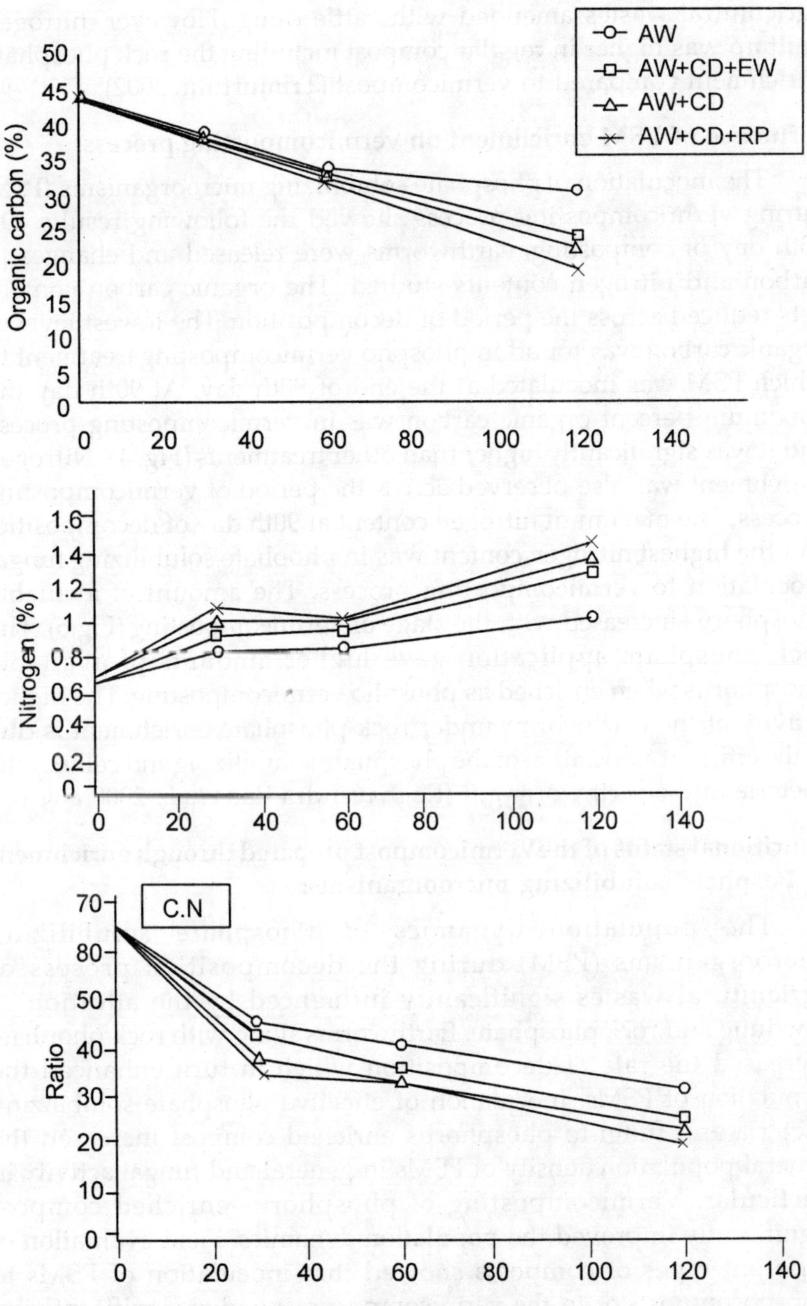

Fig. 3. Changes in Carbon, Nitrogen and C : N ratio during decomposition process. Aw: agricultural wastes, CD: cattle dung, EW: earthworms, RP: rock phosphate

agricultural wastes amended with cattle dung. However, nitrogen built up was higher in regular compost including the rock phosphate enrichment compared to vermicompost (Trimurtulu, 2002).

Influence of PSM enrichment on vermicomposting process:

The inoculation of phosphate solubilizing microorganisms (PSM) during vermicomposting process showed the following results. On 30th day of composting, earthworms were released and changes in carbon and nitrogen contents studied. The organic carbon content gets reduced across the period of decomposition. The lowest level of organic carbon was found in phospho vermicomposting treatment to which PSM was inoculated at the end of 90th day. At 90th day the maximum percent organic carbon was in vermicomposting process and it was significantly higher than other treatments (Fig. 4). Nitrogen enrichment was also observed across the period of vermicomposting process. The maximum nitrogen content at 90th day of decomposition and the highest nitrogen content was in phophate solubilizing fungal inoculation to vermicomposting process. The amount of available phosphorus increased with the stage of vermicomposting (Fig.5). The rock phosphate application gave higher amounts of available phosphorus when enriched as phospho vermicomposting. The higher activity of the earthworms under rock phosphate enrichment is due to the efficient association of the phosphate solubilizing and cellulolytic bacteria in the earthworm gut (Raghavendra Rao *et al.,* 2000 a & b).

Nutritional status of the Vermicompost prepared through enrichment of Posphate solubilizing microorganisms:

The population dynamics of Phosphate solubilizing microorganisms (PSM) during the decomposition process of agricultural wastes significantly influenced by the addition of cowdung and rock phosphate. Earthworms along with rock phophate increased the rate of decomposition which in turn enhanced the population of PSMs. Inoculation of effective phosphate solubilizing bacteria and fungi to phosphorus enriched compost increased the general population density of PSMs in general and fungal activity in particular. Vermicomposting of phosphorus-enriched compost significantly improved the population dynamics. Field evaluation of different types of composts showed that inoculation of PSMs to phospocomposts or to the vermicompost responded significantly on plant growth and pod yield of French beans. This study indicates the technology to be adopted for all leguminous crops with phosphorus requirement.

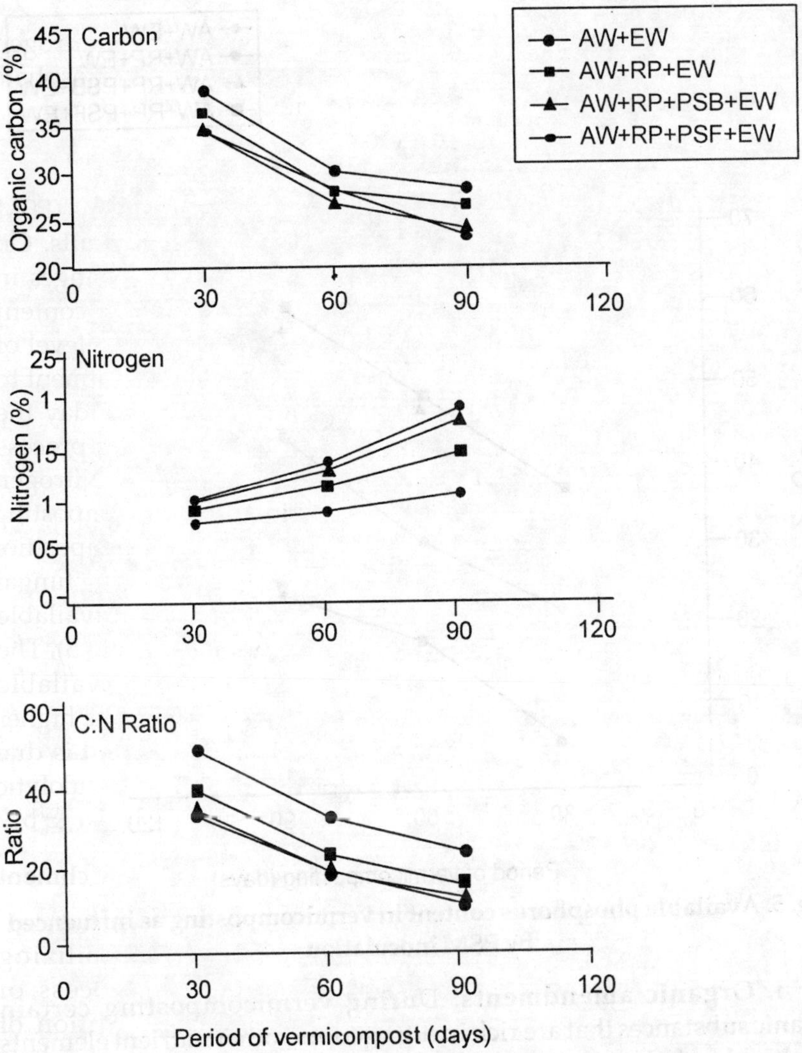

Fig. 4. Effect of PSM inoculation on chemical composition of vermicomposting process.

Enrichment of Vermicompost: During vermicomposting different types of enrichment techniques such as organic amendments, mineral additives and microbial inoculation can be taken up for improving the quality and quantity of the vermicompost produced.

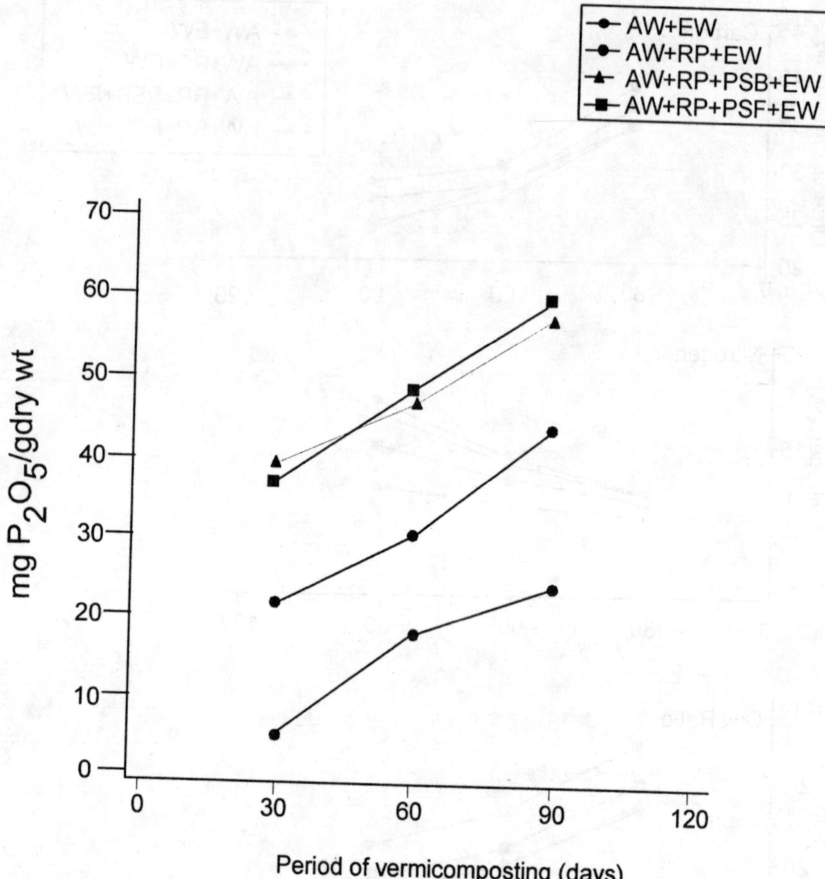

Fig. 5. Available phosphorus content in vermicomposting as influenced by PSM inoculation

i. Organic amendments: During vermicomposting certain organic substances that are rich in nitrogen and other nutrient elements can be blended a proper C:N ratio to improve the quality of the vermicompost to be used as soil conditioner and as a source of nutrients for crop production.

ii. Mineral additives: Different minerals like rock phosphate can be added layer by layer during composting to get posphorus enriched compost. The level of RP may be 12.5% to 25% depending on the P enrichment. Earthworm activity was not affected under these levels of rock phophate. Along with addition of rock phosphate, phosphate solubilizing microorganisms either *Bacillus megaterium* or *Aspergillus awamori* is inoculated at the rate of one or two kg per ton of wastes for solubilization of insoluble phosphates.

iii. Microbial inoculation: Microbial inoculation during vermicomposting is done for two reasons.

(a) Inoculation of lignin and cellulolytic fungi for hastening the decomposition process are *Phenerocheate chrysosporium, Pleurotus sp., Pacelomyces fuscisporus, Trichurus spiralis* and Municipal solid wastes in addition to fungal inoculants, bacteria such as *Bacillus subtilis, Acetobacter aceti* and *Lactobacillus* sp., that are proteolytic and amylolytic are added as process activators. These culture mass multiply in these organic matter and at vermicomposing phase provide a bioactive substrate for earthworms which in turn stimulates the growth and biochemical activities of the earthworms.

(b) Microbial inoculation for quality improvement: The low nutrient status of the compost improved by inoculation of bacterial and fungal culture. Bacterial inoculants such as *Azotobacter, Azospirillum* are added to decomposing materials after a period of 30 days of vermicomposting. These nitrogen-fixing cultures increase in population and enhance the nitrogen content. The fungal culture such as *Trichoderma harzianum, T. viride* or bacteria like *Bacillus coaugulan* are also inoculated after 30 days of vermicomposting. These cultures multiply and improve the qualtiy of the final product by producing antimicrobial metabolites and plant-growth promoting substances. These microbial inoculants are added at the rate of 2 kg/ton impart biocontrol character to the vermicompost.

Compost maturity

Maturity of the vermicompost critically affects the successful application in agriculture, especially as on organic manure and soil conditioner. Immature compost with high C/N ratio when applied to soil results in the immobilization of mineral nitrogen causing nitrogen deficiency to the plants. Compost with very low C/N ratio causes ammonium toxicity and interferes with plant growth (Inbar *et. al.*, 1990).

Conclusion:

The management of organic matter decomposition process for the production of compost is very much significant in various ways. Enrichment of vermicompost for enhanced plant nutrients supply is one of the primary supplements to inorganic fertilizers. Microbial inoculation to the vermicompost necessitates the introduction of microbial diversity to the soil ecosystem, which in turn takes part in soil mineralization activities, and sustenance of soil fertility. The additional benefits of the enriched vermicompost are to maintain the physical, chemical and biological properties of soil and to improve the soil fertility level. Proper composting of city garbage, crop residue, farm wastes and food processing wastes by regulating substrate composition under controlled environmental conditions.

References:

Bagyaraj, D.J. and Radhakrishna, D. 2000. Recent advances in composting. In "Vistas in Mycology and plant pathlogy. eds. Gangawane, Commonwealth pub. p. 88-100.

Balakrishna, A.N. Radhakrishna, D. Srinivas K.N. Gowda. T.K.S. 1991. Enrichment of municipal waste compost with urea, Curr. Res. 20: 161-162.

Berendsc, F., Berg. B. and Bosatta, E. 1987. The effect of lignin and nitrogen on the decomposition of litter in nutrient-poor ecosystem: a theoretical approach. *Can. J. Bot.* 65 : 1116-1120.

De Bertoldi, M., Ferranti, M.P., L' hermite, P., and Zucconi, F. 1987. Compost: Production quality and use. Elsevier, London.

Inbar, Y., Chen, Y., Hadar, V. and Hoitink, HAJ. 1990. New approaches to compost maturity. Biocycle (12): 64-69.

Gowda, T.K.S., Radhakrishna D., Balakrishna, A.N., and Srinivas, K.N., 1991. Studies on the manorial value and nutrient enrichment of municipal waste compost. In proceedings of National seminar on organic farming., Pune. p. 39-41.

Patil, C.R., Radhakrishna, D., Mallesha, B.C and Kale, R.D. 1999. Use of mushroom spent material and earthworms for recycling coirpith.J. Coconut, 29: 7-15.

Patil, C.R., Radhakrishna, D., and Kale, R.D., 1998. An insight on the microbial association with Eudrilus eugeniae-A promising species of earthworm in organic waste recycling. 6th International Symposium on Earthworm Ecology, 1998, Vigo (Spain).

Radhakrishna, D. and Bagyaraj D.J., 1998, Microbial degradation of solid wastes as a source of nutrients. In: "New trends in Microbial Ecology" eds. Bharat Rai and Dkhar, ISCNR, N.E. Hill University, Shillong. p. 108-117.

Raghavendra Rao. B, Radhakrishna, D, and Kale, R. D. 2000, Phosphate solubilizing efficiency of microorganisms isolated from earthworm gut. Vermillennuium, Kala Mazoo, *MI USA, S6-6.*

Radhavendra Rao. B, Radhakrishna, D. and Kale, R.D. 2000. Cellulolytic microbial isolates from gut of Eudrilus eugeniae. Vermillennium, Kala Mazoo, *MI USA-S6-6.*

Trimurtulu, N. 2002. Dynamics of Phosphate solubilizing microorganisms in organic matter decomposition and its impact on plant growth. Ph. D Thesis, University of Agricultural Sciences, Bangalore.

Chapter **4**

Earthworms and Vermicomposting Techniques in Re-cycling of Organic Wastes

R.S. Giraddi

Department of Agricultural Entomology, University of Agricultural Sciences, Dharwad 580 005.

Bio-degradation of organic wastes by earthworms (vermicomposting) is one of the important recent development in biological sciences. Earthworms are responsible for the breakdown of complex organic residues into simple water soluble substance called "Vermicompost".

Vermicompost is chiefly the fecal matter of worms obtained in organic matter recycling. It is a rich source of plant nutrients such as macronutrients (NPK), micronutrients (Fe, Zn, Cu,Mo, B), plant promoter substances and beneficial microflora.

Earthworm species and preferred wastes in vermicomposting

Though more than 12 species of earthworms are used in the world for vermicomposting, the African night crawler, *Eudrilus eugeniae* (Kinberg), the tiger worm, *Eisenia fetida* (Savigny) and compost worm, *Perionyx excavatus* (Perrier) are the prominent species utilized in Karnataka and other parts of the country (Kale and Bano, 1988; Sunitha *et al.*, 1997; Giraddi *et al.*, 2002 and Giraddi and Lingappa, 2002). These species are more preferred in organic wastes management due to their better reproductive traits and adaptability to diverse food substrates.

In India, annually more than 2002 million tons of animal waste, 250-300 million tons of agricultural crop waste besides huge amount of agro-based industrial waste is produced (Ramaswamy, 1998). Earthworms indicated as above, bio-degrade various organic wastes such as agricultural wastes, animal droppings, forest litter and agro-based industrial wastes (Kale *et al.*, 1982, Giraddi *et al.*, 2002). They are known to exhibit preferential acceptability to various organic wastes. Crop wastes such as soybean harvest waste, potato and peanut halms, vegetable waste, crop trash and straw viz., paddy straw, sugarcane and banana trash are known to be more preferred than other wastes such as crop stalks and stubbles which are rich in lignin. Among the animal droppings, cowdung accounts for greater acceptability followed by others; while poultry droppings are not preferred. Status of various key organic wastes in relation to earthworm development and vermicomstability (Giraddi *et al.*, 2000) is presented in Table 1.

Table 1. Earthworm preference to farm wastes and vermicompostability

Sl No.	Type of waste	Cocoon Numbers*	Worm biomass	Vermi-compost (kg)	Waste: Vermi-compost ratio
1.	Potato	15.3	600.5	13.7	1:0.68
2.	Peanut halms	13.6	590.7	11.4	1:0.57
3.	Rice straw	17.0	551.0	12.0	1:0.60
4.	Sugarcane trash	11.0	501.3	11.7	1:0.58
5.	Soybean harvest waste	17.7	704.9	13.6	1:0.68
6.	Maize ear pith	10.0	279.0	10.3	1:0.51
7.	Sunflower head pith	10.4	303.7	10.0	1:0.50
8.	*Parthenium* weed	9.8	255.0	8.4	1:0.42
9.	*Eupotorium* weed	8.5	250.4	8.0	1:0.40
10.	Poultry dropping	2.7	27.0	1.5	1:0.07
11.	Sheep dropping	9.5	310.5	7.5	1:0.37
12.	Cow dung	16.4	820.3	14.3	1:0.71
13.	Control**	20.5	890.0	15.1	1:0.75
	SE ±	1.01	20.8	0.60	-
	CD@ 5%	3.10	63.3	1.80	-

* Nos. per sample size of 50 x 50 x 10 cm.

Initial release of 50 worms per 1.0 x 1.0 x 0.5 cm.

** Mixture of organic wastes (litter: animal dung: green leaves in 65:20:15 ratio)

Soybean waste, potato halms that is produced in large amount after the harvest of tubers, rice straw, sugarcane trash and peanut halms resulted in a better waste:vermicompost ratio than others. Similarly cow dung was more acceptable to worms than other animal droppings.

Presence of toxic chemical, coarse substrate texture, higher amount of cellulose and lignin with lesser water holding capacity etc. are the limitations for vermicomposting of agro-based industrial wastes. However, it is possible to accelerate the vermicompostability of these wastes by adding a palatable and other additives that give the substrate acceptable physical structure. An example of a case study (Giraddi *et al.*, 2002) is given below to explain how good additives accelerate vermicomposting of agro-industrial wastes.

Table 2: Bio-conversion of agro-industrial wastes using peregrine earthworm, *E. eugeniae* in greenhouse

Sl. No.	Treatment	Worm biomass (g)	Cocoon numbers	Vermicompost (kg)
1.	Distillery waste in Pressmud 100%	140.00 (11.85)*	3.1 (1.89)	1.97 (1.57)
2.	Distillery waste in Pressmud 80% + Coir waste 20%	125.83 (12.23)	2.8 (1.81)	2.06 (1.60)
3.	Distillery waste in Pressmud PM 90% + Coir waste 10%	212.50 (14.59)	5.3 (2.40)	3.06 (1.88)
4.	Distillery waste in Pressmud 80% + Sugarcane trash 20%	297.00 (17.23)	6.9 (2.72)	3.60 (2.02)
5.	Distillery waste in Pressmud 90% + Sugarcane trash 10%	271.00 (16.47)	5.9 (2.52)	3.03 (1.87)
6.	Pressmud 100%	100.00 (10.01)	3.0 (1.87)	1.76 (1.50)
7.	Pressmud 80% + Coir waste 20%	123.33 (11.12)	3.3 (1.94)	1.96 (1.57)

Sl. No.	Treatment	Worm biomass (g)	Cocoon numbers	Vermicompost (kg)
8.	Pressmud 90% + Coir waste 10%	143.33 (11.98)	3.6 (2.02)	1.90 (1.54)
9.	Pressmud 80% + Sugarcane trash 20%	279.00 (16.70)	6.5 (2.64)	3.10 (1.89)
10.	Pressmud 90%+ Sugarcane trash 10%	185.15 (13.62)	5.4 (2.42)	2.50 (1.73)
11.	Bagasse 100%	16.66 (4.12)	0.0 (0.07)	0.46 (0.98)
12.	Bagasse 80% + Cow dung 20%	131.66 (11.49)	2.3 (1.67)	1.90 (1.54)
13.	Bagasse 90% + Cow dung 10%	84.16 (9.19)	2.0 (1.58)	1.16 (1.28)
14.	Bagasse 80% + Press mud 20%	41.73 (6.48)	0.5 (1.00)	0.63 (1.06)
15.	Bagasse 90% + Pressmud 10%	31.20 (5.62)	0.0 (0.07)	0.40 (0.94)
16.	Check (Standard recepi)	409.00 (20.23)	7.8 (2.88)	3.90 (2.09)
SE ±x		0.27	0.09	0.03
CD @ 5%		0.76	0.24	0.08
CD @ 1%		0.90	0.31	0.10

$\sqrt{x + 0.5}$ transformations

The data (Table 2 and 3) implies that agro-based industrial wastes and agricultural industry bye-products could be re-cylcled at varying degrees. Pressmud, a chief waste from sugar factories, could be a good substrate to absorb liquid distillery waste which eventually aids in biodegradation of liquid distillery effluent waste.

Similarly, small amounts of coir waste when added gives a good physical structure to pressmud which is otherwise a fine powder-like material. Addition to cow dung to rice husk increases degree of acceptability of substrates by the worms.

Vermicomposting Techniques

Till the early 90's, vermicomposting was restricted to indoor situations with output of vermicompost in small quantities. Sustainable agriculture strategies with emphasis on organic farming, which are in vogue in many regions of the country, necessitate large scale

Table 3: Bio-conversion of agro-industrial wastes using peregrine earthworm *E. eugeniae.*

Sl. No.	Treatment	Worm biomass	Cocoon numbers	Vermicompost (Kg)
1.	Rice milk husk 100%	13.80 (3.76)*	0.0 (0.07)	0.26 (0.87)
2.	Rice millhusk 80% + Cow dung 20%	30.13 (5.53)	0.5 (1.00)	0.46 (0.98)
3.	Rice mill husk 90 % + Cow dung 10%	25.83 (5.11)	0.0 (0.07)	0.40 (0.94)
4.	Rice mill husk + Rice straw 20%	35.96 (6.02)	1.5 (0.41)	0.36 (0.92)
5.	Rice mill husk + Rice straw 10%	24.86 (5.02)	1.5 (1.41)	0.46 (0.98)
6.	Peanut shell 100%	9.00 (3.02)	0.0 (0.07)	0.16 (0.81)
7	Peanut shell 80% + cow dung 20%	30.5 (5.55)	0.5 (0.70)	0.33 (0.91)
8.	Peanut shell 90% + cow dung 10%	24.26 (4.96)	0.0 (0.07)	0.23 (0.85)
9.	Peanut shell 80% + Rice straw 20%	24.76 (5.10)	0.5 (1.00)	0.30 (0.89)
10.	Peanut shell 80% +Rice straw 10%	24.56 (4.99)	0.0 (0.07)	0.23 (0.85)
11.	Check (Standard recepi)	409.00 (20.23)	7.8 (2.88)	3.90 (2.09)
12. SE ±		0.27	0.09	0.03
CD @ 5%		0.76	0.24	0.08
CD @ 1%		0.90	0.31	0.10

$\sqrt{x + 0.5}$ transformations

vermicompost production so as to substitute part of inorganic fertilizers in crop husbandry. In this context, field vermicomposting assumes greater significance.

It is possible to re-recycle large amount of organic wastes such as farm wastes in various field structural designs. Broadly three types of vermicomposting designs (Sunitha and Giraddi 1997., Giraddi 2000 and Giraddi 2004) are practiced.

1. **Vermicomposting in field pits:** rectangular pits of dimensions 10 x 1.0 x 0.5 m (LBD) are laid out for the purpose of vermicomposting.

2. **Vermicomposting in windrows:** involves vermicomposting of organic waste heaps put on ground. Normally, series of heaps of dimensions 10 x 1.0 x 1.0 m (LBH) are laid on the ground using organic wastes and vermicomposting is taken up and,
3. **Vermicomposting in special structural designs:** This is a very popular practice where in rectangular compartments (10 x 1.0 x 0.75m (LBH) made out of earthern or cement bricks or stone slabs are used for the management of wastes. Each of these methods have their own advantage as well as limitations depending on ecological factors such as rainfall pattern, biotic stress, quality of vermicompost.

Vermicomposting Cycle

Irrespective of type of vermicomposting structure, a common procedure has to be followed for successful vermicomposting. This involves various steps explained below as a flow chart.

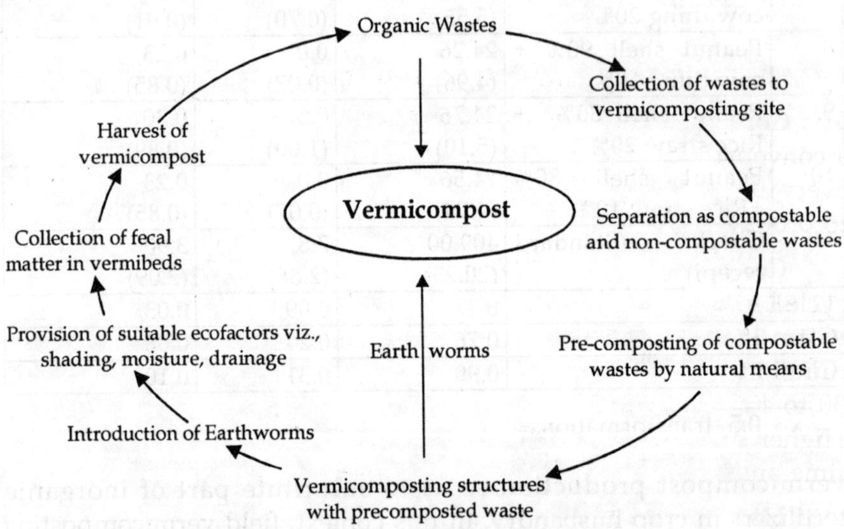

Fig. Vermicomposting cycle indicating various steps.

(i) **Organic wastes in vermicomposting**: Farm wastes *viz.*, crop wastes, animal droppings, agricultural weeds besides agro-based industrial wastes are suitable.

(ii) **Mechanical separation:** It is necessary to classify the waste and subject it to separation by physically removing non-compostable materials *viz.*, plastics, metals, stones, toxic substance etc.

(iii) **Pre-composting of wastes:** It is necesssary to pre-compost the wastes for faster biodegradation. Sun-drying, beating, chopping, dung slurry treatment etc. are some of the treatments that could be given to waste substrate before it is shifted to vermi-beds.

(iv) **Filling of vermicomposting designs with wastes:** Pre-composted organic wastes, animal droppings, green leaves are used in layers, repeatedly in the pattern of sandwich so that the wastes with differential decomposition rates are uniformly distributed.

(v) **Maintainence of optimum ecological factors:** It is essential to maintain optimum soil temperature, bed substrate moisture, drainage etc. for good vermicomposting. A temperature of 12° to 38°C is the range when worms feed and breed actively. Similarly a moisture range of 60 to 80 percent is to be maintained in the vermibeds for effective vermicomposting. In order to avoid stagnation of water in vermi beds during rainy season, and to maintain soil temperature during summer, the vermi-beds are to be thatched.

Conversion ratio: A successful vermicomposting should lead to a conversion ratio of 1.0 to 0.6 (waste : vermicompost). That means, every 100 kg of waste under normal vermicomposting, should lead to production of 60 kg of vermicompost.

Conversion duration: Different agricultural wastes could be re-cycled in 45 to 75 days depending on type of waste, pre-composting, worm loading rates etc. Hard substrates take longer composting duration v/s pre-composted wastes which could be biodegraded in 30 to 45 days. Similarly worm density influences vermicomposting. Higher the worms density in vermi-beds, lower is the composting time and vice-versa.

Harvesting of Vermicompost and Storage: Vermicompost collected in the vermibeds could be manually collected, sieved and bagged. While bagging it is essential to maintain about 25 per cent moisture in vermicompost in order to ensure good microbial activity in it. It is desired that vermicompost so produced is to be used within six months of the harvest from the beds.

References

Giraddi, R.S. 2000. Influence of vermicomposting methods and season on the biodegradation of wastes. *Indian J. Agric. Sci.* 70 : 663-666.

Giraddi, R. S. 2004. Field Vermicomposting designs for management of organic wastes using earthworms. Proceedings of 13th Southern Regional Conference on microbial inoculants, 3-4 Dec, University of Agricultural Sciences, Bijapur, p. 55.

Giraddi, R. S. and Lingappa, S. 2002. Population growth rates of three detritivore species of earthworms in field designs used for bioconversion of organic wastes. Proceedings of 6th International Symposium on Earthworm Ecology, 1-6 S ept, Cardiff University, Wales, United Kingdom, p. 247.

Giraddi, R.S., Tippannavar, P.S. and Kulkarni, K.A. 2002. Utilization of peregrine earthworm, *Eudrilus engeniae* (Kinberg) for biconversion of agriculture, animal and agro-industrial wastes in to a organic manure. *Proceedings of 6th International Symposium on Earthworm Ecology,* 1-6 Sept, Cardiff University, Wales, United Kingdom, p. 248.

Kale, R.D. and Bano, K. 1988. Earthworm cultivation and culturing techniques for production of vermicompost 83 E UAS, Vee meal 83 p UAS, *Mysore J Agric. Sci,* 22: 339-344.

Kale, R.D., Bano, K., and Krishnamoorthy, R.V. 1982. Potential of *Perionyx excavatus* for utilizing organic wastes.*Pedobiologia, 23 : 419-425.*

Ramaswamy, P.1998. Recycling of wastes as manure, potentials and prospects. In: *Summer School on Integrated Soil Productivity Management for Sustainable Agriculture.* Indian Council of Agricultural Research, New Delhi, p. 83-91.

Sunitha, N.D., Giraddi, R.S., Kulkarni, K.A. and Lingappa, S. 1997. Evaluation of methods of vermicomposting under open field conditions. *Karnataka J. Agril. Sci.* 10 : 987-990.

Chapter **5**

Vermicomposting as Biotechnology for Conversion of Organic Wastes into Organic Fertilizer and Animal Protein

P.S. Chaudhuri

Department of Zoology, M.B.B. College, Agartala (Tripura).

In India about 100,000 tons of urban solid wastes are produced daily and per capital production of solid wastes per day is about 0.5 kg. (Source: Ministry of Non-Conventional Energy Sources, NewDelhi). Under the present condition of acute energy crisis and environmental degradation, important resources like plant nutrients and biogas could be successfully recovered from the huge amount of organic wastes, which were once thought to be of no use. Earthworm is now known to be nature's best biological element for recovery of vermifertilizer and vermiprotein from organic waste to be used in agroecosystem, aquaculture and poultry respectively.

Earthworm scientists often recognize three broad ecological groups of earthworms: epigeic, anecic and endogeic. Epigeic earthworms (eg. *Perionyx excavatus*) inhabit litter heaps or any other degrading organic matter such as cow dung on soil surface.They are generally small to medium-sized, deeply pigmented, flat ventrally, tolerant to disturbance and have short life cycle, higher fecundity and regeneration capacity. Anecic earthworm (*Metaphire houlleti*) lives in deep vertical burrows in the soil and they emerge at night to draw dead leaves and other decaying organic matter down into their burrows. They are generally large, moderate to heavily pigmented, geophytophagous and intolerant to disturbance. Endogeic species (*Metaphire posthuma*) rarely come to the surface. They inhabit mineral soil horizons, feed more on soil than on organic matter and are tolerent to some disturbance. Both anecies and endogeics have long life cycles with limited regeneration capacity. The three categories of earthworms contribute differently to soil fertility and structure. Only the epigeic categories of earthworms are being utilized in vermicomposting.

VERMICOMPOSTING

Utilizing the surface feeding habit of epigeic earthworms, large masses of organic wastes can be converted into organic fertilizer within a minimum time span. Earthworm is physically an aerator, crusher, mixer and chemically a degrader and biologically a stimulator in the decomposer system (Mitchell, 1978). Microbial composting of organic wastes through earthworm activity is called vermicomposting which does not involve a thermophilic stage. Products of vermicomposting are organic fertilizer called vermicompost and earthworm biomass that form vermiprotein.

Biological conditioning of wastes through vermicomposting has the following advantages: i) reduce the pollution of organic wastes; (ii) production of vermifertilizer (worm cast) for application in agroecosystem; (iii) produce more earthworms to extend the vermicomposting areas; (iv) production of high quality protein-vermiprotein from waste and utilisation of this protein as feed for poultry, fish, pig and other domestic animals.

Worm farming does not involve a very skilled technology. Vast resources of unskilled labour and huge quantities of organic wastes could be utilized for this purpose.

Principle of Vermicomposting

1) While eating, epigeic earthworms turn and maintain the substrate in an aerobic condition and cover the surface of the substrate with their faecal matter or casts reducing bad odours.

2) As the earthworms feed on organic wastes,their muscular gizzard of the digestive tract acts as a crusher and breaks up larger particles into finer ones, thus, increasing the exposed surface area, enhancing the beneficial action of the symbiotic microbes and the enzymes present in the earthworm gut. During the process about 5% of the ingested matter is assimilated and the rest is ejected out as vermicast.

(3) Active phase of vermicomposting is characterized by mesophilic bacteria and fungi which are stimulated and encouraged by the activity of earthworms (Subler *et. al.*, 1998)

(4) Different casts mix to earthworms mucus (mucoprotein) and its excreted ammonia/urea and allow optimal combination and composition of the nutrient content, producing a much finer, fragmented and uniform material than by any other composting method. Collective mass of vermicasts is called vermicompost.

(5) Thus earthworm's major contribution is in fragmentation of the organic matter. The micro environment that they provide for the establishment of microorganisms is of utmost importance in the composting process.

Components of the Vermicomposting system

To run successfully and produce an efficient and valuable plant growth medium, four principle components are needed for vermicomposting: (i) the proper substrates; (ii) the optimum environmental conditions; (iii) appropriate species of earthworm with suitable population characteristics; and (iv) the design and operations to be implemented.

(i) Substrates

A wide variety of organic wastes for culturing earthworms are available in the tropics. These come from animal, vegetable, urban and industrial residues. Many of them are common in temperate climates also (eg. cattle, pig, horse, rabbit, sheep, turkey or poultry manures, kitchen wastes, brewery, paper pulp solids, spent mushroom substrates, trimming from floriculture industries, garden refuse, sawdust, urban and municipal solid wastes, etc.), but some others are found exclusively in tropical countries (e.g., coffee pulp, sugar cane wastes, coconut and betel-nut residues, aquatic weeds like water hyacinth, banana stems, bamboo leaf litters and other tropical plant leaves).

One of the most important characteristics of substrates supporting earthworm growth is the C/N ratio, which should be approximately 30/1. When wastes with different C:N ratio are present, an appropriate mixture (either high carbon or high nitrogen residues) is recommended to attain close to this ratio. A substrate suitable for one earthworm species may not be a food of choice for another species (Chaudhuri *et al.*, 2003).

(ii) Environmental factors

One of the basic limiting factors for earthworms activity is the heat generated during the initial decomposition of organic matter.

During processing of waste, earthworms work best at temperature 25-30°C, 50-60% moisture, pH 6.5-7.5 (Chaudhuri *et. al.*, 2001).

(iii) Composting earthworms and their selective features.

Selective features of composting worms are: (i) worms should have high adaptibility with respect to environmental factors; (ii)worms should be capable of inhabiting high percentage organic materials; (iii) they should be voracious feeder; (iv) they should be prolific breeder (high fecundity) with short incubation period (cocoon development time) and high hatching success; (v) worms should have quick maturation time (short life cycle).

The best known species, with potential for waste management under Indian conditions include: *Eisenia andrei* (European red tiger worm), *Eisenia fetida* (brandling or tiger worm), *Eudrilus eugeniae* (African nightcrawler) and *Perionyx excavatus* (Indian blue).

(iv) Method of vermicomposting (Tank System)

In a well ventilated and shaded place with facility of water, vermicompostingcan be carried out in tanks made up of bricks, cement or stone slabs. Desirable size of the container is of any convenient length with 90-100 cm width and 60 cm depth. According to Kale (1998a) a tank size of 60 x 45 x 60 cm can hold a population size of 1000-1500 adult *E. eugeniae,* 3000-5000 of *E. fetida* and *P. excavatus.* Different wastes mixed thoroughly along with 10% cowdung slurry are left for primary decomposition (precomposting) for 2-3 weeks. Moisture content of the wastes should be maintained at 50-60% by periodic sprinkling of water. The following precomposting of wastes, epigeic earthworms are released (a minimum of 1 kg earthworms for 30 kg wastes). Immediately after release, the earthworms enter the material to be composted. In order to avoid predator attack and to maintain darkness, the whole system should be covered by jute cloth or any other porous lids. Due to feeding activity of earthworms the whole material becomes sweet smelling, fine, granular and dark brown compost (now called vermicompost) with about 20-30% unfed matter within 45-60 days. The contents of the culture tank is cleared and heaped like a cone on the ground under bright light for 24 hrs. Being photonegative, all the worms move downwards and vermicompost is harvested.

Vermicomposting, for household purposes, can also be done effectively by adding the wastesfrequently in small, thin layers inside the culture chamber and allowing the earthworms to feed successive aerobic layer of wastes.

To minimize nutrient loss from the materials during vermicomposting and to provide a vent for the release of CO_2 and other gases during decompostion, Kale (1998b) recommended placing of a 2.5 cm thick mud pack on the surface of decomposing material and PVC tubes 3 cm in diameter with a series of holes or even hollow shoots of bamboo into the packed material 30 cm apart into the composting chamber. This method is very much effective in preventing the emission of bad smell and keeps away flies during composting of kitchen wastes.

During the process of vermicomposting worms multiply. The overcrowding will reduce and hamper their growth and reproduction. So once the population reaches a peak, harvesting of worms will provide scope for continuous development of progeny in the worm beds. Fastest processing of organic waste is achieved by innoculation with nearly fully grown earthworm because of their high rate of feeding activity. Culture beds should be kept free from giant flat worms, termites, rodents and centipedes. As far as possible worms should not be injured while handling.

Physical and chemical characteristics of vermicompost

The final physical and chemical characteristics of the vermicompost produced by earthworms from variety of wastes depend very much on the nature of input. However, the final product from most of the organic wastes is usually a finely divided homogeneous material with excellent structure, porosity, aeration, drainage and moisture-holding capacity (Edwards,1998). The nutrient level in the vermicompost is always at a a lower level than in the original material but the level of macro or micronutrient is higher than in the compost derived from any other method (Kale, 1998a). Most important feature of vermicompost is that, during processing of the various organic wastes by earthworms, many of the nutrients are changed to available forms that are more readily taken up by plants, such as nitrate or ammonium nitrogen, exchangeable phosphorus and soluble potassium, calcium and magnesium. So, vermicomposts have a higher level of available nutrients from the wastes from which they were formed (Buchanan *et. al.*, 1988). Humic acid is a very important constituents of vermicompost. A few among many of its important properties are slow release of plant nutrients, improvement of soil physical properties, enhancement of micronutrient element nutrition of plants through chelation reactions etc. (Martin and Focht, 1986). Plant growth regulators, belonging to the auxin, giberellin and cytokinin groups present in the worm-worked materials are produced by a wide range of soil microorganisms, many of which live in the guts of earthworms or within the castings (Tomati *et al.*, 1983; Tomati and Galli, 1995; Atiyeh *et al.*, 2000). Another important feature is that during production of vermicompost bioavailable heavy metals (like Cd, Pb, Zn etc. generally found in pig manures) and pathogens are eliminated (Dominguez *et al.*, 1997). Major nutrient contents in the vermicompost derived from various organic wastes and effect of earthworm activity on nutrients in organic wastes are given in Table 1 and Table 2, respectively.

Table 1 : Major plant nutrient elements in earthworm-processed wastes.

Waste material	NUTRIENTS					References
	N	P	K	Ca	Mg	
Cattle solids	2.20	0.40	0.90	1.20	0.25	Edwards and Burrows (1998)
Pig solids	2.60	1.70	1.40	3.40	0.55	"
Cattle solids + straw	2.50	0.50	2.50	1.55	0.30	"
Pig solids + straw	3.00	1.60	2.40	4.40	0.60	"
Chicken solids + wood shavings	1.80	2.70	2.10	4.80	0.70	"
Leaves	0.80	0.34	0.82	1.96	0.53	"
Sugarcane	2.67	2.11	0.40	4.08	1.89	Romon and Romero (1993)
Banana stems	2.50	0.56	3.74	2.36	1.50	"
Coffee pulp	2.01	0.27	2.14	1.96	0.37	"
Kitchen wastes	1.81	1.12	0.87	2.95	0.41	Chaudhuri *et al.* (2001)
Paper waste	1.10	0.57	0.29	8.02	0.53	Piccone *et al.* (1987)

Table 2: Effect of earthworm activity on nutrients in organic wastes (Edwards, 1998)

Organic waste	Nitrate nitrogen (ppm)	Readily soluble P (% d.m.)	Exchangeable (% d.m.)		
-	-		K	Ca	Mg
CATTLE WASTE	-	-	-	-	-
Unworked	8.8	0.11	0.19	0.35	0.05
Worm-worked	259.4	0.18	0.41	0.59	0.08
PIG WASTE	-	-	-	-	-
Unworked	31.6	1.05	1.49	1.56	0.45
Worm-worked	110.3	1.64	1.76	2.27	0.72
POTATO WASTE	-	-	-	-	-
Unworked	74.6	0.19	1.94	0.91	0.24
Worm-worked	1428.0	0.22	3.09	1.37	0.34

ROLE OF VERMICOMPOST IN PLANT GROWTH

Vermicompost has been shown to promote growth of a wide range of cereals, vegetables, ornamental plants etc. (Kale, 1998 b; Edwards, 1998; Ghosh *et al.*, 1999). Kale, *et al.*, (1992) carried out field trials on application of vermicompost to rice fields and observed increase in population of beneficial microbes like N-fixing bacteria and mycorrhizae over control plots. Ghosh *et al.*, (1999) reported that integration of vermicompost with inorganic fertilization tended to increase the yield of crops *viz.*, potato, rape seed, mulberry and marigold over that with traditional compost prepared from the same substrate. A field trial conducted on upland rice (var TRC-87-251) using different doses of vermicompost revealed significant increase in both grain and straw yield coupled with improvement in soil aggregation, water use efficiency and nutrient uptake in vermicompost treated plots compared with the control and NPK treated plots (Bhattacharjee *et al.*,2001). Recommended doses of NPK along with 5 to 10 tons of vermicompost led to high increase in the uptake of nutrients in the paddy. Application of vermicompost reduces the dosage of NPK for crops. Vermicompost along with judicious use of chemical fertilizers will not only bring down the cost of cultivation but also present unique opportunities for sustainable agriculture (Bhattacharjee *et al.*, 2001).

Effect of vermicompost on crop production is not solely nutritional. Application of vermicompost increase the soil aggregation with concomitant increase in soil aerobicity and water holding capacity,thus providing the characteristics of a healthy soil, which ultimately increase the water use efficiency of the plants. Besides these, biologically active plant growth influencing substances/ phytohormones (auxin, giberellin and cytokinin) released by beneficial microorganisms in the vermicompost are also involved in the growth of plants (Scheu, 2003).

NUTRIENT VALUE OF EARTHWORMS AS ANIMAL FEED

The high biomass production capacity of earthworms can be used to prepare animal protein. From 1 kg of fresh earthworm biomass, the dry matter recovery will be about 200g. Worm tissue contains 50-70% protein and 7-10% fat, and its protein content is significantly positively correlated with body weight (Patra and Dash,1973). Vermiprotein has been used as an excellent food additive for fish, poultry, pigs or domestic animals. After worms are collected, they must be washed thoroughly and left standing in water for several hours in order to evacuate the residual waste particles from their guts completely. When the guts are evacuated completely, earthworms are taken out, washed thoroughly in water and later washed in 0.5 to 1% sodium chloride solution (Kale, 1998a). When narcotised due to osmotic stress, they are removed and air dried in the plastic sheets in shade. When almost dry, they are to be sun dried or dried in oven at 60°C till the earthworms turn crisp. The crisp worms can be ground in a grinder to get the earthworm meal (Kale,1998a). Apart from having high protein level not much variation in the nature of amino acids including the essential amino acids was observed in a earthworm (Table 3a and 3b) and other good animal feed, when compared with the recommendation of FAO/WHO (Edwards and Bohlen, 1996). Predominance of poly unsaturated fatty acids with significant amount of linoleic and linolenic acids (essential for increasing egg size in poultry birds) and an adequate mineral contents are other characteristic components of worm meal. Worm meals have an excellent range of vitamins and are rich in niacin, which is a valuable component of animal feeds and an unusual source of vitamin B_{12} (Edwards and Bohlen, 1996). Use of earthworm as fish bait is known to all. According to Tacon *et al.*, (1983), earthworms have good potential both as complete food or protein supplement for trout or other fish. Guerrero (1983) reported that *Tilapia* fish grew better on diets containing earthworm protein supplements from *P. excavatus* than those provided with other fish meal supplements. Jin-

Table 3a. Chemical composition of earthworm (*Eudrilus eugeniae*) meal (Kale, 1998a)

Chemical constituents	Constituents (in %)
1. Moisture	7.70
2. Crude protein	56.27
3. Total ash	10.49
4. Crude fibre	0.56
5. Calcium	1.01
6. Phosphorus	1.25
7. Fat	6.05
8. Silica	3.76

Table 3b. Amino acid contents of earthworm (*Eudrilus eugeniae*) meal (Kale, 1998a)

Amino acid	in g/100g. protein
Aspartic acid	10.3
Threonine	4.8
Serine	4.8
Glutamic acid	13.8
Alanine	5.2
Cysteine	1.6
Valine	5.0
Methionine	2.0
Isoleucine	4.5
Leucine	7.2
Tyrosine	3.4
Phenylalanine	4.1
Lysine	7.1
Histidine	2.6
Arginine	6.1

you *et al.* (1982) reported that chicken fed on earthworm increased weight faster than those given other diets (including fish meal) and had more breast muscles. The same authors further reported that piglets grew better on diets with earthworm protein supplements than on other protein supplements, weaning was accelerated, estrus in sows was earlier, and there was increased disease resistance and a decreased incidence of white diarrhea.

Earthworms have also been used as food for humans in some parts of New Zealand and South Africa. In Japan, earthworm pies have been made, and there are special restaurants with worm-based dishes. Primitive natives from New Guinea and parts of Africa have been reported to eat raw earthworms (Edwards and Bohlen, 1996).

MEDICAL APPLICATION OF VERMICULTURE BIOTECHNOLOGY

Earthworms have been used in medicine for various remedies since 1340 A.D.(Stephenson, 1930). There have been many reports of earthworms being eaten or applied to humans to relieve or cure illness like stones in the gall bladder, jaundice, piles, fever, and small pox. Earthworm ashes have been applied to the head to make hair grow (Stephenson, 1930). It has been suggested that earthworms might contain a substance effective in curing rheumatism (Weisbach, 1962) and asthma (Reynolds and Reynolds, 1972). According to Vohora and Khan (1978) earthworms have largely been used internally, as well as externally as powerful aphrodisiacs and thus cure impotency. Japanese put earthworms in to sake (wine made from rice), allowing them to secrete a milky liquid and then drink the potent bur (Ghatnekar *et. al.*, 1998). There are recent reports on earthworm extract to have spermatocidal, anti-hypertensive, anti-allergic, anti-inflammatory and anti-blood coagulatory effects (Zhang *et al.*, 1992; Ismail *et al.*, 1992; Popovic *et al.*, 2002).

Conclusion

In India, a megadiversity country with rich earthworm resources, vermitechnology has a bright future as it concerns with waste management, resource recovery and environment conservation. Mass rearing and maintenance of selective species of earthworms on organic wastes has a good scope for developing it as cottage industry in India having available organic residues, suitable climatic conditions and required manpower. Research work must continue on discovery of more new earthworm species especially from forest areas, their proper identification and selection of appropriate species for vermicomposting biotechnology, "in-soil earthworm technology" and environmental monitoring. Pharmacological use of earthworm is also a promising line of future research.

References

Atiyeh, R.M., Subler, S., Edwards, C.A., Bachman, G., Metzger, J.D. and Shuster, W.2000. Effect of vermicompost and compost on plant growth in horticultural container media and soil, *Pedobiologia* , 44: 579-590.

Bhattacharjee, G., Chaudhuri, P.S. and Datta, M. 2001. Response of paddy (var. TRC-87-251) crop on amendment of the field with different levels of vermicompost. *Asian J. Microbiol, Biotech. Env. Sci.* 3 (3): 191-196.

Buchanan, M.A., Russell, E. and Block, S.D. 1988. Chemical characterization and nitrogen mineralization potential of vermicompost derived from differing organic wastes. In: *Earthworm in Enviromental and Waste Management* (eds. Edwards C.A. and Neuhauser E.F.) SPB Academic Publishing, The Netherlands, p. 231-240.

Chaudhuri, P.S., Bhattacharjee, G., Pal, T.K. and Dey, S.K. 2001. Chemical characterization of kitchen waste vermicompost processed by *Perionyx excavatus. Proc. Zool. Soc.* Cal. 54: 81-83.

Chaudhuri, P.S., Pal, T.K. Bhattacharjee, G. and Dey, S.K. 2003. Rubber leaf litter (*Hevea brasiliensis,* var RRIM 600) as vermiculture substrate for epigeic earthworms, *Perionyx excavatus, Eudrilus eugeniae* and *Eisenia fetida, Pedobiologia* 47 : 796-800.

Dominguez, J., Edwards, C.A. and Subler, S.1997. A comparison of vermicomposting and composting. *Biocycle.* 38: 57-59.

Edwards, C.A. and Bohlen, P.J. 1996. Biology and Ecology of Earthworms. Chapman & Hall, London.

Edwards, C.A. 1998. The use of earthworms in the breakdown and management of organic wastes. In:*Earthworm Ecology* (ed. Edwards, C.A.) CRC Press LLC, Florida, p. 327-354.

Edwards, C.A. and Burrows, I. 1988. The potential of earthworm compost on plant growth media. In: *Earthworms in Environmental and Management* (eds. Edwards, C.A. and Neuhauser, E.F) SPB Academic Publishing, The Netherlands, p. 211-220.

Ghatnekar, S.D., Kavian, M.F., Ghatnekar, G.S. and Ghatnekar, M.S. 1998. Management of solid wastes through vermiculture biotechnology. In: *Ecotechnology for pollution control and Environemntal management* (eds. Trivedy, R.K. and Arvind Kumar). Enviro Media, Maharashtra, p. 59-67.

Ghosh, M., Chattopadhyay, G.N. Baral, K. and Munsi, P.S., 1999. Possibility of using vermicompost in Agriculture for reconciling sustainability with productivity. *Proc. Seminar or Agrotechnology and Environment.* p. 64.68.

Guerrero, R.D. 1983. The culture and use of *Perionyx excavatus* as a protein resources in the Philippines. In: *Earthworm Ecology from Darwin to Vermiculture* (ed. Satchell, J.E.) Chapman and Hall, London, p. 309-313.

Ismail, S.A. Pulandiran, K. and Yegnanarayan, R. 1992. Anti-inflammatory activity of earthworm extracts. *Soil Biol. Biochem.* 24 (12): 1253-1254.

Jin-you, X., Xian-kuan, Z. and Zhi-ren, P. 1982. Experimental research on the substitution of earthworm for fish meal in feeding broilers. *Journal of South China Normal College* 1: 88-94.

Kale, R.D. 1998 a. *Earthworm: Cinderella of Organic Farming*. Prism Books Pvt. Ltd., Bangalore.

Kale, R.D.1998 b. Earthworms: natures' gift for utilization of organic wastes. In: *Earthworm Ecology* (ed. Edwards, C.A.). C.R.C. Press LLC, Florida.

Kale, R.D., Mallesh, B.C. Bano, K, and Bagyaraj, D.J.1992. Influence of vermicompost application on the available macronutrients and selected microbial population in a paddy field. *Soil Biol. Biochem.* 24 : 1317-1320.

Lofs-Holmin, A. 1985. Vermiculture, Present knowledge of the Art of Earthworm Farming, Institute Ekologie Miljovard, Swedish University Agronomic Sciences.

Martin, J.P. and Focht, D.D. 1986. Biological properties of soils. In: *Soils for Management of Organic wastes and waste water.* ASA, Madison, Wisconsin, p. 115-169.

Mitchell, M.J. 1978. Role of invertebrates and microorganisms in sludge decomposition. In: *Utilization of Soil Organisms in Sludge Management* (eds. Hartenstein, R.) . Natl. Tech. Inf. Services, PB 286932, Springfield, Virginia, p. 35-50.

Patra. U.C. and Dash, M.C. 1973.Changes in the body weight and protein content during developmental stages of *Lampito mauritii* (Oligochaeta: Megascolecidae). *Indian J. Exp. Biol.* 11 : 357-358.

Piccone, G., Biasiol, B., Deluca, G. and Minelli, L. 1987.Vermicomposting of different organic wastes. In: *Compost Production Quality and Use* (eds. Bertoldi De, Ferranti, M.P., L, Hermite, P. and Zucconi, F). Elsiver, London, p. 818-821.

Popovic. M., Grdisa, M. and Hrzenjak, T. 2002. Biological activity of tissue homogenate extract of Eisenia fetida. *The 7th International symposium on Earthworm Ecology* (Abstract), Wales, p. 196.

Ramon, C.J. and Romero, G.A. 1993. La lombricultura una opeion technologica. In: *Manejo y Disposicion Final de Residuos Solidos Municipales.* Congreso Regional del Sureste, SMISAAC y AIDIS, Merida, Mexico, p. 110-117.

Reynolds, J.W. and Reynolds, W.M. 1972. Earthworms in medicine. *Am. J. Nursing.* 72: 1273.

Scheu, S. 2003. Effects of earthworms on plant growth: pattern and perspectives. *Pedobiologia* 47: 846-856.

Stephenson, J. 1930. *The Oligochaeta.* Clarendon Press, Oxford.

Subler, S., Edwards, C.A. and Metzger, J. 1998. Comparing vermicompost and Compost. *Biocycle* 39: 63-66.

Tacon, A.G.J., Stafford, E.A. and Edwards, C.A. 1983. A Preliminary investigation of the nutritive value of three terrestrial worms for rainbow trout. *Aquaculture.* 35 : 187-199.

Tomati, U. and Galli, E.1995. Earthworm, soil fertility and plant productivity. *Acta Zoologica Fennica.* 196:11-14.

Tomati, U., Grappelli A and Galli, E. 1983. Fertility factors in earthworm humus. *Proc. Int. Sym. on Agricultural and Environmental Prospects in Earthworm Farming.* Publ. Minist. Ric. Sci. Tec., Rome, p. 49-56.

Vohora, S.B. and Khan, M.S.Y. 1978. *Animal Origin Drugs Used in Unani Medicine.* Institute of History of Medicine and Medical Research, Tughlaquabad, New Delhi.

Weisbach. W.W. 1962. Regenwurmer und Essbare Erde, *Biol. Jaarb. Dodonea.* 30: 225-238.

Zhang, F.X., Guo, B.Z. and Wang,. H.Y. 1992. The spermicidal effects of earthworm extract and its effective constituents *Soil. Biol. Biochem.* 24 (12):1247-1251.

Chapter **6**

Role of Earthworms in Converting Domestic Organic Wastes with Special Reference to Local Species

A. Misra

Zoological Survey of India, 27 J.L. Nehru Road, Kolkata-700 016

Earthworms have been on the earth for over 120 million years. In this time they have faithfully done their part to keep the cycle of life continuously moving. Their purpose is simple but very important. They are playing a great role in nature's way of recycling organic nutrients from dead tissues back to living organisms.The value of these worms has been recognized by many. Ancient civilization, including Greece and Eygpt valued the role of earthworms play in the formation of rich agricultural soil. They recognized the important role, the worms played in fertilizing the Nile Valley croplands after annual floods. However, the beneficial effects of earthworms in increasing soil fertility was documented since the time of Darwin (1881). Referring to an earthworm Darwin said, "It may be doubted whether there are many other animals in the world which have played so important a part in the history of the world." The earthworm is a natural resource of fertility and life. They are popularly known as **'Friends of Farmers'**. Considering their importance in maintaining a balance in the soil ecosystem and in managing organic wastes, they could be referred as **'Friends of People'**.

E-mail: zsi_gnc@rediffmail.com

During the last three to four decades, agricultural production has dramatically increased in our country due to use of high-yielding crops, multiple cropping and enhanced consumption of chemical fertilizers and pesticides. But the dark side of this high chemical input intensive agriculture is the rapid fall of fertilizer response, the rapid destruction of soil structure and microbial nutrient recycling system, which resulted in the decline of the soil productivity. The organic matter has also been gradually decreasing.

Humus loss is the main cause of serious problem of soil compactness, which results in lower crop yield. According to an estimate, the humus contents of the average top soil has dropped from seven percent to three percent. At two percent or less, plants can hardly grow, even with additional chemical fertilizers. Along with this, the average population of earthworms has also gradually been decreasing. The loss of earthworms and organic matter have been proved to be interrelated, resulting in reduced water-holding capacity of some agriculture farm soils by 70% or more, which facilitate increased runoff.

Every year, the organic matter level in our agricultural soils drops another fraction of a percent. Crop rotation and other sustainable practices may decrease the rate of soil organic matter loss, but they do little to built it back. Like falling leaves, feeding a forest floor (soil) every year with a layer of organic material, we also need to feed our agricultural soil with an annual load of organic matter, a loading rate which exceeds the oxidation rate. Organic material increased soil productivity to the extent that people will be able to produce more food on less ground. Earthworm cultivation may be considered as a component in deriving added value from the process of maximizing organic matter potentials.

Role of Earthworms

Earthworms live in the soil and feed on decaying organic material. They can rightly be considered tiller of the soil. As it tunnels through the soil, the active worms can eat nearly equal of its own weight of soil and organic matter every 24 hours (Hartenstein, 1981). However, Kale (1998) reported that one kilogram of epigeic earthworms can ingest and digest about 4 to 5 kilogram of organic wastes having 40%

to 50% moisture content. They ingest food through their mouth and pass it to gizzard. Small grains of sand and mineral particles in the gizzard grind the material into fine particles. When the material leaves the gizzard, it enters the worm's intestine. The intestine secretes digestive enzymes to chemically breakdown molecules of food particles even farther. After absorbing a very little amount of nutrients,the undigested particles of the food material is passed through anus in the form of castings. These castings are very important to the fertility of the soil. The studies show that castings contain five times nitrogen, seven times potash, and one and a half times calcium that can be found in good top soil. Moreover, the carbon and nitrogen ratio is also found to be very convenient (20: 1 or less than this) for the absorption by the plants.

Earthworms are also the great incubators for beneficial microorganisms as they travel through the earthworm's intestine. Some people refer to it as a 'tubular bioreactor'. The oxygen-rich micro environment created by the earthworm is also intolerable to human pathogens which are for the most part anaerobic. They enhance decomposition process by 25 to 40 per cent by ensuring an anaerobic environment and by increasing the surface area of litter available for the activity of microbes through fragmentation, feeding and casting activity (Dash and Senapati, 1986). In moderate temperature, earthworms work primarily in the top 10 to 12 inches of soil. The remarkable tunneling done by the earthworms is of great value to the gardens where they live. These tunnels aerate the soils and also improve drainage. Roots have been found to travel down worms' holes in their search for water and nutrients. Since deep burrowing earthworms have the habit of pulling leaf litter and other organic matter on the surface deep into their burrows, they effectively improve soil structure by boosting humus levels.

Earthworms and People

Rapid growth of population, urbanization and industrialization have caused generation of large quantity of wastes everyday which finds its way mostly into the local environment leading to increased levels of environmental pollution and spreading of diseases due to lack of treatment and proper waste management facilities. In India,

Municipal Solid Waste (domestic and commercial) is produced at an average rate of 300-600 g/capita/day. The production of urban Municipal Solid Waste in India is increasing at a faster rate. Collection and disposal of urban and solid waste is one of the major problem areas for the local authorities all over India (Shuchi, *et al.*, 1998). Indian cities and adjoining suburban areas have poor standard of service in respect to the collection and disposal of daily wastes. According to the official estimation of Kolkata Municipal Corporation (KMC), City of Kolkata generates approximately 2500 MT of garbage per day. The average quantity of the solid waste generated is 300-450 g/capita/day. The total garbage is disposed at the site as open dumping. Approximately 500 trips are needed per day to transport the waste to the dumping ground.Though the Supreme Court gave a three year notice to implement the Rule – "**Municipal Solid Waste (Management & Handling Rules, 2000,** nothing substantial has happened so far. Though there are stray instances across the country including West Bengal that several communities have initiated door-to-door waste collection and segregation. In Delhi, the recycling of MSW (Municipal Solid Waste) is currently carried out by an informal sector comprising recyclists at the lowest end and a succession of dealers (Agarwal *et al.*, 2005). Owing to lack of financial and human resources, Municipal Corporations fail to oganize timely lifting, transportation and disposal of solid waste. All these result in spreading of pollution and the situation, causes major threat to public health.

Every household generates a considerable amount of waste, which generally, contains organic (kitchen waste) and inorganic waste (plastic, metal, leather, glass etc). It has been estimated that Indian cities and rural areas produce nearly 7000 million metric tons of organic waste every year. In order to reduce the pollution hazards, it is needed to have effective management system to minimize the solid waste generation as well as maximize the effective disposal techniques. The problem is severe in the urban areas, now a days, due to attainment of better standard of living. Hence, it is highly essential for the Municipal Corporations and local Management Committee to adopt a systematic method of collection, transportation, disposal and processing of solid waste to prevent environmental hazards. An overview of the waste management and disposal options with a comprehensive and up-to-day analysis of how recycling could develop is detailed by Waite (1995).

With increasing environmental awareness, the problem of disposal of solid waste in environment-friendly fashion is also receiving a higher level of attention from several environmentalists. One of the options of the effective solid waste management is bio-conversion of organic wastes and making organic manures to encourage organic farming, which is the need of the hour for sustainable agriculture. One of the most efficient ways of converting this bio-degradable waste resource on a small scale, at domestic and also at cmmunity level, is through composting with the help of earthworms (Vermicomposting). Certain species of earthworms are known to be most efficient in this bio-coversion process.

Earthworms provide the essential conditions for transforming agro-based and other forms of organic wastes (kitchen waste, municipal wastes, market wastes, etc.) into recyclable micro-nutrients and essential manures. It is rather an approach of biological burning in aerobic media. Earthworms in a sense, create the basic grounds for the aerobic bacteria to play its role in an enhanced rate in the process of decomposition of organic wastes. Dash (1978) has highlighted first in our country the role of earthworms in the degradation of organic matter and stimulation of microbial activity in the soil. On the contrary, absence of earthworms creates a ground for anaerobic bacteria, which create the bad odour in the environment. Therefore, earthworm encourages the cultivation and growth of aerobic bacteria by inhibiting the growth of anaerobic bacteria, which releases noxious gaseous substances into the surrounding environment. Its constant burrowing action allows air to penetrate to a much greater depth, providing in the process sufficient organic carbon, which gets converted into useful energy to create kinetic actions in the media. Humus is the by-product of the process without which soil gets blown off.

Earthworms occur in diversified habitats from organic heaps (manure, compost, litter, humus, kitchen drainage etc.) to forestland, grassland, agricultural land, plant nursery, etc. Earthworms inhabit different layers of soil are generally categorized into three groups: surface or litter dwellers (Epigeics,) topsoil inhabitants (Endogeics) and subsoil dwellers (Anecics). Litter dwelling are the more active and deeply pigmented than others. These are the most suitable species for vermicomposting purpose. The topsoil dwellers are tolerant to some disturbance and weakly pigmented. Whereas, the subsoil dwelling forms are intolerant to disturbance and slightly pigmented at anterior and posterior ends only. All of them are omnivorous, but most of them derive nutrition from dead organic matter. Presently, earthworms is not restricted as basic biology material but is being established as basic material for biotechnology (vermitechnology). Considering the significant role of some of the species of earthworms in organic matter decomposition and mineral cycling, they are selected for waste utilisation and vermicomposting (Edwards and Lofty, 1977; Julka, J. M. 1986; Julka, J. M. 1993; Senapati, B.K. and Julka, J.M.1993; Kale, R.D. 1998; Prabhu, 1998; Ismail, 1997).

Earthworm species suitable for Vermicomposting

It is not very difficult to rear and maintain earthworms. However, the capability of decomposing organic matter varies from species to species. Therefore, it is essential to select species for vermicomposting purpose. From literature, it appears that out of about 3627 global species (Reynolds, 1994) including over 500 reported from India (Julka, 1993), only three species, *Eisenia fetida, Eudrilus eugeniae* and *Perionyx excavatus,* are recognized in order of preference for their ability to degrade organic matter and are utilised for vermicomposting purposes throughout the world, However, some other species of earthworms are reported in literature (Julka, 1993 and Senapati & Julka, 1993; Misra & Halder, in press) for consideration regarding vermicomposting. Moreover, there are several attempt to study the efficacy to local species of earthworms in degrading organic wastes (Ismail, 1995; Kaviraj & Sharma, 2003; Tripathi & Bhardwaj, 2004; Chaudhuri, *et al.,* 2001 a, b; Chaudhuri, *et a.,* 2002; Chaudhuri & Bhattacharjee, 2002).

In the present paper an attempt has been made to include a taxonomic key for the identification of 14 litter-dwelling species of earthworms belonging to 10 genera and 5 families prospective for use in vermicomposting activities. It is expected that the present paper will be very helpful to the students and the future workers to get the composting species identified at their own level.

Systematic list of earthworm species suitable for vermicomposting

Taxa	Distribution
Phylum: Annelida	-
Class: Oligochaeta	-
Order : **Moniligastrida**	-
Family: **Molinigastridae**	-
1. *Drawida willsi* (Michaelsen)	*U.P. M.P., Orissa, Andhra Pradesh,*
Order : **Haplotaxida**	-
Family : **Eudrilidae**	-
2. *Eudrilus eugeniae* (Kinberg)	Tropical West African species (not reported in nature from India, but a local strain of the species is available at Kerala)
Family: **Lumbricidae**	
3. *Eisenia fetida* (Savigny)	European species, but not recorded from Western & Eastern Himalayas (Simla, Kashmir, Sikkim, Darjeeling, etc.)
4. *Lumbricus rubellus (Hoffmeister)*	Himachal Pradesh
Family : **Megascolecidae**	
5. *Amynthas alexandri* (Beddard)	Maharashtra (Mumbai), Assam, and W.B. (Kolkata)
6. *A. diffringens* (Baird)	Western & Eastern Himalayas, Palni Hills, Bababudan Hills, S. India
7. *Metaphire anomala* (Michaelsen)	U.P. W.B. (Sibpur, Darjeeeling,), (Dehradun), Nilgiri Hills, S. India
8. *M. birmanica* (Rosa)	U.P.
9. *Polypheretima elongata* (Perrier)	M.P., Maharashtra (Pune, Mumbai), W.B. (Kolkata, Namkhana,), Karnataka, Andhra Pradesh, Tamil Nadu
10. *Lampito mauritii* (Kinberg)	Widely distributed in India
11. *Perionyx excavatus* (Perrier)	Widely distributed in India
12. *P. sansibaricus* (Michaelsen)	U.P. M.P., Gujarat, Maharashtra, Orissa, Andhra Pradesh, T.N., Kerala,
Family: **Octochaetidae**	-
13. *Dichogaster bolaui* (Michaelsen)	U.P., M.P., Arunachal Pradesh Meghalaya, W.B., Orissa.
14. *D. modiglianii* (Rosa)	Meghalaya, W.B., Orissa, Andamans

Key to the identification of eartworm species suitable for Vermicomposting

	Characters	Result
1.	Male pores paired in 10/11 (intersegmental furrow between segment X & XI); clitellum in X-XI; dorsal pores absent;	Drawida willsi (Family-*Moniligastridae*)
	Male pores paired behind 10/11; clitellum in XIII and posterior segments; dorsal pores present or lacking	2
2.	Male pores in front of female pores, dorsal pores present, clitellum saddle-shaped	3 (Family-Lumbricidae)
	Male pores behind female pores, dorsal pores present or lacking, clitellum annular	4
3.	Setae 8 in four pairs per segment (lumbricine); spermathecal pores 2 pairs near mid-dorsal line; male pores on XV; colour purple or red or brown, usually with mid-segmental bands dorsally	*Eisenia fetida*
	Setae lumbricine; spermathecal pores 2 pairs ventrolaterally At C D; male pores on XV; colour ruddy brown or red-violet and without mid-segmental bands dorsally	*Lumbricus rubellus*
4.	Setae limbricine; male pores lights in front of 17/18 dorsal pores absent, colour red dorsally	*Eudrilus eugeniae* (Family- Eudrilidae)
	Setae lumbricine or unpaired and more than 8 per segment (perichaetine); male pores not in 17/18; dorsal pores present, colourotherwise	5
5.	Setae lumbricine; prostates tubular; male pores on XVIII; prostatic pores 2 pairs on XVII and XIX	6 (*Dichogaster*) (Family-Octochaetidae)
	Setae perichaetine; prostates racemose; combined male and prostatic pores (paired) on XVIII	7 (Family- Megascolecidae)
6.	Female pore single and median on XIV	*Dichogaster bolaui*
	Female pores paired on XIV	*Dichogaster modiglianii*
7.	Spermathecal pores at least 2 pairs and closely paired; male pores closely paired on XVIII; female pore single on XIV: meganephridia present-nephridium large and one pair per segment; colour purple dorsally and pale ventrally	8 (*Perionyx*)

	Spermathecal pores at least one pair and widely paired; male pores widely paired; female pores one pair or single on XIV; micronephridia present–nephridium small and more than one pair per segment; colour otherwise	9
8.	Spermathecal pores 2 pairs at 7/8 and 8/9; penial setae present on XVIII; nephridiopore in one rather irregular rank on each segment	*Perionyx excavatus*
	Spermathecal pores 3 pairs at 6/7, 7/8 and 8/9; penial setae lacking; nephridiopores in two series on each side alternating dorso-laterally and dorso-ventrally	*Perionyx sansibaricus*
9.	Male pores on XVIII; female pores paired; gizzard in V; penial setae present on XVIII	*Lampito mauritii*
	Male pores on XVIII or more behind; female pore single and median; gizzard in VIII; penial setae absent	10
10.	Polythecal (spermatheca more than one pair per segment), spermathecal pores at 5/6-6/7; male pores on XVIII: copulatory papillae widely paired, 3-7 pairs on XIX and successive posterior segments	*Polypheretima elongata*
	Not polythecal; male pores on XVIII or more behind; copulatory papillae either lacking or present with their number and arrangement otherwise	11
11.	Spermathecae 4 pairs, spermathecal pores at 5/6; 6/7, 7/8 and 8/9; male pores on XVIII	12
	Spermathecae 3 pairs; spermathecal pores at 5/6, 6/7 and 7/8; male pores on XVIII or more behind	13
12.	Copulatory papillae present on preclitellar segments	*Amynthas diffringens*
	Copulatory papillae lacking on preclitellar segments	Amynthas alexandri
13.	Male pores on XVIII; copulatory papillae absent	*Metaphire birmanica*
	Male pores on XX; copulatory papillae present, 3 pairs on XVII to XIX	*Metaphire anomala*

Comparative taxonomic accounts of all the three commonly used species of earthworms and one locally abundant species (*Lampito mauritii*) also used in open system of vermicomposing are given in Table-1 for easy identification.

Table: 1: Comparative accounts of four commonly used species of earthworms in vermicomposting activities.

Characters	*Eisenia fetida* family Lumbricidae	*Eudrilus eugeniae* Family Eudrilidae	*Perionyx excavatus* Family Megascolecidae	*Lampito mauritii* Family Megascolecidae
Length	27-130 mm	90-185 mm	30-180 mm	95-155 mm
Diameter	3-5 mm	5-8 mm	3-7 mm	3-6 mm
Setae	Lumbricine	Lumbricine	Perichaetine	Perichaetine
Clitellum	Saddle-shaped, XX-XXXIV	Annular, intersegmental, furrows, faintly demarcated, XIII, XIV-XVIII	Annular, XIII-XVII	Annular, XIV-XVII
Male pore	Paired, large glandular papillae on XV	Paired, transverse slits, slightly in front of 17/18	Closely paired, on small papillae in single male field on XVIII	Paired, XVIII on slightly raised porophores
Female pore	Paired on XIV	Paired, transverse slits on XIV	Single, mid-ventral on XIV	Paired, presetal on XIV
Colour	Purple, red to reddish brown, usually in transverse mid sigmental bands alternating with white or yellowish bands	Brown or red to bark violet	Deep purple to reddish brown dorsally, pale ventrally	Grayish yellowish or brownish

Vermiculture

It is the process of culturing or rearing of earthworms in natural/ semi-natural conditions for multiplication with the objective of using them in time of need (composting/poultry feed/fish bait). In natural and man-made agro-ecosystem/forest land, the earthworms remain active only for a short period of time, as their activity is limited by a number of factors (temperature, moisture, pH, availability of food, predators, etc.). However, some of them can multiply very fast and remain as active feeders throughout the year in semi-natural or even artificial environments with optimal conditions. Considering this amenability for culturing, these worms are cultured for mass multiplication and utilised throughout the year effectively by the vermicomposting practitioners. The worms can be easily propagated fast in a mixture of animal dung and compost, properly mulched with decaying straw or grasses. Addition of locally available cheap nutrient supplements such as, oil cakes, rice/wheat bran or gram powder will enhance the multiplication rate. Multiplication rate reduces with increasing density and to avoid this, large plastic or cement tubs with ample space may be used for the purpose.

Vermicomposting

It is the process of the biodegradation of waste biomass (organic) with the help of earthworms. This process produces organic manures. The technology is very simple and available within our country. It requires more manual labour. Though, it is suitable for rural areas, it could be tried in urban areas at domestic and also at community level.

Principle of Vermicomposting

As the earthworm feed on organic wastes, their muscular gizzard of the digestive tract acts as a crusher and break up larger particles into finer ones. This degradation process is further enhanced by the symbiotic microbes and enzymes available in the gut of the worms. During this process, about 5% of the ingested matter is assimilated and the rest is ejected out as vermicast. Thus the main basis of the vermicomposting technology lies on the voracious feeding habit and high fecundity of the earthworms.

Essentials for Vermicomposting:

- Suitable species of earthworms (epigeic) in sufficient number
- Organic wastes, *viz.*, kitchen wastes, leaf litter, any green wastes of the garden, weeds, husk, straw, etc.
- Culture tank/pit/vat made up of bricks and cement, plastics or earthen material.
- Well-ventilated and shaded place with facility of water.

- Optimum temperature (20°-30°C), Optimum pH (6.5-7.5).
- Predators, like ants, rats, termites etc. are to be carefully avoided.

Techniques of Vermicomposting

All sorts of organic wastes (kitchen wastes, household wastes, market wastes, leaf litter, etc) could be tried initially. The waste materials are to be mixed with cow dung after thorough sorting and shredding and kept for 2 to 3 weeks with periodical turning. Moisture content of the wastes is to be monitored carefully so as to maintain 40% to 50% by regular sprinkling of water at 2 to 3 days interval. This process of bacterial decompostion is called **primary decomposition.** After this process, selected species of earthworms are released at the rate of 15 to 20 g/kg of pre-decomposed wastes at the surface. Immediately after the release, the earthworms enter the material to be composted. In order to avoid predator attack and to maintain darkness the whole system is system is to be carefully monitored for temperature, pH and moisture for a period of one and half months or so. At the end of the composting process, it appears that the contents become sweet smelling, fine, granular and dark/light brown with 10% to 20% unfed waste material. Finally, the compost is harvested for storing, and the worms are reused for further composting purpose.

Flow Diagram of Vermicomposting:

Collection of wastes (domestic/municipal) - -→sorting of organic wastes - -→shredding- -→ chopping - -→air drying (two or three days) - -→primary decomposition (12-15 days) - -→ inoculation of selected species of earthworms - -→ monitoring of temp., pH & moisture - -→ sampling at 15 days interval for chemical analysis (mainly for C/N ratio) - -→ Harvesting after one and a half months)

Domestic Vermicomposting:

A working model for domestic vermicomposting has been developed by the present author. (Misra & Kaustuv, 2004) for the individuals interested in practising vermicomposting at household level.

Aims of the project: To design domestic Vermi-composting kits and standardising the operational methods, which will be small and easy to use but effective for individual family.

Objective: To inculcate the belief in Vermicomposting

methodologies among the general public at household level with an aim to conserve and improve the degrading soil and to discourage deleterious chemical farming practices.

Methodology

(i) Designing of the bins

Various pots like earthen pots, earthen tubs, plastic bins of various sizes, were tried. Finally, earthen pots (12 inch size) were selected. (It can manage kitchen wastes of a family of 2 to 3 persons for 15 days). Three such pots, marking as Bin -I, Bin-II and Bin-III, were taken for continuous running of the vermicomposting process.

(ii) Designing the operational flow chart

(Please refer to the chart enclosed, **Table -II**)

Main aspects

i) In the Bin-I, daily waste dumping and turning (DWD/T) was done for 15 days. [During this time Bin-II and Bin-III remained empty]

ii) Primary decomposition was allowed for another 15 days in Bin-I. [During that period waste material were dumped in Bin-II, and the Bin- III remained empty.]

iii) Final weight of the decomposed waste in Bin-I was measured

iv) Inoculation by earthworm was done in the Bin-I on the 31st day

Report on the Experiment on Domestic Vermicomposting

Two preliminary trial runs were performed with a set of three bins, as mentioned above, and a 10 days cycle of dumping (D), Primary decomposition (PD), and Turning (T) for vermicomposting with two refills. But it was found that composting of the material was not up to the mark. Later, a 15 days cycle with similar set of three bins was adopted successfully as described below:

1. A family near Golf Green Urban complex having 3 adult members, 2 males and one female, was selected for the test run of domestic vermi-composting. Domestic waste was collected from the family everyday at 1.00 a.m. on and from 15.4.2005, sorted and deposited in Bin-I for 15 days.

2. Paper, plastic, metal foils, coconut shells, etc. were discarded. The remnant contained mainly vegetable peels, fruit rinds, meal leftovers, used tea leaves etc.
3. Fresh weight of the waste was recorded as provided in the Table No. III for Bin-I. Total weight of the dumped waste at the end of 15th day was obtained by adding the daily data and found to be 8263 g.
4. But the actual weight of the accumulated waste measured on the 15th day i.e. on 29.04.2005 was found to be 5364 g.
5. The material was left for primary decomposition in Bin I for the next 15 days with two turnings per week. At the end of primary decomposition for 15 days (on 14.05.2005) the weight was found to be 4373 g. The waste material was deposited in Bin-II from 16th days onwards for a period of 15 days, and kept for primary decomposition for the next 15 days.
6. Adult *Perionyx excavatus* was inoculated in Bin-I @ 20g of earthworm per kg of waste material (i.e., in all 85 g (105 worms) of earthworm was inoculated in 4373 g of waste).
7. Another set of experiment was done with *Lampito mauritii* for the sake of comparison between two native species regarding their efficacy in vermicomposting (pl. see **Table- IV**).
8. A cup full of water was added every third day. Temperature was recorded before inoculation. It was found to be 28.5° C in the waste and air temp. being 29° C. The pH was also measured and found to be a 6.5. Few egg shells were crushed and added to the waste to raise the pH level, and it was found to be increased up to 7 within 15 days.
9. First refilling of decomposed waste from Bin -II was done on the 46th day and second refilling was done from Bin-III on the 61th day of the experiment.
10. Harvesting from Bin-I was done on the 75th day. 368 earthworms were harvested having a weight of 184 g on 28.06.2005.
11. For details of waste dumping, primary decomposition, earthworm inoculation and harvesting, please see the Operational Model (**Table-II**).

12. Another set of three bins were kept as control (without earthworms) for noting the changes in NPK and C:N ratio.

Table-II. Domestic Vermicomposting: Operation Model (Flowchart)

Phases	Days	Bin-I	Bin-II	Bin-III	Remarks
I	1st 15th	Daily waste dumping + Turning (DWD/T)	-	-	
II	16th 30th	[Primary decomposition] [PD]	Daily Waste Dumping + Turning (DW D/T)	-	
III	31st 45th	Earthworm Inoculation	[PD]	Daily Waste Dumping + Turning	
IV	46th 60th	Refil-I (from bin-II)	Transferred to Bin-I (DWD & T)	[PD] trans. to Bin-I	
V	61th 75th	Refil-2 (from bin-III) <u>Harvesting</u>	[PD]	[DWD/T]	
VI	76th 90th	(DWD/T)	Earthworm Inoculation	[PD] trans, To Bin-II	
VII	91st 105th	[PD] trans. To bin-II	Refil-01 (tear Bin-III)	DWD/T)	
VIII	106th 120th	(DWD/T)	Refil-02 From binI <u>(Harvesting)</u>	[PD]	
IX	121st 135th	(PD) trans, To bin-III	(DWD/T)	Earthworm Inoculation	
X	136th 150th	DWD/T	[PD] trans. to Bin-III	Refil-01 (from Bin-I)	
XI	151th 165th	[PD]	DWD/T	Refil-02 From bin- II <u>Harvesting</u>	
XII	166th 180th	Earthworm Inoculation	[PD]	(DWD/T)	

Table: III- Data for Waste Dumping in Bin-I.

DAYS	DATE	WEIGHT (g)
01	15.04.2005	490
02	16.04.2005	560
03	17.04.2005	619
04	18.04.2005	495
05	19.04.2005	527
06	20.04.2005	605
07	21.04.2005	540
08	22.04.2005	527
09	23.04.2005	620
10	24.04.2005	465
11	25.04.2005	520
12	26.04.2005	495
13	27.04.2005	630
14	28.04.2005	540
15	29.04.2005	630
TOTAL WEIGHT 8263 g		
Actual weight 5364 g on 29.04.2005 and 4373 g on 14.05.2005		

Summary: During the study the weight of the daily waste was noted carefully. Thus in the first 15 days total weight of dumped domestic waste was revealed 8263 g (Table III). Actual weight of the accumulated waste measured on the 15th day was found 5364 g, while after another 15 days, it reduced to 4373 g only. Initally the pH of the waste was found 6.5. To increase the alkalinity, crushed eggshells were added in the waste and the pH was raised to 7 within 15 days.

Table: IV- Experimental set-up with two local species of earthworms

Species	Code No.	No. of worms		Weight of the worm (g)		Weight of the wastes (g)	
		Initial	Final	Initial	Final	Initial	Final
P. excavatus	SP	105	368	85	184	4373	1976
L. mauritii	SL	130	158	125	145	1000	445
Control	SC	-	-	-	-	1000	510

Table V Results of the chemical analysis recorded during experiment with two local species of earthworms

Date	Sample	Total Carbon (%)	C:N ratio	Total Nitrogen (%)	Total Phosphate (%)	Total Potash (%)
14.05.05	On the day of inoculation	20	41.6	0.48	0.50	0.53
10.06.05	*P. excavatus*	12.8	10.7	1.19	1.46	1.00
	L. mauritii	15.4	14.6	1.05	1.25	0.98
	Control	Not determined				
28.06.05	*P. excavatus*	10.5	6	1.75	2.06	1.50
	L. mauritii	12	9.6	1.25	1.95	1.50
	Control	15	8.3	1.10	1.75	1.25

Note:

i) Domestic vegetable waste during primary decomposition releases a large volume of water. A better result was obtained with 2 days of pre-drying.

ii) The bins were covered with nets to avoid flies and other predators.

iii) During harvesting, the compost was sieved with a 2 mm sieve to separate out the earthworms and also the unfed material from the compost material.

iv) The weight of the separated castings was recorded as 1,976 g.

Results and Discussion

Regular monitoring of temperarture, moisture, pH, and analysis of sample for NPK and organic carbon at cerain interval was done. The chemical analysis was carried out from Nitofix Laboratory, Kolkata. The results along with a short discussion is given below.

Temperature, moisture and pH

Temperature between 45°C and 65°C, a range which is considered as optimum by the scientists, accelerates composting process. The highest temperatrue reached during the early phases of composting process ensured inactivation of any pathogens expected to be present intially in the substrate.

During the present study periods, temperature in the primary decomposition pot (Bin-I) increased rapidly reaching values between

50° and 60°C in the first five to ten days. The temperature drop and gradual stabilisation to ambient level, about 28°-30°C was found to reach within 15 to 20 days. Moisture level was maintained between 40% and 50% by periodic sprinkling of water. A non-formal way of measuring the moisture level was followed. This is simply by taking a small sample of substrate and squeezing with fingers so that water does not come out in drops. It indicates the level of moisture is optimum. The pH is a parameter, which greatly affects the composting process. The optimum range of pH for bacterial development is a 6.0 to 7.0 and for fungi the preferable range is 5.5 to 8.0 Addition of crushed egg shells or diluted lime water is followed in cases of low pH only.

During the present work, the inital pH value remains between 5 and 6. However, during later stage of composting, pH increases up to 7.5. The pH stabilisation was observed within 25 to 35 days.

Chemical Changes

The analyses of the chemical constituents of the compost samples collected on the day of earthworms inoculation revealed high carbon content and also high C:N ratio. Gradually, NPK level increases during the process of decomposition, and C/N ratio comes down and stabilizes.

Nitrogen Content:

During composting the complex organic compounds of the substrate are used by the micro-organisms to meet their energy demands. The total nitrogen was observed to be increased even in the first week of primary decomposition. A continuous increase was observed throughout the vermicomposting period, except in a few cases, where immobilization was observed. Gradual increase of nitrogen content (mineralisation) was observed for both the species used here. It was observed that initial content of 0.78% raised to 1.75% and 1.25% within one and a half months time in case of *P. excavatus* and *L mauritii* respectively, while 1.10% in control (without worms).

Carbon/Nitrogen Ratio

The carbon/nitrogen ratio is considerd to be an important parameter to assess a successful composting process. To accelerate the biodegradation process, small amount of cow dung was added during primary decomposition. There was a gradual increase in nitrogen content and decrease in carbon content to have C:N ratio from initial 41.6 to 6, 9.6 and 8.3 in case of *P. excavatus, L. mauritii* and control respectively. Hence, C/Nratio was narrowed down gradually during the composting process. However, a low but more or less stable C/N ratio indicates optimum availability of nutrients for all the cases.

Phosphorus and Potassium Content

The Phosphorus and Potassium play a vital role in plant nutrition, but its concentration in soil solution is only approximately 0.05 mg/l. During the present work, the Phosphorus level was increased to a greater extent i.e., from 0.50% to 2.06% and 1.95% within the composting period for *P. excavatus, L. mauritii* respectively. Whereas, the potassium level is also gradually increased from 0.53% to 1.50% and 1.50% in both the cases.

General Discussion

The earthworms not only create nutrient rich soils but safer soils. When the earthworms ingest raw organic material they also take in the pathogens, harmful fungi, nematodes, and harmful bacteria. When earthworm ingest these parasites they are destroyed through its digestive process. This creates soil less harmful to plants and animals. The earthworms also help to neutralize the pH level in the soil. It does not matter what the pH of the soil is that goes into the earthworm, regardless it comes out at a neutral pH of 7. This neutralization is obtained by the calciferous glands of the earthworm and the buffering action of the carbonic acid. This addition of calcium carbonate that is produced by the worms is nature's way of soil neutralization. Today, because of the decline of earthworms in the soil, outside elements such as lime has to be added to do what earthworms do naturally, neutralize the soils.

The content of earthworm castings, along with the natural tillage by the worms' burrowing action, enhances the permeability of water in the soil. Worm castings can hold close to nine times their weight in water. The burrowing of the worms through the soil lossens the soil creating a lighter and more porous texture that can retain water easily. If the soil is too compact and dense then no water could be absorbed and erosion would occur. If the soil is too porous and cannot hold on the water molecules, then the water may not stay in the soil long enough for the plants to absorb it. In worm-worked soil, the combination of light density soils from the burrowing and casting's ability to hold the water creates the optimum water availability for plant growth.

The burrowing action of the earthworm through the soil is very beneficial to the land. Along with the increase in the soil's ability to retain water, it naturally mixes and aerates the soil. As the worms move through the soil they may bring minerals from lower regions of the soil up to the surface and topsoil, and organic materials to the lower levels. This mixes and evens out the nutrient levels of the soil. The aeration of the soil helps the decomposition of organic material and provides oxygen for other decomposer organisms in the soil.

Agricultural practices have had a major affect on the earthworm population and natural fertility of the land. Plowing and tilling of the land kills the worms directly and destroys their habitat. The plowing and tilling of the soil exposes the worms to predators and dry conditions along with destroying their complex system of burrows through the soils. The destruction of the worm burrows reduce the soil's capacity to retain water, increasing the chances of flood and erosion. When plowing the land, nature's own way of keeping the soil light and porous is destroyed, or more the land is plowed the more worms are killed that naturally till the land, therefore the more plowing is needed the next time.

Pesticides and chemical fertilizers also disrupt the natural cycle of the worms. Pesticides used to kill parasitic animals not only kill the parasites but all the other organisms that inhabit that land as well, including the earthworms. When they kill organisms such as the earthworms, that naturally kill bad parasites they again enter the cycle of having to use more and more pesticides to maintain the same outcome. Chemical fertilizers is increase the salinity of the soil causing the worms and microorganisms that naturally fertilize the land, to die off or migrate out of the area. Yet again, they enter the vicious cycle. Use of chemical fertilizers useless as compared to that produced by worms. The United States Department of Agriculture tested the effect of chemical fertilizer vs. earthworms on plant growth. They started with two containers of poor soil. To container 1, they added dead worms, chemical fertilizer, and grass seed. To container 2, they added live worms, grass seed, and no fertilizer. The result was that the effect of the worms strongly outweighed that of the chemical fertilizer on the growth of the grass. The grass seed in container 2 containing the worms and no chemical fertilizer grew four times faster than the grass seed in container 1. Earthworms till the soil, fertilize crops, condition soil, and decompose organic waste and yet society continues to use industrial and chemical methods to less productively achieve what worms do naturally.

Although the agricultural society has not yet made its move in the direction of the earthworm, the general public has slowly begun to move to use earthworms for waste management. As environmental stresses on the earth increase, awareness of the earthworm's beneficial effects on the environment has expanded. Because earlier societies trends would throw out all waste that our produced. Landfill clogging and overloading quickly became a problem. Over 4,000 landfill sites have closed in the U.S. California has mandated a State law to reduce their waste dumped in the landfill by 50% of the 1994 levels by the year 2000. If this quantity reduction is not met there will be penalties up to $10,000 a day to enforce it. People have began to look to new ways to waste disposal because of mandates like this and their growing concern for the environment. Some people have started to use worms to reduce the amount of organic waste sent to the landfills. In San Jose California over 1,200 residents used discount vouchers distributed by the city to purchase composting worms. Seventy percent of the material sent to the landfills can be fed to worms. Through the process of using earthworms to decompose organic material the organic waste is decreased in volume by 60% and a highly nutrient high rich fertilizer is produced. Earthworm composting is a more efficient method of composting compared to composting without worms. This is because they decompose the organic material faster and turn it back into reusable nutrients for plants. Composting units depending completely on heat of bacteria to break down organic material take several weeks to produce a low-quality compost from one pound of organic material. One pound of worms on the other hand will break down that one pound of organic material and produce a nutrient rich castings in 48 hours. Using worms to compost organic material contributes to water conservation. Rotting organic waste in the landfills are polluting the underground water supply. When worms break down that material the only thing that seeps into the underground water supply are reusable nutrients that continue the cycle of life.

Earthworms are wonderful creatures that do so much for land and organisms that inhabit it. They provide us with fertile lands, waste reduction, and continue the cycle of the life on Earth. They are simple organisms that ask nothing of us and faithfully do what they can in the fight to save the earth's environment.

Conclusion

Municipal Solid waste (MSW) available at roadside vats/dumps as such is not suitable for vermicomposting purpose. Sorting out of only decomposable materials, keeping aside all other non-degradable components including toxic ones, is the key to the Vermicomposting process. The first step in starting Vermiculture cum vermicomposting process is to procure suitable species ofs earthworms in sufficient number and also to arrange for regular input of partly decomposed raw materials (feed) for the worms. The supply of nitrogen-rich material like cattle dung, pig dung or goat dung is to be ensured for maintaining desirable C: N ratio (40:1). All organic inputs are to be added, after primary decomposition of 15 to 20 days, only in the layers of not more than 5 to 10 cm thickness, otherwise excess amount of heat expected to be generated may kill the worms.

The vermicomposting technology is very simple and of low-cost nature, and does not require any sophisticated instruments. However, its acceptance by society depends on continuous awareness cum educative programmes with scientific information. In tropical and sub-tropical conditions, *Eudrilus eugeniae* and *Perionyx excavatus* are the best vermicomposting worms. The applicaton of epigeic species of earthworms in combating organic pollution and producing high quality organic soil additives and earthworms biomass is moving at a very slow pace in most scientific laboratories compared to the enthusiastic group of entrepreneurs who have been successful in promoting the technology. It is a challenging field for scientists to bridge the gap between the laboratory and field" (Kale, 1998).

References

Agarwal, A., Singhmar, A., Kulshrestha, M. & Mittal., A.T. 2005. Municipal solid waste recycling and associated markets in Delhi, India, *Resources, Conservation and Recycling*, 44 : 73-90.

Chaudhuri, P.S., Pal, T.K. Bhattacharjee, G., & Dey, S.K. 2001. Nutrient changes during vermicomposting by *Perionyx excavatus* of the aquatic weed *Trapa bispinosa. Philippine J. Sci,* 130 (2) : 127-133.

Chaudhuri, P.S. Bhattacharjee, G., Pal, T.K. & Dey S.K. 2001. Chemical characterization of Kitchen waste vermicompost processed by *Perionyx excavatus. Proc. Zool. Soc. Calcutta,* **54** (2): 81-83.

Chaudhuri, P.S. & Bhattacharjee, G., 2002. Capacity of various experimental diets to support biomass and reproduction of *Perionyx excavatus. Bioresource Technology,* 82: 147-150.

Chaudhuri, P.S., Pal, T.K. Bhattacharjee, G. & Dey, S.K. 2002. Rubber leaf litters (*Hevea brasiliensis,* var RRIM 600) as vermiculture substrate for epigeic earthworms, *Perionyx excavatus, Eudrilus eugeniae and Eisenia fetida. Pedobiologia,* 47 : 796-800.

Darwin, C. 1881. *The formation of vegetable mould through the action of worms with observations of their habits,* p. 298 Murry, London.

Dash, M.C. 1978. Role of earthworms in the decomposer system. In *"Glimpses of Ecology"* (eds, J.S. Singh and B. Gopal) India International, Scientific Publication, p. 399-406.

Dash, M.C. 1994. Earthworm Ecology to vermitechnology. Changing Villages 13: 18-26.

Dash, M.C. & Senapati, B.K. 1986. Vermitechnology: potentially of Indian earthworms for vermicomposting and vermifeed. In: *Soil Biology* (Mishra, M.M. and Kapoor, K.K., eds.) Department of Microbiology, HAU, Hisar p. 61-70.

Edwards, C.A. and Lofty, J.R. 1997. *Biology of earthworms,* 2nd edition, p. 333 Chapman and Hall, London.

Ghosh, M, Chattopadhyay, G.N. and Baral, K. 1998. Transformation of Phosphorus during Vermicomposting. *Bioresource Technology,* 69: 149-154

Hartenstein, R. 1981. *Use of Eisenia fetida* in organic recycling based on laboratory experiments, *Proc. Workshop on the role of earthworms in the stabilization of organic residues,* Kalamazoo, Mich, p. 155-157.

Ismail, S.A. 1995. Earthworms in soil fertility management. In: Thampan, P.K. (ed.) *Organic Agriculture,* Peekay Tree Crops Development Foundation, Cochin, India, p. 77-100.

Ismail, S.A. 1997. Vermicology: the Biology of Earthworms, Orient Longman Ltd., Hyderabad, p. 92.

Julka, J.M. 1986. Earthworm Resources of India. *Proc. Nat. Sem. Org. waste Utiliz. Vermicomp.* Part B, *Vermes and Vermicomposting,* M.C. Dash, B.K. Senapati and P.C., Misra (eds.): 1-7.

Julka, J.M. 1993. Earthworm Resources of India and their utilisation in vermiculture, p. 51-56. *Earthworm Resources and Vermiculture.* Zoological Survey of India, Kokata.

Kale, R.D. 1998. *Earthworms: Cinderella of Organic Farming.* Prism books, Bangalore

Kaviraj & Sharma 2003. Municipal solid waste management through vermicomposting employing exotic and local species of earthworms.

Bioresource Technology, 90: 169-173.

Misra A. and Basu, K. 2004. Earthworms– Friends of People: with notes on Domestic Vermicomposting. *Proc. State level Workshop on Vermitechnology for eco-friendly waste management*, p. 35-41. Dept. of Zoology & Biochemistry, Konganadu Arts & Science College, Coimbatore, Tamilnadu, 5-7 August, ed. R. Jeyaraaj & Indira A. Jayraaj

Misra, A. and K.R. Halder. 2005. Notes on the identification of earthworm species suitable for Vermicomposting purposes in India. *Rec. Zool. Surv. India* (in press)

Prabhu, S.R. 1998, Earthworms : the best waste managers for coconut plantations. ***Tree World*** 8 (4): 3-4.

Reynolds, J.W. 1994. Earthworms of the world. *Global Biodiveristy*, 14: 11-16.

Senapati, B.K. and Julka, J.M. 1993. Selection of suitable vermicomposting species under Indian conditions, p. 113-115. *Earthworms Resources and Vermiculture*. Zoological Survey of India, Kolkata.

Shuchi Gupta, Krishna Mohan, Rajkumar Prasad, Sujata Gupta & Arun Kansal 1998. Solid waste management in India: options and opprortunities. ***Resources, Conservation and Recycling,*** **24** : 137-154.

Tripathi, G. & Bhardwaj, P. 2004. Comparative studies on biomass production, life cycles and composting efficiency of *Eisenia fetida* (Savigny) and *Lampito mauritii* (Kinberg). *Bioresource Technology*, 92: 275-283.

Waite, R. 1995, Household Waste Recycling. Earthscan Publications Ltd, London.

Chapter 7

Biotechnological Developments in Solid Industrial Waste Treatment

Sudhir D. Ghatnekar and Sumukh S. Ghatnekar

Biotechnology Resource Centre, G/I Adinath, Shaikh Misry Road, Antop Hill, Mumbai- 400 037

e-mail: brc_suvash@hotmail.com

Industrial processes developed in the early part of this century relied greatly on natural resources and the products of these industries were largely biodegradable. However, with an increase in demand for industrial goods, these manufacturing industries could no longer depend only on natural raw materials.Thus research was directed to the development of artificial or synthetic raw material.

This marked the beginning of the modern industrial revolution.With industrialization came urbanization leading to a concentration of human population in a small area. Activities allied to modernization like power generation (thermal, hydro and nuclear power plants), modes of transportation etc. developed rapidly.

All these events had a detrimental effect on the environment. In recent years, repercussions of these developments have been felt and research has been directed to tackle these problems. Public awareness for the need to avoid endangerment of the natural systems that support life on earth i.e. the atmosphere, water, soil, and living things has also intensified.

Thus the need of the hour is sustainable development in the manufacturing processes and designing of eco-friendly products, which can be derived from the vast diversity of life forms on the earth, making them bio-compatible.

India consists of 65 crore acres of land, of which 35 crore acres is under agriculture. Of the remaining of 30 crore acres, 4 crore acres are barren steep rocks where the possibility of cultivation of crops is quite remote. Normally an industry situated on an acre of land can produce goods and earn revenue sufficient to manage bread and butter for a minimum of 100 families. Our strengths are land, water, sunlight and manpower, but our weakness is overpopulation. As a result we are constantly facing the problem of increasing targets of food production for the growing masses.

In these circumstances, what is needed is to increase the productivity of every acre of existing agricultural land and we have to make serious efforts to convert the so called non agricultural land into agricultural one. Our objective, therefore, should be to consider every acre of land under agriculture as a factory. Presently, the gap between input and output in the agriculture sector is very narrow. Improving the productivity of land and minimizing the cost of production can increase this gap.

The existing industrial sector which has higher productivity, normally caters to the demand of the elite population, which is only 15-18% of our total population. On the contrary, we need to cater to the demands of the remaining 82-85% of the population. This could be achieved only if we diversify our industries in agro-sector.

Though industrial productivity in India is much higher than agricultural productivity in relation to other developing countries, it is quite low. The main reason for the low productivity is the old and obsolete technologies that many of the industries use, often leading to alarming and perpetual deterioration as well as problems of population.

Every industry whether chemical, mechanical or even agricultural, creates pollution either in liquid, gaseous or solid form. Quite a few of these industries are facing closure because they fail to abate pollution and maintain safety standards. Their immediate need is to acquire appropriate and cost effective technology, which will take care of their effluents. Further, if these wastes are recycled into useful products or formulated with some renewable cheap raw materials into value-added products, it would precisely serve the need of the industry. Thus, in the circumstances what is needed is a safe technology, which can utilize the wastes of the existing industry and then convert it into useful products to again increase the productivity of our land.

Vermiculture based biotechnology for waste treatment has been developed at the **Biotechnology Resource Centre (BRC)** and implemented in several industries like food processing, wood based solvent extraction (soyabean oil), pulp and paper, textile, pesticides, and petroleum based chemical industries.

Conventional Waste Treatment Methods

The treatment of industrial wastes can be broadly classified into two groups: 1) Primary treatment (physio-chemical treatment) and 2) Secondary treatment (aeration tank, trickling filters, clarifiers, etc.). Industrial wastes can be treated by seveal means like physical, chemical, biological.

Among physical treatments given to industrial effluents, the more popular ones are: 1) Incineration (for hazardous chemical and biological waste), 2) Adsorption (on resins or other adsorbents for removal of color and odor), 3) Filtration (for removal of insoluble matter), 4) Precipitation (for removal of soluble matter), 5) Physical segregation (separation of treatable and non-treatable waste), 6) Evaporation.

The chemical treatment of industrial waste involves: 1) Neutralization of acidic or alkaline waste, 2) Coagulation or flocculation by the addition of flocculating agents, (3) Oxidation of metals and oxidizable matter, 4) Denitrification, 5) Chlorination, etc.

Conventional biological treatment is given as a secondary to tertiary treatment and uses the following treatment methods: 1) aerobic treatment (aerated lagoons, activated sludge process, fluidized bed reactors, biodiscs or rotating biological contactors 2) anaerobic process (anerobic upflow reactors, anaerobic filters), 3) bioleaching (for removal of trace metals from effluent streams) , 4) composting.

Thus in general, an industrial effluent treatment plant is a complex maze of the above mentioned activities arranged in series depending upon the characteristics of the effluent.

In industrial waste treatment, conventional biological waste treatment is expensive as far as capital and running costs are concerned. Such systems can be converted into technologically feasible and economically viable systems. Their benefits include the utilization of gas produced from digestion of sludge, and the utilization of treated sewage on land for irrigation, industrial cooling, etc.

The wastes, which are concentrated, (i.e. contributing to high pollution levels, e.g. dairy waste, distillery waste and sugar wastes) are first treated by anaerobic methods and are further treated by aerobic methods. In aerobic treatment the choice can be among aerated lagoons, activated sludge process, extended aeration and trickling filters, etc. The choice of treatment scheme depends upon the availability of land, capital and operational costs, site conditions, and skilled supervision and final disposal points.

Recent trends in waste treatment are the use of fluidized bed reactor, anaerobic upflow filters, biodiscs and contact stabilization. Fluidized bed reactors have proved useful in treating domestic and industrial wastes. This process provides greater biomass levels than the conventional activated sludge process at much lower detention times. The system can provide efficient secondary treatment as well as nitrification and denitrification.

Anaerobic filters are efficient in treating domestic waste water as well as certain industrial waste waters like vegetable, tanning, coffee pulping wastes, distillery wastes, slaughter house wastes etc. Anaerobic filters also serve as energy producing units through generation of methane. The use of pure oxygen as a substitute for air in the activated sludge process has gained in popularity where the available space for the construction of treatment facilities is limited.

Vermiculture Based Waste Treatment Methods

Vermiculture is nothing but growing or "culturing" earthworms for various uses. Researchers from all over the world have found that earthworms can play an important role in digesting wastes and improving soil fertility. The lowly earthworm not only helps in treating wastes from several industries inexpensively but can turn these wastes into premium commercial products in the form of biofertilizers, soil conditioners and plant tonics. Vermiculture biotechnology for industrial waste treatment is particularly suited for developing countries.

In Mumbai, vermiculture biotechnology has been developed at BRC to convert industrial wastes into biofertilizers and plant tonics and has been implemented successfully in several industries on large scale. This technology has proved to be a much better alternative to the conventional methods of effluent treatment.

There are several advantages of this biotechnology like 1) the technology is inexpensive and comprehensive in that it involves very little capital and operational costs and it can be applied to solid as well as liquid effluents. 2) the products of this technology, unlike most of the conventional methods, is clean and safe value-added biofertilizer or plant tonic which can be sold in the market, 3) it is relatively a low-technology which does not require highly skilled supervision once the treatment plant is optimized, 4) it requires $1/4^{th}$ to $1/5^{th}$ the space versus conventional effluent treatment plants, 5) it is very well suited for developing countries, 6) the earthworms, which form the biomass, can also be sold at high profit margins for a variety of uses such as bait for freshwater sport fishing, high value protein for animals and humans, pharmaceuticals, etc. And above all the most coveted advantages is that the cost of implementing this biotechnology is hardly 1/4th to 1/5th of a conventional treatment plant.

The only snag appears to be that the vermiculture biotechnology effluent treatment plant must be "tailor-made" to suit the specific properties of the effluent from each individual source. Essentially, the worms required for culture must be of very superior quality and they should remain in the confined area only.

Waste Management and Resource Recovery

A large number of industries generate massive quantities of solid and liquid wastes. The most undesirable pollutant effects are:

1. Oxygen demand: There are pollutants which deplete the dissolved oxygen content of natural waterways and hence cause damage to all life forms.
2. Toxicity: Contaminants such as, arsenic, cyanide etc. are toxic not only to aquatic life but to human life as well.
3. Taste and Odor: There are contaminants which impart highly undesirable taste and odors to natural environment.
4. Color and Turbidity: These damage the aesthetic values of the waterways and impede photosynthesis.
5. Corrosion and Silting: Causes damage to public sewer systems.
6. Fire and explosive hazards: Are caused by excessive discharge of flammable material.
7. Temperature: High temperatures can be harmful to aquatic life and decrease the capacity of waterways for dissolving oxygen.

Some of these wastes might be more appropriately called "misplaced resources." These can be considered as rich carbohydrate, protein or mineral-based resources that are currently being wasted. Vermiculture aids in disposal by significantly improving the qualities of wastes and reducing smell and putrescent potential. Such culture also recaptures much of the viable products in the form of vermi compost and the worms theselves.

Criteria for Treatment

As mentioned earlier, in the last fifteen years biotechnologists have dealt with effluents generated by 1) Paper mills 2) Soyabean Oil extraction plants 3) Naptha based organo chemical industries 4) Dairy and cheese industries 5) Tannery 6) Sewage systems 7) Uses of Pesticides 8) Hospital and Surgical Wastes 9) Enzyme production units 10) Textile industries and Processing Houses 11) Refinery and 12) Slaughter House Wastes.

Apparently there is no criterion as to which wastes can be treated with worms. However, it can be generalized that pH of the effluents should be with 5-10 and the solid content should be around 35-40 percent (semi solid). Where the solid content is less, it can be made up by adding in-house wastes including boiler waste or fly-ash, lime sludge, paper clippings and canteen, other debris, kitchen, even toilet wastes.

Other cheap materials that could be mixed to increase the solid contents are any cellulosic wastes like old newspapers, sawdust, fresh cattle dung etc. The technology is not useful to convert wastes containing plastics, polythene and polystyrene foam, glass pieces, and iron fillings or steel scraps. In fact, broken glass pieces and iron filllings present in most industrial waste need to be manually separated before inoculating earthworms and relevant biocultures to digest them.

The Treatment Protocol

Normally earthworms need to be acclimatized to particular wastes in stages and at times it may take 4-8 months before the earthworms start digesting them. Afterwards however, the retention time or cycle period is reduced to 40-45 days. Whenever the earthworms cannot act alone, the wastes can be seeded or inoculated with specific microbes like cellulose degraders or others depending on the composition of wastes to be treated. For example, some species of bacteria and fungi work very well with earthworms to degrade paper mill wastes. Hence paper mill effluents must be seeded with these cellulose degraders to stimulate biodegradation by earthworms, then bring about complete degradation of the waste sludgeby a series of chain reactions. This also leads to a prolific increase in the counts of nitrogen fixers, phosphate solubilizers and potassium enrichers.

The resultant product is a biofertilizer of excellent quality.

Two-Tier System

Recently, a new two-tier technology has been developed by BRC wherein the vermiculture-based treatmentof cellulose-based industry sludge is coupled with culture of oyster mushroosm on the surface of the sludge. This technology has also been applied commercially and the oyster mushrooms thus cultured are of superior quality and are rich in lysine and leucine, two essential amino acids, which are normally lacking in a vegetarian diet.

An important factor, which must be considered by the industries that wish to make use of vermicultrue biotechnology, however, is the space requirement. It could be generalized that to treat 5-7 tons of wastes every day one needs an open space 700-1000 sq. metres. In this open space series of trenches, cemented of plastered tanks could be made depending upon the convenience and type of wastes.

Apart from the space the other important factor in favour of vermiculture is the overall cost of treatment. Against a conventional biodegradation or chemical treatment plant, the initial capital cost will be 1/5th or 1/6th only. Another advantage is that the running cost of the vermiculture effluent treatment plant is almost negligible in terms of power consumption.

On the other hand, the value-added biofertilizer produced is a saleable product ranging from Rs. 5/kg to Rs. 20/kg. Liquid formulation for mixing with a drip irrigation or for use as a foliar spray can be also made from culture earthworm biomass and is also saleable from Rs. 90-140/litre. Many industries where this vermiculture biotechnology has been transferred are selling 5-6 tons of bio-fertilizers daily.

Other Biotechnological Waste Treatments

BRC has also developed a technology to culture *Spirulina*, the algae that can end malnutrition, in liquid effluents generated by cellulose-based industries. For example, the liquid effluent from a primary clarifier can be utilized in the form of lagoons to culture *Spirulina* species.

Spirulina is a protein rich blue-green alga which polishes the secondary and tertiary liquid effluents but also can be given to poor people as a nutritional food supplement and can at the same time reduce infectious disease.

In developed countries like the USA, Japan, Germany, and France. *Spirulina* is sold in health food stores in the form of tablets, powders, and even pasta. As much as 50 tons of protein per hectare per year can be produced by cultivating *Spirulina*. Producing *Spirulina* on treated effluents of cellulose-based industries can not only solve environmental problems but also help in enhancement of the economic viability of the developing world through better health and conservation of resources.

The polished secondary and tertiary effluents treated with *Spirulina* cultures can then be utilized for *Tilapia* and Carp culture which is also another protein rich source. Mallard Ducks also thrive in such treated lagoons and purify the water.

Conclusion

In brief, vermiculture biotechnology now developed in Mumbai converts high cost pollution into twin benefits by fertilizing non productive land to ensure bumper crop yields and increase protein biomass to remove malnutrition of the ever-increasing population. Thus unwanted pollution is converted into coveted prosperity.

References

Beychok, M.R. 1973. In. Aqueous Wastes from Petroleum and Pharmaceutical Plants, John Wiley and sons.

Gadkari, S. K., Badrinath, S.D., Deshpande, V.P. and Kaul, S.N. 1986. Problems on process waste treatment technology in India–Some case studies, Indian J. Environ Protection. 6 (1): 41-46.

Ghatnekar Sudhir, D., 1984. Growing greenbacks from worms, Science Today, 18 (4): 34-38.

Ghatnekar Sudhir D. 1988. Bioenergy from vermiculture in Maharashtra: Problems Potential and Prospects, Gadgil Gangadhar and Deshpande Arvind (eds.), Somaiya Publications Pvt. Ltd. Bombay :154-158.

Ghatnekar Sudhir, D. and Ghatnekar Anjali, S., 1990. State-of-the-art: Biotechnology development in India. Monograph published by MVIRDC, World Trade Centre, Bombay.

Ghatnekar Sudhir D. and Kavian Mahavash F., 1991. Biofertilizers–Novel venture for industry, World Trade Review, 40: 15-19.

Ghatnekar Sudhir D. and Kavian Mahavash F., 1992. New spin-offs of biotechnology after the Rio-Earth Summit, Proceedings of Inaugural Session of Biotech India October 28-31., Bangalore.

Ghatnekar Sudhir D. and Kavian Mahavash F. 1994, The application of vermiculture in Indian industries. Proceedings of Middle East Agriculture-Dubai, Organized by Arab Exhibition Services and Overseas Exhibition Services Ltd. England, April 17-20, Dubai.

Ghatnekar Sudhir D., 1994. Industrial waste treatment with worms, Indian Industrial Sources. 9(5): 37-40.

Ghatnekar Sudhir D. and Kavian Mahavash F., 1995. The application of vermiculture in Indian industries, In. Microbes and Man, Chandra Sudhir, Khanna, R.K and Kehri, H.K. and Bishen Singh, Mahendra Pal Singh, (ed.) Dehradun, India. p. 137-149.

Ghatnekar Sudhir D., Kavian M.F., Ghatnekar, G.S. and Ghatnekar, M.S., 1998. Management of solid wastes through vermiculture biotechnology. In: Eco-technology for pollution control and environmental management, Trivedy, R. K. and Kumar A., (eds.) Envrio. Media, Karad, India p. 59-67.

Kavian Mahavash F, Ghatnekar Sudhir D., 1991. Bio-management of dairy effluents using red earthworms (*Lumbricus rebellus*), Indian J. Environ. Protection, 11 (9): 680-682.

Kavian, M.F., Ghatnekar Sudhir D. and Kulkarni Pushpa R., 1997. Biodegradation studies of soybean oil extraction sludge waste by *Lumbricus rubellus*, J. Industrial Pollution Control, 13 (2): 177-183.

Kavian, M.F., Ghatnekar, S.D. and Kulkarni, P.R. 1997. Biodegradation studies on onion sludge at pilot and plant level using vermiculture biotechnology. Indian J. Environ. Protection, 17 (8). 605-609.

Satchell, J.E. 1983. Earthworm Ecology- from Darwin to vermiculture, Chapman and Hall, London.

Chapter **8**

Biomanagement of Paper Mill Sludge using Vermitech and its Field Application

M. Gobi and G.S. Vijayalakshmi

Sri Paramakalyani Center for Environmental Sciences, Manonmaniam Sundaranar University, Alwarkurichi 627 412 (Tamilnadu)

Human and animal acivities generate large quantites of organic residuals. In India a large fraction of these residuals are wasted and dumped into the environment, thus causing overloading on land and in water bodies. Overloading, in turn leads to environmental pollution.

It is estimated that about 60 billion tons of organics are produced globally every year. Much of this is wastefully respired through man made processes as well as litter respiration in nature. The value of these organics is about 10 times the fossil energy consumed in 1995. (Meili, 1995).

Agriculture provides employment for about 60% of the population (Onayemi, 1981). However, there is a wide gap between food production and need of the population. FAO projection shows that there is going to be an additional 2.6 billion mouths to feed by 2025. The demand for basic staple food is expected to increase at an annual rate of 2.6% over 20-30 years. Shrinking sources of available farmland compounds is the problem. It is mainly through sutainable farming we can solve this global problem.

Sustainable Agriculture

Sustainability concept is based on equity between intra-generational and inter-generational equity issues. The inter-generational issues deal with dispersion of technology democratically, so that, all the farmers no matter the size of their holdings get the full benefits. Inter-generational issues involve utilization of resources at present without destroying future prospects (Swaminathan, 1992;

Agunwamba, 1993).

In the sustainable Agriculture, robust, healthy and vibrant topsoil is most important in soil-based agriculture for sustainable and economically viable production programmes. Topsoil is a living complex referred to as Bioplex, wherein a number of micro flora and fauna live in a biotic equilibrium within the framework of natural law. SOIL means SOIL OF INFINITE LIFE. But now we have turned SOIL into SOUL or INERT LUMP.

Chemical fertilizers, which are much popularized these days, are not only expensive and hazardous but also deleterious to environmental cleanliness. The excessive use of chemical fertilizer, which is characteristic of modern farming, creates pollution of soil and surface water bodies. The economic and environmental costs of excessive use of chemical fertilizers in arable farming are of global concern. How are we going to tackle this? It is only through evolving a sustainable ecosystem that is ecologically sound which means dependence on naturally-occurring nurient cycles mediated by soil macro fauna and microbes in an economically viable way for which vermi technology provides an answer. When water-soluble fertilizers are applied to the soil, a sizable portion of the added nutrients does not become available to plants but is lost either to the atmosphere or hydrosphere.

So biologists and agriculturists concentrate more on producing manure of biological origin and from waste materials in recent days.

Paper Mill Sludge

The problem of environmental pollution is mainly due to industrialization. The major industries that pollute the rivers include pulp and paper, textile, tannery, sugar, vegetable oil, plastic, fertilizer and petro-chemicals (Murugesan, 1998). The growth of pulp and paper industry is an index of the social, cultural, technical, industrial and economic development of the nation. There are about 305 paper mills in India with an installed capacity of 3014 lakh tons (Trivedi and Gurudeep, 1992). The volume of water consumed by paper industry is next to agriculture and being highly water intensive it becomes a major polluter of water resources. Pulp and Paper industry is one of the largest consumers of water, consuming about 250-350 m^3 of water/ ton of paper produced and generates about 225-275 m^3 of waste water/ ton of paper and produce huge volume of sludge. (Raghuveer and Sastry, 1995). The paper mill sludge-a cellulosic waste introduced into the water body further degrades more slowly thus increasing the BOD level of the water body.

Physical, chemical and biological processes bring about the treatment of wastewater. The physical and chemical processes although can be designed for any degree of purification are highly expensive (Gohil, 1995). Worldwide, the most commonly used waste treatment method by paper mills is by "activated sludge process". This process is not acceptable since it results in the formation of excessive active sludge. Hence these are usually dehydrated to cake and then discarded off in landfill sites or at times incinerated. Both these methods lead to the loss of profitable cellulose-based resource and have obvious environmental and economic disadvantages.

Paper mill sludge cannot be applied directly to the soil since the soils become overloaded leading to soil sickness and pollution of soil and ground water. Therefore biological treatment methods have received much attention and are considered as an efficient low-cost treatment. Biologists and agriculturists concentrate more on producing manure of biological origin from waste materials in recent days.

Applications of vermibiotechnology for conversion of paper mill sludge into a useful biomass would not only solve the waste disposal problem but would also indirectly meet the growing energy crisis of developing countries (Jeslyn Vijayakumari *et al.*,1988). Hence this material here was subjected to biological treatment.

Vermiculture biotechnology is a dynamic process brought about by the earthworms with the aid of mixed microbial population with specific function. The end product is called humus, which is enriched with essential micro and as well as macro nutrients. Adding casts to soil not only improves soil structure and fertility but also leads to improvement in the overall plant growth and thusincrease their yield (Kavian, 1997). Vermicompost not only improves and protects the fertility of the soil but also enables the soil to improve the productivity by 40% to 60% (Ranganathan and Christopher, 1996).

In the present studies, proper managment of one of the industrial solid wastes i.e., paper mill sludge through vermitechnology by employing exotic species of earthworm *Eudrilus engeniae* was undertaken.

COLLECTION OF WASTES

The industrial waste viz., paper mill sludge was collected and transported to the working unit at Sri Paramakalyani Centre for Environmental Sciences, Manonmaniam Sundaranar University, Alwarkurichi. The paper mill sludge was collected from the Sun Paper Mill Ltd, Cheranmahadevi. The bulking agent saw-dust was collected from nearby sawmills. The sludge since freshly collected had high water content. To reduce the excess heat and volatile matter, the heaped sludge was well spread and sun dried.

VERMICOMPOSTING

The freshly collected and dried industrial waste material paper mill sludge was mixed with bulking (Sawdust) at 2:1, 1:1 and one served as control, in which 4 kg of sawdust mixed with 2 kg of sludge (2:1), 2 kg of sawdust mixed with 4 kg of sludge (1:2), 3 kg sawdust mixed with 3 kg of sludge (1:1) and sludge was only used as control.

The above mixed waste material were placed in 125 X 62.5 X 25 cm size vermi pits. The exotic earthworm, *Eudrilus eugeniae* was inoculated, in which, 5 earthworms/kg were inolcuated and the whole setup was replicated.

EXPERIMENTAL SETUP

Sawdust: Sludge 2:1 (4 kg : 2 kg)	Sawdust: Sluge 1:2 (2 kg: 4 kg)	Sawdust: Sludge 1: 1 (3 kg : 3 kg)	Sludge Control

POT CULTURE STUDIES FOR BLACK GRAM

The present study was carried out to determine the impact of vermicompost prepared from paper mill sludge on the morphological and yield characteristic of black gram in earthen pots. Based on the nutrient status present in the composted paper mill sludge (viz., 2:1, 1:2 and 1:1), only one concentration 1:2 was selected and applied for field studies. The plants were cultivated in the medium designed with the following permutation and combinations.

SELECTION AND TREATMENT OF SEEDS FOR BLACK GRAM

The certified seeds of the pulse crop (*Vigno mungo*) variety CO-1 was selected for the study were procured from the regulated market. The selected seeds were washed with deionised water and surface sterilized with 0.1% mercuric chloride solution to keep off from spores of fungi and was sown in pots.

MORPHOLOGICAL CHARACTERISTICS OF THE PLANT

The experiment was run for a period of 60 days. Plants cultivated in the pots were watered regularly and from the wet medium five plants were removed gently from each treatment. The plants were washed in clean water to remove the adhered soil particles and the excess water was removed with the help of a filter paper and the following morphological characteristics were measured every fortnight:

Root length and Shoot length (cm)

With the help of a long thread, the length of the shoot (from the tip of young leaf to the base) and root length (from the base to the tip of the longest root) were measured.

Leaf area index (cm^2)

The total leaf area index was measured by the formula described by Puttaswamy *et al.,* (1976)

LAI = K (L x W)

Where, LAI-Leaf Area Index

K-Correlation factor

L-Length of the terminal leaflet (cm)

W-Maximum width of the terminal leaflet (cm)

Number of nodules

The total number of nodules present in the roots of the plants were counted and recorded.

Fresh and dry weight (g)

The total fresh weight of the plant was recorded using a manopan balance. For observing the dry weight the plants were dried in the hot air oven at 60°C for 48 hrs and the readings were tabulated.

Number of pods

At every fortnight for a period of 60 days, the total number of pods per plants was counted and recorded.

Number of seeds per pod

The total number of seeds unsheathed in each pod was counted and recorded.

Weight of seeds (g)

The weight of the seeds in each pod was weighted and taken into account for analysis.

⁻SULTS

Physico-chemical parameters of paper mill sludge

pH

The pH of the paper mill sludge mixed with bulking agent saw dust in the ratio 2:1, 1:2, 1:1 and control sludge was 7.40 ± 0.04 before composting. After composting the values were observed to range from 7.97 ± 0.19, 7.98 ± 0.08, 7.84 ± 0.10 and 7.28 ± 0.14 in 2:1, 1:2, 1:1 and control of *Eudrilus eugeniae* sludge respectively.

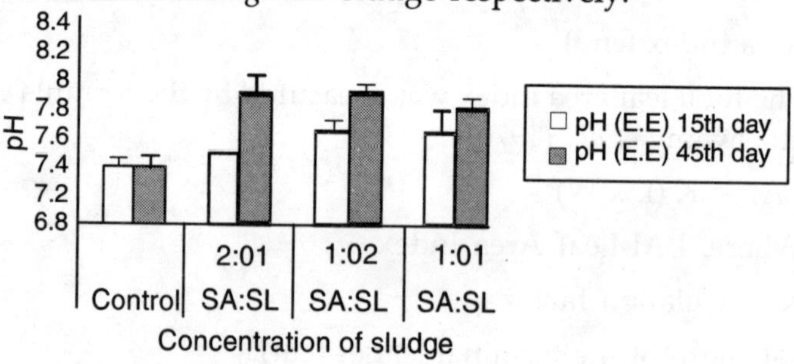

E.E- ***Eudrilus eugeniae***

Fig.1 pH of different concentration of paper mill sludge

Electrical Conductivity

The mean electrical conductivity of the initial substrate was 1.90±0.08 mS/cm in control paper mill sluge. A gradual decrease of EC was observed in all the treatments from the initial value. The final EC of the *Eudrilus* compost recorded was 1.64 ± 0.06, 1.68 ± 0.05, and 1.70 ±0.01 in 2:1, 1:2 and 1:1 concentrations, respectively.

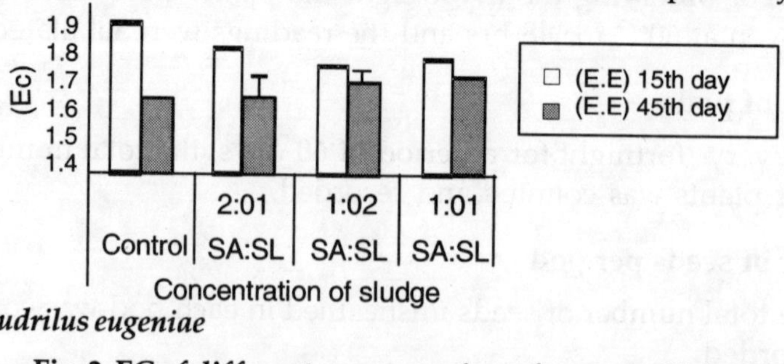

E.E- ***Eudrilus eugeniae***

Fig. 2. EC of different concentration of paper mill sludge

Water-holding Capacity

The initial and final water-holding capacities of the substrates before and after composting are presented in Figure-3. The water holding capacity of the paper mill sludge in the control was 48.51. After composting, the water-holding capacity was found to be increased in all the compost. A maximum increase of 67.91% was noted in 2.1 sludge.

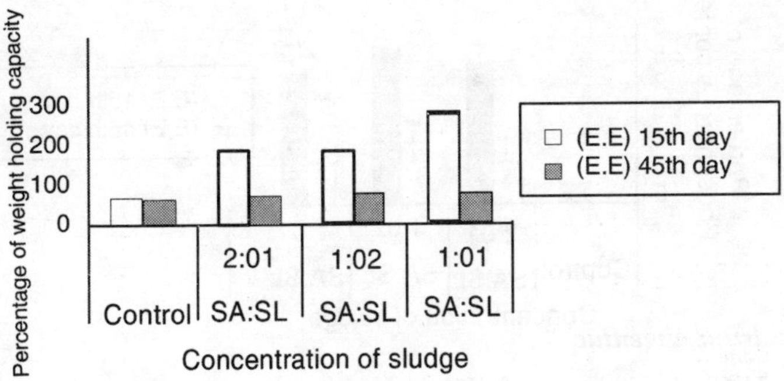

E.E- *Eudrilus eugeniae*

Fig. 3. Water Holding Capacity of different concentrations of paper mill sludge compost

Pore Space

The pore space of the different concentrations of paper mill sludge before and after composting is shown in Figure-4. The pore space of the paper mill sludge in the control compost was 66.31%. Pore space value was found to increase in all the treatments gradually, during the experiment. The maximum percentage increase was observed in *Eudrilus* worked sludge.

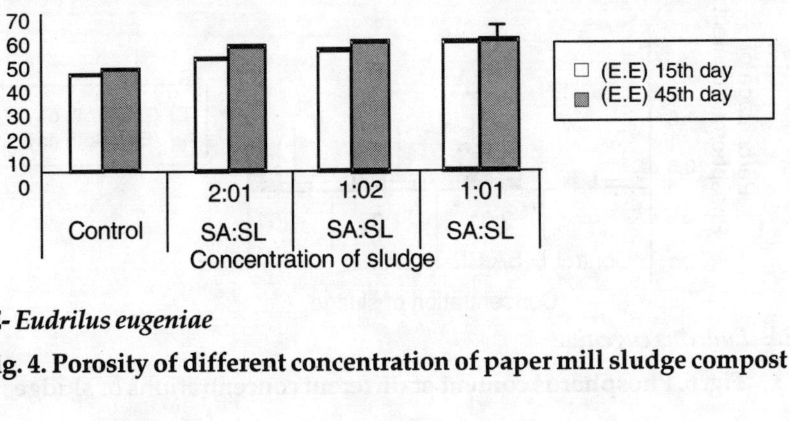

E.E- *Eudrilus eugeniae*

Fig. 4. Porosity of different concentration of paper mill sludge compost

Nitrogen

The nitrogen content of different concentrations of paper mill sludge before and after composting is shown in Figure-5. In all the four concentrations of paper mill sludge, increase in the nitrogen content was noted in *Eudrilus* worked compost. In general, with the increase in the concentration of sludge a corresponding decrease in nitrogen content in the compost was observed.

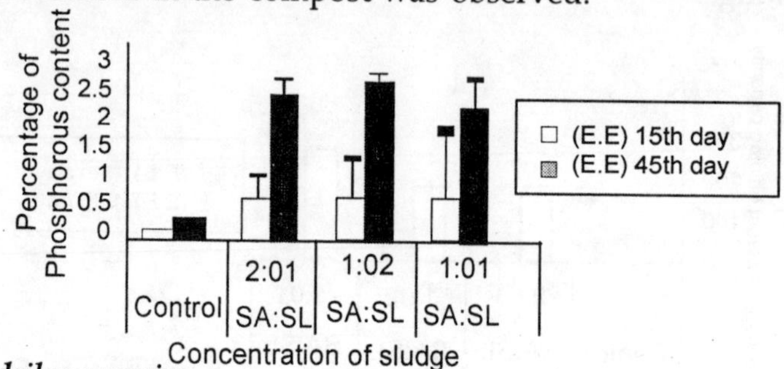

E.E- *Eudrilus eugeniae*

Fig. 5. Nitrogen content of different concentrations of paper mill sludge

Phosphorus

The phosphorus content of the substrates before and after composting is presented in Figure-6. The vermicompost produced by the *Eudrilus* showed significant difference between treatments. The maximum phosphorus content was recorded in all the four concentrations of paper mill sludge under study than the control. Increased phosphorus content was observed in the *Eudrilus* experimental tub with increased concentrations of sludge (0.924±1.04 in 2:1 sludge, 0.987±1.00 in 1:2 sludge and 0.955±0.144 in 1:1 sludge respectively on 60th day of composting).

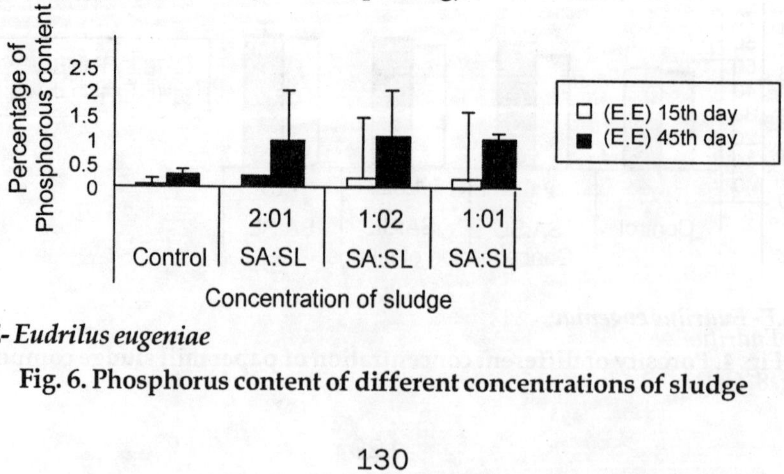

E.E- *Eudrilus eugeniae*

Fig. 6. Phosphorus content of different concentrations of sludge

Potassium

The potassium content of the substrates during composting is shown in Figure-7. Significant increase between treatments and control was noted in all the concentrations of paper mill sludge on the 60th day of composting. Maximum increase was observed in 2:1 (1.05±0.54), 1:2 (1.26±0.33) and 1:1 (1.18±0.42) in *Eudrilus* worked composts.

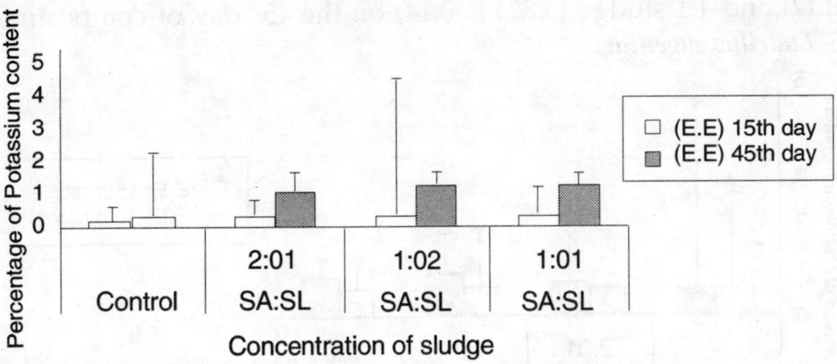

E.E- *Eudrilus eugeniae*

Fig. 7. Potassium content of different concentrations of paper mill sludge compost

Calcium

Figure-8 shows the mean values of calcium in different concentrations of paper mill sludge. In general, significant increase in calcium content was observed in all the concentrations of paper mill sludge composts on 60th day over control. The calcium content was recorded to be maximum in *Eudrilus eugeniae* worked compost (3.907±0.34) in 1:2 sludge.

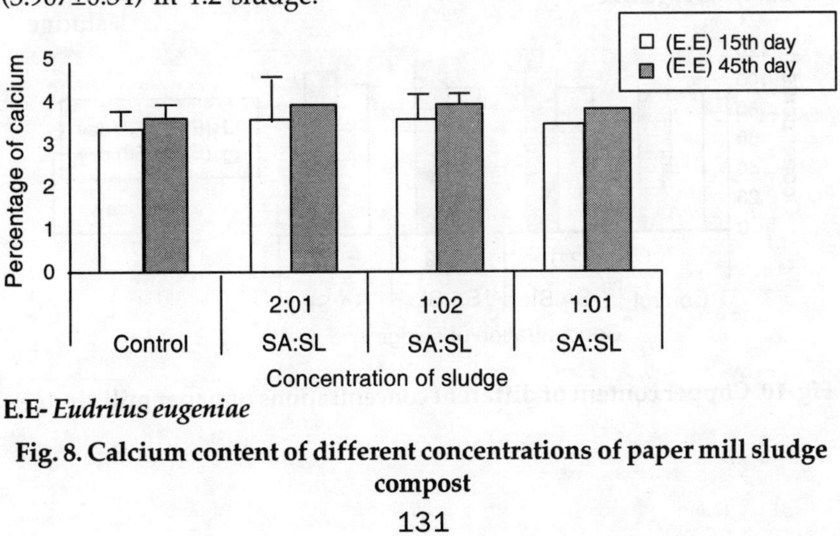

E.E- *Eudrilus eugeniae*

Fig. 8. Calcium content of different concentrations of paper mill sludge compost

Magnesium

The initial and final levels of magnesium present in the different concentrations of paper mill sludge are given in Figure-9. After composting the magnesium values increased in all the composts over initial and control. In the *Eudrilus* worked composts, the maximum percentage increase was recorded in 2:1 (3.907 ± 0.04), 1:2 sluge (4.01 ± 0.12) and 1:1 sludge (3.821 ± 0.14) on the 45th day of composting.

E.E- *Eudrilus eugeniae*

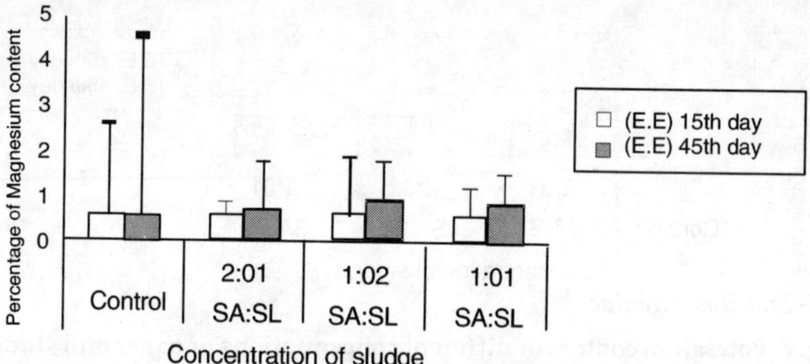

Fig. 9. Magnesium content of different concentrations of paper mill sludge compost

Copper

Figure-10 shows the inital and final amount of copper present in the compost under study. In the *Eudrilus* worked compost the increase in copper content was observed in 108 ± 0.08 in 2:1, 114 ± 0.04 in 1:2 sludge and 106 ± 1.00 sludge.

E.E- *Eudrilus eugeniae*

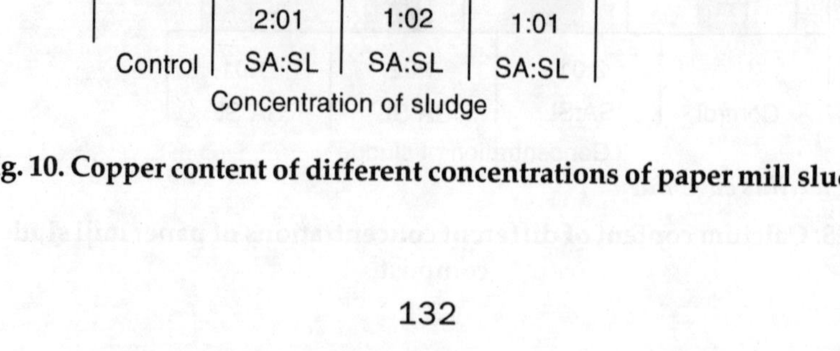

Fig. 10. Copper content of different concentrations of paper mill sludge

Iron

The initial and final iron content in the waste substrate under investigation is given in Figure 11. Control beds had more iron than in the initial stage of composting. In the paper mill sludge treated with *Eudrilus* earthworms, an increase of iron over control was found to be 0.51 ± 0.77 in 2:1 sludge, 0.58 ± 0.21 in 1:2 sludge and 0.54 ± 0.11 in 1:1 sludge.

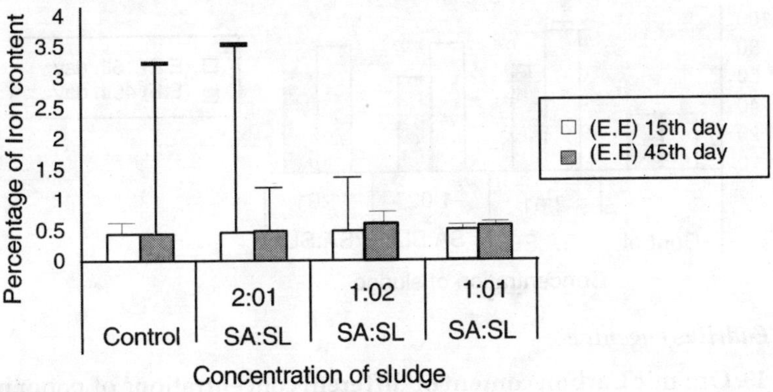

E.E- *Eudrilus eugeniae*

Fig. 11. Iron content of different concentrations of paper mill sludge compost

Zinc

The zinc content of paper mill sludge mixture before and after composting is presented in Figure 12. There was a significant increase over initial and control in all the treatments. Among treatments, maximum increase was observed in *Eudrilus* worked composts in 2:1 sludge (216±0.09), 1:2 sludge (235±1.80) and 1:1 sludge (227±0.64), respectively.

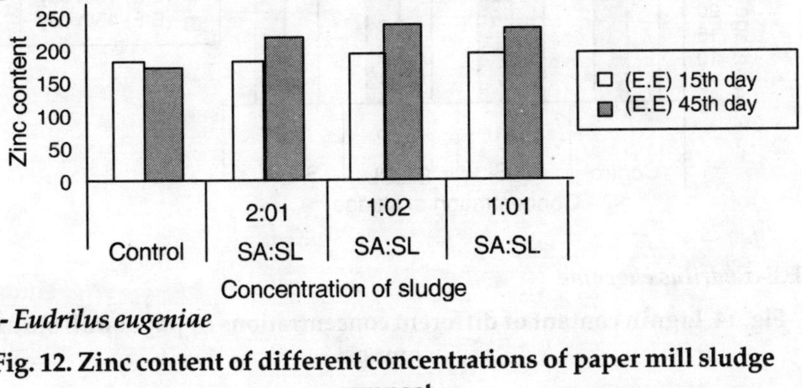

E.E- *Eudrilus eugeniae*

Fig. 12. Zinc content of different concentrations of paper mill sludge compost

Organic Carbon

The amount of organic carbon in the initial and final composted sludge mixed well with sawdust at 1:1, 1:2, 2:1 and control is given in Figure 13. Significant reduction over initial and control was observed in all the treatments. The maximum reduction in 62.31±2.04 in 1:2 sludge was recorded in *Eudrilus* worked composts.

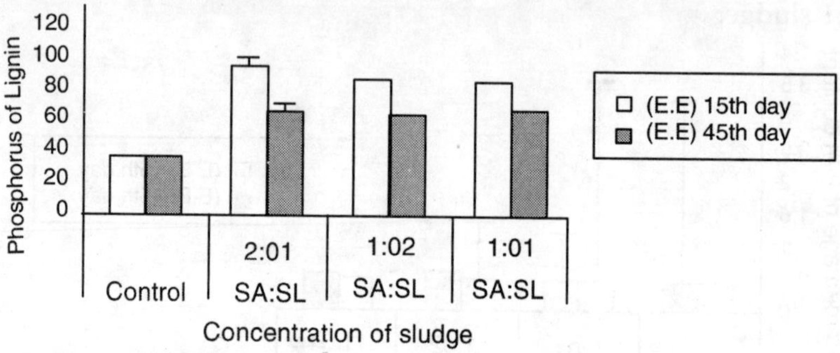

E.E- *Eudrilus eugeniae*

Fig. 13. Organic Carbon content of different concentrations of paper mill sludge compost

Lignin and Cellulose

The initial and final lignin and cellulose content before and after composting are reported in Figure 14 & 15. After composting significant reduction in cellulose and lignin in 2:1, 1:2 and 1:1 sludge was observed. The maximum percentage reduction of cellulose was

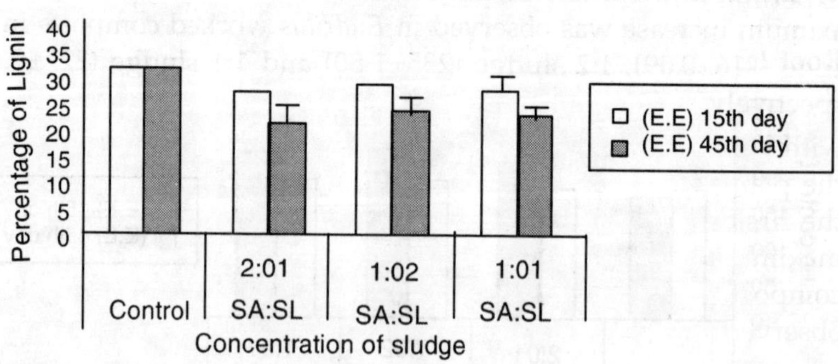

E.E- *Eudrilus eugeniae*

Fig. 14. Lignin content of different concentrations of paper mill sludge compost

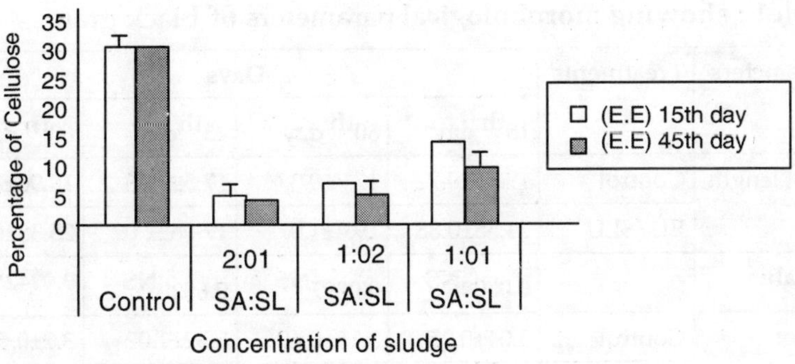

E.E- *Eudrilus eugeniae*

Fig. 15. Cellulose content of different concentrations of paper mill sludge compost

observed in the compost of the different econcentrations of paper mill sludge obtained from *Eudrilus eugeniae* over control. The percentage reduction of lignin at four different concentrations of paper mill sludge was found to be maximum in *Eudrilus* worked composts (22.06 in 2:1, 24.18 in 1:2 and 23.48 in 1:1 sludge mixture) over control. Highest reduction is lignin content was observed to be proportional to decrease in the concentration of paper mill sludge.

POT CULTURE STUDIES FOR BLACK GRAM

Effect of vermicompost on the growth and yield of black gram (*Vigno mungo* L) as well as the quality of the compost was tested using them as organic fertilizer for black gram. A pot culture experiment was carried out for growth studies.

Root length (cm)

The average root length (cm) of the plants grown in pots applied with vermicompost is given in Table-1. In general the root length of the plants grown with vermicompost has increased gradually from the first day to 60 days and it was more than that of control. The maximum root length 25.38± 0.59 was recorded in *Eudrilus eugeniae* compost on 60th day and the minimum root length 18.96±1.31 was observed in the control of their respective treatments.

Shoot length (cm)

The average shoot length of the plants was recorded once in every fortnight and presented in table-1. The shoot length was found to increase gradually in all the experiments. The maximum shoot

Table1 : showing morphological parameters of black gram

Parameters	Treatments	Days			
		15th day	30th day	45^{th}day	60th day
Root length	Control	19.66±0.72	17.7±0.37	17.5±1.46	18.96±1.31
	EU/SLU	24.58±0.88	19.4±1.07	17.06±2.02	25.38±0.59
F-Value	-	**0.0000^{NS}**	**0.0097^{NS}**	**0.6620^{NS}**	**9.9242***
Shoot Length	Control	3.04±0.25	3.16±0.40	5.52±1.02	3.2±0.51
	E/SLU	3.04±0.24	3.22±0.45	4.5±0.72	5.26±0.40
F-Value	-	**18. 5064***	**2.2230^{NS}**	**0.0310^{NS}**	**19.8442***
Leaf area index	Control	2.63±0.61	10.29±0.12	17.94±2.36	16.25±1.00
	EU/SLU	3.74±0.15	12.3±1.57	16.33±2.58	19.57±1.84
F-Value	-	**9.3570***	**0.1536^{NS}**	**2.4567^{NS}**	**0.4243^{NS}**
No. of Nodules	Control	26.0±3.21	27.6±1.94	30.0±2.19	12.4±2.04
	EU/SLU	31.0±3.45	26.6±2.42	28.4±2.86	20.4±2.66
F-Value	-	**1.1261^{NS}**	**0.1039^{NS}**	**0.1975^{NS}**	**5.7041***
No of leaves	Control	5.00±0.00	8.2±0.37	11.2±1.91	12.6±1.12
	EU/SLU	8.00±0.00	9.8±0.80	16.0±1.26	16.4±1.66
F-Value	-	**6553***	**3.2820^{NS}**	**4.3969^{NS}**	**3.5920^{NS}**
Internodal Length	Control	2.58±0.37	1.86±0.08	3.24±0.27	2.32±0.29
	EU/SLU	4.64±0.20	2.84±0.26	4.88±0.82	2.54±0.34
F-Value	-	**23.5755^{NS}**	**12.6036***	**3.5765^{NS}**	**0.2360^{NS}**
Fresh weight	Control	0.62±0.08	1.21±0.15	2.97±0.30	3.28±0.37
	EU/SLU	1.20±0.13	1.39±0.07	3.26±0.51	4.47±0.85
F-Vaue	-	**13.2406***	**0.9904^{NS}**	**0.2323^{NS}**	**1.6547^{NS}**
Dry weight	Control	0.39±0.03	0.19±0.03	2.02±0.21	2.29±0.41
	EU/SLU	0.54±0.03	0.54±0.03	2.44±0.40	3.18±0.81
F-Value	-	**10.9030***	**6.2741***	**0.8300^{NS}**	**0.9524^{NS}**

MEAN ±SD; * - Significant at 0.05; NS - Not Significant at 0.05 level length of the plants grown in the *Eudrilus* compost was recorded on 30th and 60th day; it was 3.22±0.45 and 5.26±0.40 respectively. Control plants had minimum growth rate i.e., 18.96±1.31 on 60th day.

Leaf Area Index (cm^2)

The data on leaf area index on different stages of growth are listed in table-1. The maximum leaf area of 19.57±1.84 was recorded in the leaves of plants growth in *Eudrilus* compost on 60th day. But the plants grown control pot recorded the maximum leaf area index which was found to be 16.25±1.00 on 60th day.

Number of Root Nodules

The number of nodules found in the roots of the plants in the vermi compost is tabulated in table-1. The maximum root nodules were found on 60th day in *Eudrilus* compost (20.4±2.66) and it was found to gradually increase from the first day onwards nodule number was counted in the control treatment on 60th day and it was 12.4±2.04.

Number of Leaves

The number of leaves in each plant is shown in table-1. A gradual increase from 15th day till the completion of the experiments was observed. The maximum number of leaves was found in *Eudrilus* sludge compost on 60th day (16.4±1.66). Likewise the control showed increased leaf numbers 8.00±0.00 on 15th day, 8.2±0.37 on 30th day, 11.2±1.91 on 45th day and 12.6±2.04 on 60th day respectively.

Internodal Length

The mean internodal length of the plants in each treatment is given in table-1. The internodal length of all the plants was higher on 45th day. Plants grown in vermicompost the internodal length was found to be 4.88±0.82 and 3.24±0.27 for control treatment, but it was gradually reduced at 60th day.

Fresh Weight (g)

The mean fresh weight of the plants in each treatment is given in table-1. The fresh weight increased gradually during the growth studies in respect of the root length and shoot length. Plants grown in *Eudrilus* compost showed increase of fresh weight (4.47±0.85) on 60th day. Likewise plants grown in control exhibited increased fresh weight in (3.28±0.37) on 60th day.

Dry Weight (g)

The dry weight of the plants cultivated with two different composts is tabulated in table-1. The data on dry weight revealed that as in fresh weight the maximum dry weight was recorded in all the three composts. Generally, plants in paper mill sludge compost showed increased dry weight on 15th and 30th day of all the treatments.

No. of flowers

The number of flowers, which emerged from each plant is presented in table-2. The first flower emerged after 45 days in all treatments. But the total number differed with each other. Generally, the total number of flowers recorded on 60th day was 1.4±0.24 for vermicompost, and 0.2±0.20 for control.

Table 2 : showing no. of flowers, pods and seeds of black gram

Parameters	Treatments	Days	
		45 th day	60 th day
No of flowers	Control	0.6±0.24	0.20±0.20
	EU/SLU	0.6±0.40	1.4±0.24
F-Value	-	0.0000NS	14.4000*
No of pods	Control	0.00±0.00	1.8±0.80
	EU/SLU	0.00±0.00	3.2±0.37
F-Value	-	0.0000NS	2.5128NS
Total no of seeds	Control	4.77±0.31	5.17±0.22
	EU/SLU	5.37±0.16	5.37±0.28

No of pods/Plant

Total numbers of pods per plant in relation to the vermi compost and control treatments are given in table-2. On 60th day the number of pods per plant was found to be more in *Eudrilus* compost (3.2±0.37) and 1.8±0.80 for control. The number of pods was found to be the minimum in the control pots in all the treatments.

Total number of seeds per pod

The total number of seeds per pod in each treatment are listed in table-2. The maximum number of seeds was observed in *Eudrilus* compost (5.37±0.28). Likewise the number of pods was found to be 5.17±0.22 in control.

Total weight of yield (g)

The average weight of seeds in each treatment is presented in table-3. Plants grown in *Eudrilus* compost applied pots showed a maximum yield (17.14). But in control grown plants recorded total weight of yield (9.08) only. Similarly, percentage of yield increased over control was 88.76%.

Table 3 : Average total weight of yield of *Vigno mungo* in two different treatments

Days	Control	EU/SLU
Total weight of yield (g)	9.08	17.14
% of yield increase over control		88.76

DISCUSSION ON NUTRIENT CONTENT

INFLUENCE OF EARTHWORMS ON THE PHYSIO-CHEMICAL AND MICROBIAL PROPERTIES OF THE PAPER MILL SLUDGE

pH

Earthworms are directly affected by low pH. Each species showed a specific tolerance to acidity that influenced the distribution of that species in soils (Laverack, 1963). The distribution of the earthworm species is influenced by the native soil pH. (Piearce, 1972). Haimi and Huhta (1987) stated that the decrease of pH towards neutral is an important factor to be considered influencing retention of nitrogen. The lower pH recorded in the final products might have been due to the production of CO_2 and organic acids by microbial activity during the process of bioconversion of the different substrates in the beds (Haimi and Huhta, 1986).

High solubility of nutrients in earthworm casts increases the pH of cast (Barley, 1961). This could be another reason for the rise in pH of the substrates observed in the present study. Bhatnagar and Palta (1996) stated that preference of neutral soils by most earthworm species expecting *Eisenia fetida* that tolerates slightly acidic soils. Several workers reported that earthworm's casts are found to be more neutral than the soil in which the worms live (Salisbury, 1925; Puh, 1941; Nye, 1955; Ramalingam, 1997). One possible reason for this may be the neutrilization of soils as it passes through the earthworms gut, through secretion of the calciferous glands. On the contrary, Edwards and Lofty (1977) are of the view that neutralization of soil is due to secretions from the intestine and ammonia excretion. El Duweini and

Ghabbour (1965) observed that the population can be adversely affected by high salt concentrations. Springett and Syers (1984) found that the production of cast increased with increasing pH and calcium level, but not with increasing calcium when pH was constant. Observance of collections of castings of *Metaphire posthuma* and *Eutyphoeus woltoni* was found in soils having pH of 5.9 than 7.8 and 8.4. (Singh, 1989)

The observed pH of 7.33 to 8.27 in the present study was found to be at par with the above results, supporting increase in biomass, fecundity and cast production of the earthworms.

Electrical Conductivity

Electrical conductivity is an indicator of concentrations of soluble salts. The electrical conductivity of the vermicompost produced was more than the substrates and control. Bhatnagar and Palta (1996) suggested that the ionic conductivity below 3.0 mS/cm was found to be optimum for earthworms. Electrical conductivity of 1.5-3.0 mS/cm supported the weight gain of earthworms (Kaplan *et al.*,1980). The increase of electrical conductivity in vermicompost when compared to the control might be due to the presence of exchangeable calcium, magnesium and potassium in worm casts than the soil (Bhatnagar and Palta, 1996). Balamurugan *et al.*, (1999) have also obtained similar results withs pressmud composted by *Eisenia fetida, Eudrilus eugeniae* and *Trichoderma harzianum*. The observed EC in the present study was in agreement with the reports of Bhatnagar and Palta (1996), Balamurugan *et al.*, (1999) and Balamurugan (2002).

Pore Space

The maximum percent increase of pore space was observed in the *Eudrilus* worked paper mill sludge. An increase of pore space from 52.31% in the initial litter waste to 150.7% was observed in the *Lampito* compost by Umamaheswari *et al.*,(2003a), which is in agreement with the present study. Observation of an increase in pore space from 52.34% to 144.10% in the *Eudrilus* worked compost of vegetable waste was recorded by Selvakumar *et al.*,(2003).

Water-Holding Capacity

The values of water-holding capaicty in the final composts were found to be more than in the control. *Eudrilus* worked compost recorded maximum water-holding capacity in all the four different concentrations of paper mill sludge and sugar factory pressmud under study. Venkatraja *et al.*, (2001) recorded similar increase in water holding capacity in the *Lampito* worked compost obtained from leaf litter. Similar results were obtained by Umamaheswari *et al.*, (2003b) in the mango litter waste composted by *Perionyx sansibaricus*. These findings agree with the present research work.

Nitrogen

After composting, the nitrogen values significantly increased over control in all the experiments. The increasing trend in nitrogen in the vermibeds was also reported by Dash and Patra (1979); Curry *et al.*, (1995), Ramalingam (1997) and Balamurugan (2002. Of the total nitrogen excreted by worms, about another half is secreted as mucoproteins by gland cells found in the epidermis, and half in the form of ammonia, urea and possibly uric acid as allantoin in a fluid excreted from the nephridiopores (Edwards and Lofty, 1977). Dash and Patra (1979) analysed the nutrient status of the *Lampito mauritii* worked soils and observed that the cast contained 0.47% N compared to 0.35% in the surrounding soil. They also estimated that the increase in nitrogen in casts was equivalent to 9.29 $g^{-2}y^{-1}$ and some of them probably from excretion of urine.

Graff (1971) too reported that the excreta of earthworms had more nitrogen considerably in casts than in the surrounding soil. The reason for the increase of nitrogen in the present study might have been due to the addition of mucoproteins secreted from the body wall of the earthworms. Mucoproteins secreted from the body surface found in drilosphere were reported by Lee (1985). A net mineralization of nitrogen occurred due to earthworm activity, whereas a net loss of mineral nitrogen was observed on exclusion of earthworms (Opperman *et al.*, 1987). Blair *et al.*, (1997) have observed that the earthworm might increase nitrogen availability by reducing microbial immobilization. Therefore the variation in increased percentage of nitrogen over control in composts with each different species of earthworm could have been due to the varying number of microorganisms present in the different concentration of the substrates and the palatability of the substrates by earthworms.

Curry *et al.*, (1995) observed that the earthworms would contribute an addition of 3.4-4.1g of mineral nitrogen to the soil through excretion, mucus production and soil ingestion. Bhatnagar and Palta (1996) revealed that about 6% more nitrogen was made available to plants by worm excreta. These documents are in conformation with the present study. Selvakumar *et al.,* (2003) have also observed results when they analysed the nitrogen content of the vegetable wastes composted by *Eudrilus eugeniae.*

Phosphorus

In the present study the phosphorus content increased in the earthworm treated waste when compared with the initial and control. The initial and final phosphorus content in the three concentrations of paper mill sludge composting has increased over control in all the experiments. The uptake of bacteria and fungi followed by grazing microorganisms by the earthworms, excretion and decomposition might result in release of phosphorus compounds that can be cycled through plants and back again to the soil biota as observed by Coleman *et al.,* (1983). Similar results were reported by Mansell *et al.,* (1981) with regard to the increase of short-term plant availability of phosphorus derived from plant litter by two or three fold by the earthworms. The uptake of the proliferated fungal species was found to be more in the beds treated with *Eudrilus,* which might account for enhanced phosphorus content in the *Eudrilus* composts, Phosphorus was found to be more in casts than the surrounding soil (Lunt and Jacobson, 1944; Graff, 1971). Bhatnagar and Patra (1996) repported that 15-30% more phosphorus was made available to plants by worm activity. Vermicompost obtained individually from cow dung, sugarcane trash, pig manure and horse manure had increased level of phosphorus compared to control (Jambhekar, 1992). Gunjal and Nikam (1992) observed similar findings in grapevine under drip irrigation system, Ramalingam (1997) in pressmud mixed with organic waste and Selvakumar *et al.,* (2003) in vegetable waste vermicompost. The present study also lends support to the above results.

Potassium

The initial and final values of potassium in different concentrations of paper mill sludge revealed that potassium increased progressively more than the control. Gunjal and Nikam (1992) also found that water-soluble potash of grapevine increased more than 8.4 times in vermicompost over control. Jambhekar (1992) observed considerable increase in available potassium than the initial and control treatments in different animal residues and agricultural wastes. Graff (1971), Nijhawan and Kanwar (1952), Watanabe (1975), Buchanan *et al.,* (1988) and Ramalingam (1997) reported similar trends. The findings of the present studies are also in conformity with the above-mentioned results.

Calcium

The increase of calcium in the vermicompost might be due to the excretion of calcium from the calciferous glands. The value of calcium at the end of compost formation was more than the control. The soil particles in the worm intestine are found to be cemented by calcium humate formed from the intestine organic matter and calcite excreted by the calciferous glands (Satchell, 1967). In the present study, calcium was found to increase over the initial value. A report that the cast contained 1.3 times more calcium than the surroundings soil was provided by Kale and Krishnamoorthy (1980). They also found that the excess of calcium gets excreted in concretions formed in the calciferous glands. Occurrence of enough calcium in available form in the calciferous glands with the primary role of secreting calcium and secondarily excreting wastes was reported by Jamieson (1981). Similar results were observed by Watanabe (1975), Dash and Patra (1979), Buchanan *et al.*, (1988), Bhatnagar and Palta (1996) and Ramalingam and Thilagar (2000) whose findings corroborates with the present one. Kavian and Ghatnekar (1991) observed increased clacium content in 25% soyabean oil extraction sludge waste when subjected to treatment by *Lumbricus rubellus.*

Micronutrients

The initial and final values of the micronutrients such as magnesium, manganese, copper, iron and zinc revealed that the main reason for the increase in the micronutrients in the vermicompost in the present study might be due to the release of the excess amount of micronutrients and heavy metals from the earthworm's body into the environment through the calciferous glands. Ireland (1975) suggested that the chemical changes that occur in the alimentary tract of earthworms might enable various metals more readily available to plants and mineralization of dead earthworms would release accumulated heavy metals into the environment. The chemical properties of earthworm casts, termite, mould and ant gallery were compared by Reddy and Dutta (1984) who found that the earthworm casts had increased nutrient than the others.

The availability of metals such as Pb, Cu, Cd, Zn, Mn and Ca in the tissues of earthworm was reported by Ireland (1979). Ionic regulatory mechanism in earthworms involves uptake of Fe, Mn and Na from ingesta and its excretion via calciferous glands (Bouche, 1983). Ash and Lee (1980) found Pb, Cd, Cu and Fe concentration in the tissue of *L. terrestris. L. rubellus* and *A. chlorotica.* The concept of incrase in the rate of heavy meal accumulation with addition of compost was provided by Mba and Wei-Chun (1982) on examination of the body content for Cd, Pb, Cu, Ni, Mn, Fe and Cr in *A. caliginosa.* Kale *et al.,* (1994) observed insignificant increase of Fe and Cu in *Eudrilus eugeniae* worked compost, which coincides with 100% sludge in the present study. Ramalingam (1997) recorded both increase and decrease in the level of Fe and uniform decrease in the level of Cu in the *Eudrilus eugeniae* worked compost. These two metals are required for haemoglobin formation (Maynard *et al.,* 1983).

Anderson and Laursen (1982) observed the excretion of Zinc, Manganese and Iron through the calciferous glands in *L. terrestris,* which coincided with the present study in *Eudrilus eugeniae* in different concentrations of paper mill sludge. Ramalingam (1997) and Balamurugan (2002) observed similar findings in differet organic wastes. The differences of micronutrients and metals in the different concentrations of paper mill sludge may be due to the differential mineralizatioin rates due to the combined effect of earthworms and microorganisms.

Organic Carbon

The level of organic carbon in the four different concentrations of paper mill sludge after composting was found to decrease from its initial value in both control and treatments.

Microorganisms have the capability of utilizing carbon as their energy source and nitrogen for growth during the process of decomposing materials in which carbon is released as CO_2. During the respiration of earthworms, combustion of carbon into CO_2 brings down the amount of carbon (Bhatnagar and Palta, 1996). A similar trend was observed in the present study too. The respiration of earthworms and growth of microorganisms might have been responsibile for the reduction of organic carbon. Bhandari *et al.,* (1967) found that the worm casts were significantly richer in polysachharides than the soil. Hand *et al.,* (1988) recorded a decrease in the organic carbon content of the peat and slurry mixture at the beginning of the experiment which got stabilized after 21 days and was observed to be lower than in the control at the end of the experiment. This finding strongly supports the present work in the paper mill sludge compost.

In the present study, the amount of organic carbon was found to be reduced a little from its initial value and it was within the range of

27.12% to 34.05%. Satchell and Martin (1984) recorded similar results in the culture containing earthworms. Hence it could be concluded that the organic carbon in the vermi compost might be the main source of energy for microoganisms, plants and soil aggregates.

Lignin and Cellulose

The initial and final contents of lignin and cellulose of the paper mill sludge mixed with saw dust at 1:2, 2:1, 1:1 and control revealed a significant reduction of cellulose and lignin was observed in the present experiments.

Neuhauser *et al,.* (1978) found the inability of earthworm, *E. fetida* to degrade ring ^{14}C, methoxy ^{14}C and side chain ^{14}C, lignin $^{14}C_2$ over 10 days thus providing very strong evidence that the invertebrate like earthworms does not have the ability to degrade lignin. Hand *et al.,* (1988) recorded a slight increase in the lignin content in the earthworm-inoculated beds. In contrast, in the present study, a decrease in the lignin content was observed on inoculation with the earthworms. This might be due to the microorganisms present in the gut of the earthworms and in the substrates. Kale (1998b) stated that there was an increase in the the cellulolytic, hemicellulolytic and nitrifying bacteria in earthworm's cast compared to the surrounding soil. She suggested that a heterogenous substrate like a mixture of agricultural waste with more lignin content would encourage the building up of not only cellulolytic but also lignolytic micro flora in the earthworm worked soil, irrespective of the species of the earthworm. Rutigliano *et al.,* (1996) recorded decrease in lignin concentration to tune of 73 to 87 percent in beech litter and to about 60 to 67 percent in litter decomposition. The slight reduction in lignin in the present study may be due to the presence of some lignolytic bacteria present in the gut or the substrates, which is not specifically identified, in the present work.

Based on the discussion, it could be inferred that paper mill sludge available in enormous quantities could be used as an effective medium for vermiculture supplemented with sawdust and cattle dung because not only served as a suitable medium for the growth and reproduction of the earthworms but also yielded a valuable biomanure for agriculture practices. Data on the growth and reproduction of the earthworms, physico chemical and microbiological analysis of wastes before and after treatment indicated that 1.2 concentration of sludge pressmud was ideal giving the highest microbial count and reproductive ratio of the earthworms.

Finally, the use of industrial waste (paper mill sludge) as raw material in the vermi systems can potentially help to convert these wastes into value-added materials, avoid their widespread disposal and corresponding environmental and economic drawbacks, and reduce the cost related to the exclusive use of different types of farm wastes as feed for the earthworms.

EFFECT OF VERMICOMPOST ON THE GROWTH AND YIELD OF BLACK GRAM (VIGNO MUNGO)

Root and Shoot Length

The length of the root increased steadily during the growth of plants. The maximum root length was recorded in *Eudrilus* compost over control.

The growth of shoot length was also found to increase gradually in all the experiments. The maximum length of shoot among treatments was recorded (5.26±0.40) in *Eudrilus* compost on 60th day. Control plants had the minimum growth in all experiments during all the stages of growth. Significant difference was observed in control.

Nijhawan and Kanwar (1952) have observed similar results of increased root length than the control on application of earthworm compost to wheat. A similar effect in Salvia and Aster grown in the pots was observed by Grappelli *et al.*, (1985). Increase in crop growth due to the transport of minerals and other compounds from deep down to the surface soil by the earthworms were found by Sharma (1986).

In the present study, presence of cocoons and juveniles in the vermicompost might have been the reason for the transport of minerals and other compounds as described by Sharma (1986). Application of casts of *P. alexandri* showed significant increase in the length and weight of the shoot and root systems of the *V. rosea* and *O. sativa* (Raddy, 1988). Reddy *et al.*, (1994) found that the plant height and biomass of sorghum were significantly higher when earthworm casts was applied with the soil mixture than with soil alone.

The present study on black gram grown with vermicompost shows similar results. The enhancement of plant growth by the earthworm compost might be attributed to physical and chemical condition of the soil and a direct hormone-like effect on the plants. (Neilson, 1965), Grappelli *et al.*, (1985) concluded that the enhancement of root initiation, root elongation, root biomass and rooting percentage might be due to vermicompost. Zraherskii (1957) attributed the production of some pro-vitamin D by earthworms. Presence of some plant growth factors and group B vitamins in the coelomic fluid of the earthworms was observed by Gavrilov (1962). Enhancement of soil structure and improvement in water-holding capacity and porosity that facilitates root respiration and growth by vermicompost was reported by Lee (1992).

No. of Leaves

The number of leaves in each plant grown with the three composts is given in table-1. The maximum number of leaves was found on 60th day in the plants grown in *Eudrilus* compost. The statistical analysis of data shows that there is insignificant difference ($P<0.01$) in the number of leaves among the treatments.

Similar results were observed by Nijhawan and Kanwar (1952) in Wheat, Tomati *et al.*, (1988) in Petunia, Begonia and Coleus. Grappelli *et al.*, (1985) in Salvia, Aster in pot culture studies and by Nethra *et al.*, (1999) in China aster.

No. of root nodules

The maximum number of root nodules was found on 60th day in *Eudrilus* compost (20.4±2.66) and it was found that the root nodules gradually increased from the first fortnight. The minimum number of nodules was found in roots of control plants. The nodule number differed significantly ($P < 0.01$) between treatment among the three different composts.

Kale *et al.*, (1992) have also reported that the significant increase in the colonization of the microbes (total microbes, nitrogen fixers, actinomyces and spore formers) in the experimental plots, which received half the recommended dose of fertilizers and the vermicompost over control. The presence of increased number of bacterial population, in the present study, is in accordance with the above result. The soil nutrients and physical properties may be another reason for the maximum number of root nodules. Haimi and Huhta (1987) inferred that the vermicompost could be considered superior to that of conventional compost especially with regard to its physical make up. Improvement of physical properties cardinal to soil health results in better oxygen and waste supply to root system (Aina, 1984). Based on the results obtained by Chakrabarti *et al.*, (1998), vermicompost can be very well recommended as compost for container nursery. The plant roots could grow well coupled with increased microbial population and the number of nodules also enhanced significantly over the control due to the improved physical structure of vermicompost.

Fresh and Dry Weight

A gradual increase in fresh weight of the plant was recorded with respect to root length and shoot length. Plants grown in vermicompost showed an increase in fresh weight (1.20±0.13, 1.39±0.07, 3.26±0.51 and 4.47±0.85) on 15th, 30th, 40th and 60th day respectively. Likewise plants grown in control exhibited decreased fresh weight (0.62±0.08, 1.21±0.15, 2.97±0.30 and 3.28±0.37) on 15th, 30th, 45th and 60th day. Significant difference ($P<0.01$) among composts was recorded.

The data on dry weight (table-1) showed that as in fresh weight the maximum dry weight was recorded in all the two treatments. Plants grown with *Eudrilus* compost showed on increasing dry weight on 60th day (3.18±0.81). The minimum dry weight was recorded in the plants grown in control pots (2.29±0.41).

The performance of the worm cast as a manure in the nursey beds of paddy was observed by Kale and Bano (1986) and it was found that the seedlings showed significant increase in growth in plots applied with worm cast and after transplanation the vegetative growth was influenced by the worm cast in a better way than that of the chemical fertilizers. This may be one of the reasons for an increased weight of the plant on fresh and dry weight basis. Shuxin *et al.*, (1991) who studied the dry weight of the plant by applying worm cast in soybean found that 40% to 70% increase was due to the nutrient absorption by the plant and the nitrogen absorbed by the plants from soil was increased by 30 to 50%. Hence it is clear that the worm cast can boost the yield of the vegetative growth as well as the yield.

No of Flowers

The first flower emerged after 45 days in all treatments. However, the total number of flowers varied with each other. The maximum number of flowers 1.4±0.24 was recorded on 60th day with *Eudrilus* compost. ANOVA showed that there is an insignificant difference ($P<0.01$) in the number of flowers between treatments and composts.

The reason for increased crop yield due to decomposition of organic matter by earthworm that increased nitrification was reported by Russel (1909). Graff and Makeschin (1980) observed that the yield influencing substances were released into the soil by *L. terrestris, A. caliginosa* and *E. fetida* but did not speculate on the nature of the substances. The increased nutrient availability in the growth medium in vermicompost applied pots, might have been the main reason for the maximum number of flowers in the present study, which was also suported by Kang *et al.*, (1994) who studied the effect of worm casts prepared from agro forestry woody sp. *Dactyladenia barteri, Glyricidia sepium, Leucana leucocephala, Senna stamea* and *Trechlia africana.* Nijhawan and Kanwar (1952) observed that application of earthworm compost to wheat crop increased the availability of nitrogen, phosphorus and potassium and decreased the pH of the soil as compared to control. From the above validation, it can be concluded that the application of vermicompost could hasten the flowering of the plants, which leads to the increased production.

No. of Pods/Plant

The total number of pods per plant in all the treatments revealed that their number was more in vermicompost on 60th day. The minimum number of pods was found in the control pots. Hopp and Slater (1949) first quantified the improvement of crop yield due to earthworm addition. The maximum yield recorded, in the present study, in the plants grown with vermicompost coincides with the following findings:

Enhancement of the activity of selected microbes in the soil system with vermicompost application was found by Kale *et al.*, (1992). Hence, there was a high level of total nitrogen in the experimental plot, which comparatively received less quantity of fertlizers. Kale, (1998b) recommended the optimum amount of vermicompost without chemical fertilizers for some crops for optimum yield as 15 tons for tomato, 10 tons for brinjal and carrot, 8 tons for radish and coriander, 12 tons for bhendi and 3 tons for cowpea per acre. She, further stated that the combination of vermicompost with chemical fertilizers could reduce their amount of chemicals into half for field application.

Number of seeds per Pod/Weight of Seeds

The maximum number of seeds was observed in *Eudrilus* compost (5.37 ± 0.28) and the minimum was found in control plants.

The total weight of the yield (17.14g) was recorded in vermicompost. The reason that could be attributed for increased seed weight in the respective treatment is that the leaf area index was also enhanced and which subsequently resulted in elevation of photosynthesis and accumulation in the grain/pulses.

Results of similar trends i.e., maximum record on applying vermicompost alone with recommended dose of chemical fertilizer in various crops were observed by various researchers, which agree with the present findings. Increase in yield up to 40% and 36% due to the application of chemical fertilizer and vermicompost respectively over control has been reported by Gunjal and Nikam, (1992). Bawa (1995) found that application of vermicompost@ 10 tons/hectare along with recommended dose of nitrogen and phosphorus resulted in 55% increase in dry pod yield over the treatments receiving only recommended dose of nitrogen and phosphorus. Soyabean seeds pelleted with vermicompost @ 50g/Kg resulted in an increase of pod yield by 16% (Dharmalingam, 1996). Palanisamy (1996) found 40% increase in yield of wheat when he applied the worm cast in soil. Kale (1998b) concluded that the application of chemical fertilizer could be brought down by 25 to 50% when it is used along with vermicompost as organic amendment. It can also reduce 50% of the regular applications of the FYM (Farm Yard Manure).

Conclusion

Based on these present findings, it could be inferred that paper mill sludge available in enormous quantities could be used as as effective medium for vermiculture, supplemented with sawdust and cow dung. Paper mill sludge not only serve as a suitable medium for the earthworms but also yielded a valuable biomanure for agriculture. Data on the physico-chemical analysis of paper mill sludge before and after composting indicated that 1:2 concentration of sludge compost was found to be ideal considering its nutritive value.

Growth studies on black gram (*Vigno mungo*) were carried out employing 1:2 sludge vermicompost. It was observed that the morphological and yield parameters were found to increase significantly over control. Hence, it is clearly found that the paper mill sludge compost not only increase the yield of any type of plant but also reduce the recommended dose of chemical fertilizers.

References

Agunwamba, J.C. 1993. Poverty, sustainable development and enviroment technology. NSE Proceedings, p: 90-108.

Aina, P.O. 1984. Contribution of earthworms to porosity and water infiltration in a tropical soil under forest and long-term cultivation *Pedobiologia*. 26: 131-136.

Andersen, C. and Laursen, J. 1982. Distribution of heavy metals in *Lumbricus terrestiris, Aporrectodea longa* and *A. rosea* measured by atomic absorption and X-ray fluorescent spectrometry, *Pedobiologia*, 24: 347-356.

Ash, C.P.J. and Lee, W.P. 1980. Lead, Cadmium, Copper and Iron in earthworms from roadside sites, *Environ. Pollut*. 22: 59-67.

Balamurugan, V., Gobi, M. and Vijakyalaksmi, G.S. 1999. Comparative studies on degradation of pressmud using cellulolytic fungi and exotic species of earthworms with a note on its gut microflora, *Asian Microbiol Biotech. Env. Sc.* Vol. I, No. (3-4): 131-134.

Balamurugan, V. 2002. Physico-chemical and microbial perspectives of vermicompost produced by *Eisenia fetida*, Savigny, Eudrilus eugeniae, Kinberg and *Lampito mauritii*, Kinberg with a note on their fecundity and growth studies in ten different organic wastes. Ph.D. thesis submitted to Manonmaniam. Sundaranar University, Tirunelveli, India. Bangalore., p: 88.

Barley, K.P. 1961. Abundance of earthworms in agricutural land and their possible significance in Agriculture. *Adv. Agron*. 13: 249-268.

Bawa, J.N. 1995. Studies on the effect of different organic manures, chemical fertilizers and growth promoter on growth, yield and quality of Rabi-hot weather groundnut (*Arachis hypogea* L.) under later tic sols of Kongen region. M.Sc. Thesis submitted to KKU, Dapoli.

Bhandari, G.S., Randhawa, N.S. and Maskina, M.S. 1967. On the polysaccharide content of earthworm casts. *Curr. Sci*. 36:519-520.

Bhatnagar, R.K. and Palta, R.K. 1996. Earthworm-Vermiculture and vermicomposting. Kalyani Publications, Ludhiana, p-106.

Blair, J.M. Parmelce, R.W., Allen, M.F., Mc Cartney, D.A. and Stinner, B.R. 1997. Changes in Soil Nitrogen in response to earthworm population manipulations in Agro-ecosystems with different N-Sources, *Soil Biol. Biochem*. 29: 361-367.

Bouche, M.B. 1983. Ecophysiologie deslombriciens: acquis recents et perspectives. In: New Trends in Soil Biology, (eds.) Lebrun, Py., Andri, H.M. Medts, A, de., Gregorie-wibo, C. and Wauthy, G., Dieu Brichart, Louvain-la-Neuve, p 321-333.

Buchanan, M.A., Russel, G. and Block, S.D. 1988. Chemical characterization and nitrogen mineralization potentials of vermicomposts derived from different organic wastes, In: Earthworms in Waste Environmental Managment. (eds) Edwards, C.A. and Neuhauser, E.F. SPB Academic, The Hague, p: 231-239.

Chakrabarti, K., Zaidi, A. and Barari, S. 1998. Compost for container nursery. A West Bengal experience. *Indian Forester*. January, 17-30.

Coleman, D.C., Reid, C.P.P. and Cole, C.V. 1983. Biological strategies of nutrient cycling in soil systems. *Advances in Ecological Research*. 13: 1-55.

Curry, J.P., Byme, D. and Boyle, K.E. 1995. The earthworm population of a winter cereal field and its effect on soil and nirogen turnover. *Biol. Fertil. Soils*. 19: 166-172.

Dash, M.C. and Patra, U.C. 1979. Worm cast production and nitrogen availability to soil by a tropical earthworm population from a grassland site in Orissa. *Rev. Ecol. Biol.* 16: 79-83.

Dharmalingam, C. 1996. Vermicompost pelleting enhances productivity in soyabean. In: Notes on National Training on Vermiculture prepared by Directorate of Extention Education. TNAU, Coimbatore. p: 50.

Edwards, C.A. and Lofty, J.R. 1977. Biology of earthworms. Chapman and Hall Ltd., London. p: 333.

EI-Duweini, A.K. and Ghabbour, S.I. 1965. Population density and biomass of earthworms in different types of Egyptian soils *J. Appl. Ecol.* 2: 271-287.

Gavrilov, K. 1962. Role of earthworms in the enrichment of soil by biolgically active substance. *Voprosy Ekologii Vysshaya Shkola*. 7:34.

Gohil, M.B.1995. Treatment of pulp and paper mill waste-case studies in pollution management in industries. (eds.) Trivedy, R.K. Environmental Publications, Karad. p: 16-20.

Graff, O. 1971. Sticksoff, phosphor und kalium in der Regenwumbsung aif der Wiesenversuchsflache des Sollingprojektes. In: "IV Colloq. Pedobiolgia" (eds.) Agnika, D. Institut National des Recherches Agriculturelle, Publ,. Paris. p: 71-77.

Graff, O. and Makeschin, F. 1980. Bee influssung des Ertrags Von Weidegras (Lolium multiflorum) furch Ausscheidungen Von Regenwiirmen dreier verschiedener Arten, *Pedobiologia*, 20: 176-180.

Grappelli, A., Tomati, V. and Galli, E. 1985. Earthworm casting in plant propagation. *Horti. Sci.* 20: 874-876.

Gunjal, S.S. and Nikam, T.B. 1992. Grape cultivation through earthworm farming. In: Proc. Nat. Sem. Organic farming. Mahatma Phule Krishi

Vidyapeeth College of Agriculture. Pune, India. p. 48-50.

Haimi, J. and Huhta, V. 1986. Capacity of various organic residues to support adequate earthworm biomass for vermicomposting. *Biol. Fertl. Soils.* 2: 23-27.

Haimi, J. and Huhta, V. 1987. Comparison of composts produced from identical wastes by vermistabilization" and "conventional composting". *Pedobiologia.* 30: 137-144.

Hand, P., Hayes, W.A., Satchell, J.E. and Frenkland, J.C. 1988. The vermicomposting of cow slurry. In: Earthworms in waste and Environmental Management. (eds). Edwards, C.A. and Neuhauser, E.F., SPB Academic, The Hague, p: 49-63.

Hopp, H. and Slater, C.S. 1949. The effect of earthworms on the productivity of agricultural soil. *J. Agric. Res.* 78: 325-339.

Ireland, M.P. 1975. Metal content of *D. rubida* (Oligochaeta) in a bares metal mining area. *Oikos* 26: 74-79.

Ireland, M.P.1979. Metal accumulation by the earthworm *Lumbricus rubellus, D. veneta* and *Eisenia tetraedra* living in heavy metal polluted sites. *Environ. Pollut.* 13: 201-206.

Jambhekar, H.A.1992. Use of earthworms as a potential source to decompose organic wastes. In: Proc. Nat. Sem. Organic Farming, Mahatma Phule Krishi Vidyapeeth, College of Agriculture, Pure. p. 52-53.

Jamieson, B.G.M. 1981. The Ultra structure of the Oligochaeta. Academic Press, London.

Jeslyn Vijayakumari, K.M. Nirmala and K. Usha. 1988. Biodegradatioan of coir pith. *Ind. J. Agric. Sci.* 59: 316-318.

Kale, R.D. and Krishnamoorthy, K.V.1980. The calcium content of the body tissue and castings of *Pontoscolex corethrurus* (Annelida, Oligochaeta). *Pedobiologia.* 20: 309-315.

Kale, R.D. and Bano, K. 1986. Field trails with vermicompost (Vee Com. E. 83 Vas) and organic fertilizer. Proc. Nat. Sem. Org. waste. utiliz. Vermicom. Part B: Vermi and Vermicomposting. (eds). Dash, M.C., Senapati, B.K. and Mishra, P.C. p. 151-156.

Kale, R.D., Mallesh, B.C., Bano, K. and Bagyaraj, D.J. 1992. Influence of vermicompost application on the available macro-nutrients and selected microbial populations in a Paddy field. *Soil Biol. Biochem.* 24 (12): 1317-1320.

Kale, R.D. Seenappa, S.N. and Jagannatha Rao, C.B. 1994. Sugar factory refuse for the production of vermicompost and worm biomass. 5th Int. Symp. on Earthworm, Ohio University, Columbus, U.S.A.

Kale, R.D. 1998 B. Earthworm-Cinderella of organic farming. Prism Book Pvt. Ltd. Bangalore., p-88.

Kang, B.T., Akinnifesi, F.K and Pleysier 1994. Effect of agro forestry woody species on earthworm activity and physicochemical properties of worm cast. *Biol. Fertil. Soils.* 18: 193-199.

Kaplan, D.L., Hartenstein, R., Neuhauser, E.F. and Maleki, M.R. 1980. Physicochemical requirements in the environment of the earthworm, *Eisenia fetida. Soil. Biol. Biochem.* 12: 347-52.

Kavian, M.F. and Ghatnekar. S.D. 1991. Biomanagement of dairy effluent using culture of Red earthworms (*Lumbricus rubellus*). *J. Environmental Protection.* 11 (9): 680-682.

Kavian, M. F. 1997 Biotechnological and Microbiological aspects of vermiculture. Ph.D. Thesis, University of Bombay,. Mumbai.

Laverack, M.S. 1963 The physiology of earthworms, Perganoon Press, London.

Lee, K.E. 1985. Earthworms, their ecology and relationship with land use. Academic Press, Sydney.

Lee, K.E. 1992. Some trends and opportunities in earthworm research (or) Darwin's children the future of our discipline. *Soil Biol. Biochem.* 24 (12) : 1765-1771.

Lunt, H.A. and Jacobson, G.M. 1944. The chemical composition of earthworm casts. *Soil Sci.* 58: 367-375.

Mansell. G.P., Syers, J.K. and Greeg, P.E. H. 1981. Plant availability of phosphorus in dead herbage ingested by surface-casting earthworms. *Soil Biol. Biochem.* 13: 1633-1637.

Maynard, L.A., Loosli, J.K. Hintz. H. F. and Warner, R.G. 1983. Animal nutrition Tata Mc Crew-Hill Publishing Co. Ltd., New Delhi. p. 416-471.

Mba, C.C. and Wei-Chun. 1982. Utilization of *Eudrilus eugeniae* for disposal of cassava Peel. In: Earthworm Ecology from Darwin to Vermiculture. (ed). Satchell, J.E., Chapman and Hall, London p: 315-321.

Meili, M. 1995. Biogeochemical Cycles, In: Encyclopedia of Environmental biology. Vol. 1 (ed. W.A. Nirenberg). Academic Press, NewYork. p.235-248.

Murugesan, A.G. 1998. Toxicity of textile mill effluent to an air breathing fish. Ph.D. Thesis, MKU, Madurai.

Nethra, N.N., Jeyaprasad, K.V. and Kale, R.D. 1999. China aster (*Callistephus chinesis* L.). Ness cultivation using vermicompost as organic manure. *Crop. Res.* 17 (2): 209-215.

Neuhauser, E.F., Hartenstein, R. and Kaplan, D.L. 1978. Second progress report on the potential use of earthworms in sludge management. In: 8th National Conference Information Transfer, Silver Springs. p. 9.

Nielson, R.L., 1965. Response of plant growth substances in earthworms deconstructed by the chromatography and the Went Pea test. *Nature*. 208:113.

Nijhawan, S.D. and Kanwar, J.S. 1952. Physico-chemical properties of earthworm casting and their effect on the productivity of soil. *J. Indian Soc. Soil Sci.*, 22: 357-372.

Nye, P. H. 1955. Some soil forming processes in the humid tropics. IV., The action of soil fauna, *J. Soil Sci.* 6: 78.

Onayemi, O. 1981. Post-harvest of loss management in Nigeria. *Industry. Env.*, (Jan/Feb): 5-7.

Opperman, M. H., Mc Bain, L. and Wood M. 1987. Movement of the cattle slurry through soil by *E. fetida* (Savigny). *Soil Biol. Biochem.* 19: 741-745.

Palanisamy, S. 1996. Earthworms and plant interactions. In: Notes on National Training on vermiculture prepared by directorate of extension education. TNAU, Coimbatore, p. 42-46.

Piearce, T. G. 1972. The calcium relation of selected Lumbricidae, *J. Animal Ecology*. 41: 167-185.

Puh, P.C. 1941. Beneficial influence of earthworms on some chemical properties of the soil. *Contr. Biol. Lab. Sci. Soc.* China. 15: 147-155.

Puttasamy, S., Thinmagowda, S. and Krishnamoorthy, K. 1976. Determination of leaf area in pulses. *Curr. Res.* 5 (3): 47.

Raghuveer, S. and Sastry, C.A. 1995. Studies on biological treatment of pulp and paper mill waste waters. Waste treatment plants. Narosa Public. House. New Delhi. p. 401-405.

Ramalingam, R. 1997. Studies on the lifecycle, growth and population dynamics of *Lampito mauritii* (Kinberg) and *Eudrilus eugeniae* (Kinberg) cultured in different organic wastes and analysis of nutrient and microbes of vermicompost. Ph.D. Thesis submitted to Annamalai University, India.

Ramalingam, R. and Thilagar, M. 2000. Bioconversion of Agrowaste sugarcane trash using an Indian epigeic earthworm, *Perionyx excavatus* (Perrier). *Indian J. Envir. Ecoplan.* 3(3): 447-452.

Ranganathan, V. and Christopher. 1996. Vermicompost. *Kissan World* Vol. 23: no. 9: 15-17.

Reddy, M. V. 1988. The effect of casts of *Pheretima alexandri* (Beddard) on the growth of *Vica rosea*, and *Oryza sativa*, L. In: Earthworms in Waste and Environmental Management. (ed). Edwards. C. A. and Neuhauser, E.F. SPB Academic. The Haque. p. 241-248.

Reddy, M. V., Balashouri, P., Kirankumar, V.P., Cogle, A.C., Rao, K.P.C. and Rao, K.V. 1994. Sorghum plant growth in relation to earthworms castings activity in semi arid tropical alfisoils. In: Biota management in sustainable farming systems. (ed.) Fankhurst. C.E., CSIRO, Australia, p: 127-128.

Russel. E.J. 1909. The effect of earthworm on soil productivity. *J. Agric. Sci.* 3 (11): 246-257.

Rutigliano, F.A., Santo, A.V.D., Berg, B., Alfanity, A. and Fioretto, A. 1996. Lignin decomposition in decaying leaves of *Fagus sylvatica* L. and needless of *Abies alba* Mill. *Soil Biochem.* 28: 101-106.

Salisbury, E. J. 1925. The influence of earthworms on soil reaction and stratification of undisturbed soils. *J. Linn. Soc.* 46:415-425.

Satchell, J. E. and Martin, K. 1984. Phosphatase activity in earthworm faeces. *Soil Biol. Biochem.*, 16: 191-194.

Satchell, J. E. 1967. Lumbricidae, In: Soil Biology. (eds.) Burges, A. and Raw, F. Academic Press, London. p. 259-322.

Selvakumar, S. and Umamaheswari, S. 2003. Physicochemical and microbial characteristics of vermicompost produced by *Eudrilus eugeniae*, Kinberg with a note on their fecundity in vegetable waste. M.Sc. Thesis submitted to Periyar University, p: 60.

Sharma, N. 1986. Recycling of organic wastes through earthworms for crop growth. Ph.D. Thesis submittted to Indian Institute of Technology, New Delhi.

Shuxin, L., Dezhong, X. and Debing, W. 1991. Studies on the effect of earthworms on the fertility of red-arid soil. In: Advances in management and conservation of soil fauna, (eds.) Veeresh, G.K., Rajagopal. D. and Viraktmath, C.A., Oxford & IBH Publishing Co. Pvt. Ltd., New Delhi. p. 543-546.

Singh, S.M. 1989. Structure, development and ecophysiology of two species of earthworms. Ph.D. Thesis submitted to Lucknow University, Lucknow. p. 157.

Springett, J. A. and Syers, J. K. 1984. Effect of pH and calcium content of soil on earthworm cast production in the laboratory. *Soil Biol. Biochem.*, 16 (2): 185-189.

Swaminathan, M.S. 1992. The green revolution in Indian Agriculture from an environmentally technology point of view. ATAS. Bulletin Issue 7, Spring, p. 143-148.

Tomati, O., Grappeli, A. and Galli, E. 1988. The hormone-like effect of earthworm casts on plant growth. *Biol. Fertil. Soils.* 5: 288-294.

Trivedi, P. R. and Gurudeep., R. 1992. A study of the effluent of pulp and paper industry. In: Encyclopedia of Environmental Sciences, Vol. 9 (eds). Trivedy, P. R. and Gurudeep Raj. Akash Deep, Pull House, New Delhi. p-395-401.

Umamaheswari, S., Selvakumar, S. and Vijayalakshmi, G. S. 2003a. Bioconversion of *Mangifera indica* litter by *Lampito mauritii* (Kinberg). Proc. National Seminar on Global Strategies in Biological Sciences. Muthiammal College of Arts and Science, Rasipuram. p: 108.

Umamaheswari, S., Suveer, S. and Vijayalakshmi, G.S. 2003b. Vermicomposting of mango litter using *Perionyx sansibaricus* with a note on its physico-chemical features. Proc. on National Seminar on Global Strategies in Biological Sciences. Muthiammal College of Arts and Science, Rasipuram, p: 108.

Venkataraja, B., Balamurugan, V., Gobi, M. and Vijayalakshmi, G.S. 2001. Conversion of leaf litter through three different composting methods. *J. Ecphysiol. Occup. Health* 1: 59-66.

Watanabe, H. 1975. On the amount of cast production by the Megascolecid earthworm, *Pheretima hupienisis*. *Pedobiologia*. 15: 20-28.

Zraherskii, A.I. 1957. Dozhdevye Cherri Kak fakto plodorodiya lesnyki pochv., Kiew.

Chapter **9**

Vermitechnology-an Ecobiological Tool for Management of Solid Wastes, with Special Reference to Pressmud

L.S.Ranganathan

Department of Zoology, Annamalai University, Annamalainagar-608 002, Tamil nadu,

Man's progress has often been made at the expense of damage to the environment. Huge amounts of organic wastes are produced due to natural processes, increasing human population, intensive agriculture, urbanisation and industrialization. These anthropogenic activities have led to environmental degradation and the problem of waste disposal has become a major environmental issue, particularly, in developing countries. Poverty and illiteracy further complicate this problem. It should be possible with the latest technological achievements to recycle all human, animal, agricultural and industrial organic wastes and help to prevent the loss of nutrients from the land. Increasing migration of the rural population to large towns in search of employment, better opportunities and standard of living has led to huge generation of wastes, particularly in the slums of cities. Various types of wastes are generated (community wastes, agricultural wastes and animal wastes) in rural areas of India (Table 1).

Table 1 : showing estimated annual generation of various types of wastes in rural India (Jain 1994).

Types of Wastes	Estimated generation (million tons)
Animal dung	1365
Agricultural residues	322
Oil seeds	100
Agro industrial by-products	49
Community waste	15

Nearly 90% of rural wastes are used as fuel, animal feed and farm manure. Roughly 15% of rural wastes are utilized as fuel. Cattle dung, shaped into cakes and dried, is used as fuel. The excess is composted along with domestic and other wastes in a heap or pit. Apart from these, considerable amount of forest litter, sewage sludge, and domestic waste water are generated. All these waste materials have great nutrient potential (Table 2).

Table 2 : nutrient potential of some of the industrial and urban wastes (Palaniappan, 2002).

Type of waste	Total quantity available(mt.)	Nutrient potential (000, t/yr)		
		N	P_2O_5	K_2O
City refuse	14.0	98.0	84.0	112.0
Sewage sludge	0.5	5.1	2.9	2.8
Pressmud	3.2	33.3	79.4	55.4
Domestic waste water	6531*	317.6	139.7	190.5
Industrial waste water	66.2*	2.9	0.9	1.3

* Million cubic meters per annum

Table 3 : showing average per capita urban solid wastes generated in Indian towns (Jain, 1994).

Category of town	Total population (approximately)	Waste generated (tons)	Per capita waste generated (g/day)
Large	22,313,000	11,761	527
Medium	9,568,000	3,025	316
Small	425,000	148	349

The per capita generation of urban waste has phenomenally increased in the recent past. For example, per-capita of municipal solid waste (MSW) generated daily in India ranges from about 100g in a small town to 500g in large towns (Table 3) .The amount of waste generated per capita is estimated to increase at a rate of 1% -1.33% annually. It is further estimated that the total quantity of waste generated in 2047 would be above 260 million tons–more than five times the present level. The wastes largely comprise of biodegradable organics. The growth in MSW in Indian cities has out paced the population growth in recent years. It is due to the changed living standards, food habits and life style.

An integrated approach of managing the solid wastes consists of reduction, recycling and recovery of wastes. Generation of wastes has to be reduced at source by levy of tax, education and better technology. Proper segregation of wastes would help in better recycling. Land filling, composting, incineration and anaerobic digestion are some of the ways of disposal of solid wastes.

At present, insanitary methods are usually adopted for disposal of solid wastes. For example, the sites of landfill are prone to ground water contamination. In addition, garbage dumping sites are breeding places for disease vectors such as flies, mosquitoes, rats and cockroaches. The sites also occupy huge land space, emit bad odour; and emit methane which could cause explosion (Figures 1-3). Generation of methane gas from these sites of landfills is a matter of great concern, as it also contributes to global warming. Further, birds feeding on garbage at landfill sites cause problems for aircrafts.

Composting

Composting is an age-old process; and is still practised by farmers in developing countries to fertilize their soil. Composting is the ideal technology for solid waste management in India since it helps to recycle the nutrient back to land. Mechanized aerobic composting is practiced in some of the large municipalities.

Incineration is another method of disposing of the solid wastes. But it is not a complete solution in the Indian context, because the technology is not indigeneously available; its operational experience is not satisfactory and also the operational cost is heavy. Although anaerobic digestion is another option, technology is not available for processing heterogeneous solid waste material. This technique is more suitable for homogeneous materials like market, kitchen, vegetable and fruit wastes. Refuse derived fuel is yet another method of disposing solid waste where the combustibles are pelletised.

VERMICOMPOSTING

Dumping of wastes in the soil may lead to catastrophe, because only 24-27% of land on the earth is cultivable. In such a scenario, vermicomposting may form an effective, energy efficient and cheap recycling process. It is an eco-friendly, biological, socially accepted, economically viable and technologically simple, natural method of decomposing organic wastes by earthworms. The earthworms utilize organic wastes and convert them into soft nutrient rich, aggregates of small organic particles. As early as 1978, Mitchell demonstrated that *Eisenia fetida* could decompose and stabilize the aerobic sewage sludge. Due to vermicomposting, not only the bad odour disappeared but also the population of pathogenic organisms like *Salmonella enteriditin, Escherichia coli* and other *Enterobacteriaceae* were reduced. The use of earthworm in sludge disposal was referred to as management vermicomposting or vermistabilization (Loehr et al., 1984). The maximum possible reduction of volatile solid is the chief objective of most of the sludge stabilization system. *Eiseniae fetida, Dendrobaena veneta, Lumbricus rubellus* were found suitable for temperate climate; and *Eudrilus eugeniae, Perionyx excavatus* and *Polypheretima elongata* for tropical climate. *E. eugeniae* and *P. excavatus* have an optimum temperature requirement of 27° ± 2°C and *E. fetida* 25 ± 2°C for vermicomposting. Vermicomposting of solid wastes could be carried out in underground pits, windrows, waste heaps, containers and reactors. Windrows could be laid on soil or concrete floor: 3 m length, 1 m height, 1 m width. Cement tub of 2 m length, 1 m height and 1 m width was found to be ideal for small-scale vermicomposting. An improved model is the gantry-fed where the waste is added in thin layer, 1-2 cm thick, at frequent intervals.

The wide array of organic wastes composted by diverse variety of earthworms are summarized in Table 4. Vermicompost is characterized by increased content of micro and macro nutrients, microbial and enzymatic activities and nutrient mineralization that support plant growth and yield (Lavelle *et al.*, 1995; Edwards and Bohlen, 1996; Parthasarathi and Ranganathan, 1999; 2000; Benitez *et al.*, 2002; Chaoui *et al.*, 2003; Loh *et al.*, 2005). Kale *et al.* (1992), Edwards and Bohlen (1996), Buckerfied *et al.* (1999), Garg and Bhardwaj (2000); Parthasarathi and Ranganathan (2002), Ganihar (2003) and Ramamoorthy (2005) have demonstrated that application of vermicompost increases growth and yield of paddy, wheat, maize, tomato, rose, citrus, guava, curry leaf, turmeric, ornamental plants, cash crops, plantation crops, cereals, radish, pulse, oil seeds, spices., vegetables, fruits and sorghum; and also improves the physical, chemical and biological properties of the soil.

Pressmud Vermicomposting

India's agro-industrial sector contributes huge potential resource of plant nutrients in the form of wastes (Table 1, 2). However, they are either thrown away or buried or burnt, causing environmental pollution and loss of a huge resource of energy and organic manure.

Table 4 : Vermicomposting of different organic resources by diverse variety of earthworms (1986- 2005)

Organic resources	Earthworms	Reference
Poultry wastes	*Eudrilus eugeniae*	Bano and Kale (1986)
Coffee pulp wastes	*E. fetida*	Cegarra et al. (1996)
Organic waste-kitchen wastes, cowdung,green leaves, coir wastes, fresh neem leaves, dry leaf litters, Eucalyptus bark & leaves	*E. eugeniae*	Kale (1988)
Cowdung	*E. fetida* *Perionyx excavatus*	Reinecke et al. (1992)
House hold refuse	*E. eugeniae*, *Perionyx excavatus*, *E. fetida*	Kale and Sunitha (1993)
Crop residues with cattle dung Solid paper pulp mill sludges Pressmud	*E. fetida* *E. anderi* *Lampito mauritii*, *E. eugeniae*, *E. fetida*, *P. excavatus*	Bansal and Kapoor (2000) Elvira *et al.* 1996; 1998 Ramalingam (1997) Parthasarathi (1997)
Cattle solids, Pig solids, Horge Solids, Turkey waste, Shaving base and Straw base Acritic sludge	*P. excavatus*	Edwards *et al.* 1998
Agricultural organic wastes black and red gram, pod husk, gram husk and cowdung	*E. eugeniae*, *P. excavatus*, *E. fetida*	Amoji *et al.* (1998)
Leaf litters	*E. eugeniae*	Daniel and Karmegam (1999)
Kitchen wastes, cowdung, poultry droppings, municipal waste and dry leaves	*E. fetida*	Ghosh et al. (1999)
Dry olive cake with organic wastes	*E. fetida*	Nogales *et al.* (1999)
Cattle manure	*E. eugeniae*	Viljoen and Reinecke (1994)
Rubber leaf litters	*P. excavatus*, *E. eugeniae*, *E. fetida*	Chaudhuri *et al.* (2003)
Lignocellulosic waste from olive oil industry	*E. anderi*	Benitez *et al.* 2002

Aqualic weeds	*P. excavatus*	Chaudhuri *et al.* (2001)
Water hyacinth	*P. excavatus*	Gajalakshmi *et al.* (2002)
Solid textile mill sludge	*E. fetida*	Kaushik and Garg (2003)
Leaf litter	*Pontoscolex corethrurus*	Ganihar (2003)
Tomato skin seed wastes	*Pheretima elongata*	Singh *et al.* (2003)
Forest litter wastes	*E. fetida* *P. excavatus,* *Dichogaster bolaui*	Manna *et al.*, (2003)
Wood chip and sewage sludge	*E. fetida*	Maboeta and Rensburg (2003)
Municipal solid wastes	*L. mauritii,*	Kaviraj and Sharma (2003)
Solid textile milk sludge and cow dung	*E. fetida*	Kaushik and Garg (2003)
Kitchen wastes	*L. mauritii,* *E. fetida*	Tripathi and Bhardwaj. (2004a)
Ore mine waste	*P. corethrurus*	Ganihar (2003)
Biogas slurry, cowdung, wheat straw, leaf litter, sawdust and kitchen wastes	*L. mauritii* *E. fetida*	Tripathi and Bhardwaj (2004b)
Paper wastes with cowdung	*E. eugeniae, Drawida willsi* *P. excavatus, L. mauritii*	Gajalakshmi and Abbasi (2004)
Aquaculture effluent solids mixed with card borad	*E. fetida*	Mishra *et al.*, 2005
Pressmud, trash and bagasse	*L. mauritii,* *E. eugeniae,* *E. fetida,* *P. excavatus*	Ramamoorthy (2005) Manivannan (2005)
Goat and Pig manure	*E. fetida*	Loh *et al.* (2005)

Soil productivity can be maintained only by continued input of organic manure and other agricultural wastes. High costs of fertilizers and reduced availability of organic manures have necessitated the recycling of organic wastes for increasing soil fertility. Approximately 12 million tones of pressmud (filter cake), a major by-product of the cane sugar factory is produced annually in India. It contains 50% OM, 30% OC, 12-16% protein, 10-14% sugar, rich micro and macro nutrients, abundant microbial population and exhibits rich enzyme activities (Yadav , 1995; Parthasarathi and Ranganathan, 1999; 2000). There is a fear that its application may lead to crust formation and pH variation in the soil and pollute air, water and soil. The cost involved in the transport of the pressmud is also high because of its bad smell and

Table 5 : Chemical properties of pressmud and vermicomposts ($P < 0.05$)

Parameters	PM	PM vermicomposts	
		P. excavatus	*L. mauritii*
pH	7.66±0.02 (-2.6)	7.40±0.08 (-3.4)	7.40±0.08 (-3.4)
EC (mm.hos/cm)	0.29±0.10	0.23±0.09 (-20.7)	0.22±0.02 (-24)
OM (%)	53.16±0.19	26.20±1.02 (-50.7)	28.48±1.10 (-46.4)
OC (%)	31.02±1.16	25.60±1.30 (-17.5)	25.80±0.90 (-16.8)
N (%)	1.81±0.86	2.40±0.72 (-17.5)	2.55±0.66 (+94.65)
P (%)	2.41±0.26	4.72±0.20 (+95.04)	4.93±0.16 (103.7)
K (%)	2.31±0.02	4.56±0.08 (+97.4)	4.70±0.06(+103.5)
Ca (%)	2.47±0.03	3.11±0.02 (+29.9)	3.26±0.07 (+31.9)
Mg (%)	0.51±0.08	0.96±0.06 (+88.2)	1.08±0.01 (+111.8)
S (%)	0.64±0.02	0.26±0.05 (-59.4)	0.24±0.07 (-62.5)
Na (%)	0.21±0.05	0.26±0.02 (+23.8)	0.29±0.04 (+38)
CRP (%)	17.57+0.85	38.13±0.18 (+23.8)	40.94±0.60 (+133)
C/N ratio	23.67±0.36	10.66±0.33 (-54.9)	10.11±0.67 (-57.3)
C/P ratio	9.34±0.55	5.41±0.26 (-42.1)	5.22±0.31 (-44)
Zn (mg-kg-1)	62.20±1.15	419.55±2.30 (+574)	429.40±3.30 (+590)
Fe (mg-kg-1)	177.61±1.16	901.20±2.25 (+407.4)	902.26±2.65 (408)
Mn (mg-kg-1)	23.20±1.02	307.46±2.08 (+1225.3)	312.49±2.18 (+1324)
Cu (mg-kg-1)	40.00±1.13	26.86±1.20 (-32.8)	26.40±1.27(-34)

heat. Its conventional composting takes about six months, does not remove its bad odour completely and produces composts with poor nutritional value. Many sugar mills compost pressmud in huge wind rows by adding-selective microorganisms to hasten the process of humification. These are turned over often to facilitate aeration; and in a short span of few days, when decomposed fully, these are used as organic soil amendments. Some of the sugar mills compress them into pellets. Compressing and heating would kill the beneficial microorganisms; and composting in wind-rows would not have the benefits rendered by earthworms such as enhanced mineralisation, humification, chelation of trace metals and synthesis of plant growth-promoting substances. Vermicomposting of pressmud alleviates its potential pollution problems and converts into an eco-friendly, organic manure or soil ameliorant. This chapter discusses the scope and utility of using indigenous varieties of earthworms. *Perionyx excavatus* (Perrier) and *Lampito mauritii* (Kinberg) -as ecological tool in the management of pressmud.

The physico-chemical and biological properties of pressmud and vermicomposted pressmud are given in the tables-5 and 6. Fresh pressmud is not only hot (72°C) but also contains high content of water (70%). It emanates a bad smell. All these are undesirable and intolerable to the earthworms. The pressmud had to be left in an open field exposed to natural weather conditions so as to get rid off the smell and reduce the moisture. It is recommended that the heap of pressmud is often turned over to aerate it. After nearly a month, earthworms such as *P. excavatus* and *L. mauritii* are introduced into weathered pressmud in windrows or in cement tanks containing pressmud. In about two months, pressmud is completely vermicomposted.

The success of the vermicompost is dependent upon the quality of the organic waste provided as food for the earthworms and also on moisture content, temperature, pH and aeration. Chemical analysis of pressmud revealed it to contain: OM (50%), OC (30%), P (3.3%), N (2.8%), Ca (2.5%) and K (2.3%). Organic matter is the main source of energy for soil organisms, plant and animals. The growth and survival of microorganisms in the soil and organic matter depend mainly on the presence of OC (Edwards and Bohlen, 1996). Nitrogen was present in the pressmud mainly as protein, whereas phosphorus was in complex organic combination such as phospholipids, nucleo protein and calcium phosphate. The Ca level was high due to the addition of lime during the clarification of cane juice. Potassium was in a soluble and very easily leachable form (Yadav, 1995). These advantages were found to make the pressmud as a natural feed-substrate for earthworms; and therefore, it could be vermicomposted into a good manure or soil ameliorant.

Earthworms have no protective wall against changes in moisture and temperature. About 75-90% of the weight of the body is constituted by water and hence can survive only when there is sufficient moisture. Numerous studies on the biology and vermicomposting have confirmed this fact (Reinecke et al., 1992; Edwards and Bohlen, 1996; Ramalingam, 1997; Parthasarathi, 1997; Jayanthi et al., 2005). Further, fecundity, incubation and growth of

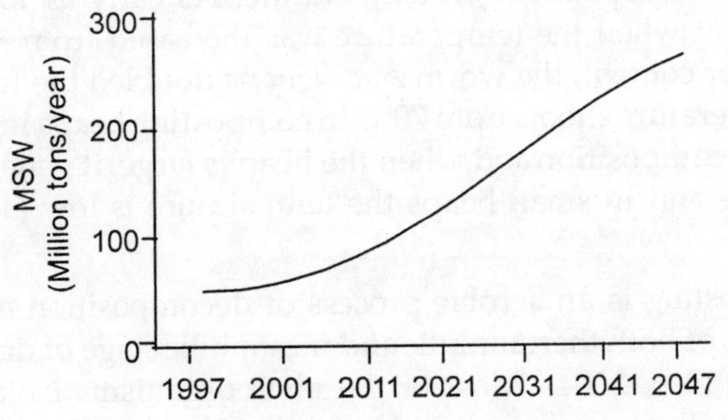

Fig. 1. Showing the likelihood of the trend in the generation of municipal solid waste (Singhal and Pandey, 2001)

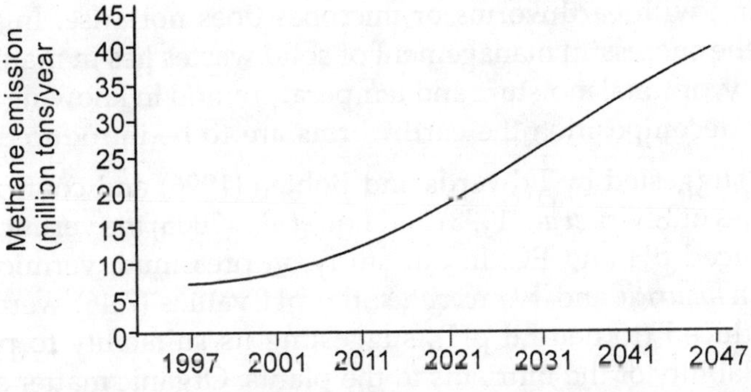

Fig. 2. Showing the trend of emission of methane from landfill sites (Singhal and Pandey, 2001)

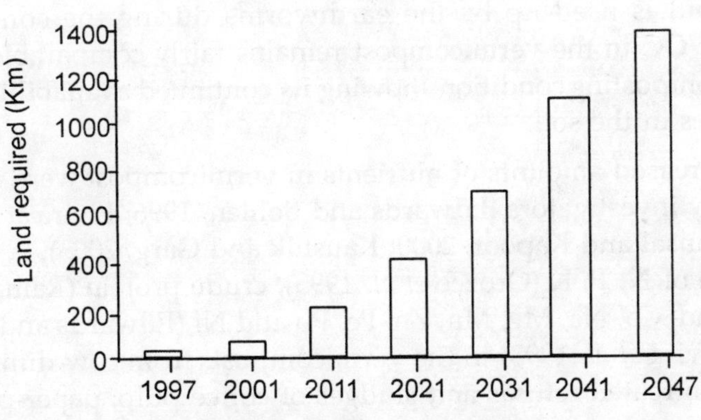

Fig.3. Showing likely trend in the cumulative land requirement for disposal of MSW (Singhal and Pandey, 2001)

earthworm are dependent on temperature. As early as 1987, Scheu observed that when the temperature was increased from 10 to 15°C at 60% water content, the worm *A. caliginosa* doubled the turnover of casts. Temperature shoots upto 70°C in composting heaps in the initial stages of decomposition and when the heap is large, it generates high temperature and in small heaps the temperature is low (Taiwo and Oso, 2004).

Composting is an aerobic process of decomposition depending on microbes of both thermophilic and mesophilic stage of degradation (Taiwo and Oso, 2004). Most of the microorganisms isolated from the gut of earthworms were reported to be thermophilic (Daniel and Anderson, 1992). Since vermicomposting of the municipal solid wastes or other agro-industrial wastes, such as pressmud, is done after few days of natural decomposition, the question of initial high heat interfering with earthworms or microbes does not arise. In fact the key for the successful management of solid wastes lies in maintaining aerobicity, optimal moisture and temperature; and in knowing at what stage of decomposition the earthworms are to be introduced.

As suggested by Edwards and Bohlen (1996) and confirmed by the studies of Elvira *et al.* (1998) and Loh *et al.*, (2005) the vermicompost had reduced pH and EC. In our study on pressmud, vermicompost of both *L.mauritii* and *P. excavatus*, the pH values (7.46) were found to be reduced (to neutral pH), suggesting its suitability to promote the availability of the nutrients to the plants. Organic matter and OC in the vermicompost are the main source of energy for both soil organisms and plants. These are helpful in the formation of top soil and soil aggregates (Edwards *et al.*, 1998). Though OM in the pressmud is used up by the earthworms during the composting process, OC in the vermicompost remains fairly comparable to pre-vermicomposting condition showing its continued availability for life processes in the soil.

Increased amounts of nutrients in vermicompost were reported by many investigators {Edwards and Bohlen, 1996; Elvira *et al.* 1996, 1998; Bansal and Kapoor, 2000; Kaushik and Garg, 2003). A uniform increase of N, P, K (Orozco *et al.* 1995), crude protein (Ramalingam, 1997) and. Ca, Na, Mg, Mn, Zn, Fe, Pb and Ni (Edwards and Bohlen, 1996; Elvira *et al.* 1998) in the vermicomposts from cow dung, sheep dung, untreated refuses and sludges of coffee pulp, paper-pulp mill and dairy industries were reported. Increased N, P and K contents in the vermicomposts from paper mills and dairy industries were found to be due to mineralization, which in turn caused decreased C/N and C/P ratios (Elvira *et al.*, 1996; 1998). Our study also revealed reduction of C/N ratio of pressmud from 23.67 to 10.66 in the vermicompost. The C/P ratio was also reduced. Increase in N, P, K, CRP, Ca, Mg, Na, Mn, Zn and Fe in the pressmud vermicompost seems to be due to effective decomposition of pressmud while passing through the gut of earthworms leading to an enhanced mineralization rate, higher microbial and enzymatic activities in the gut as well as in the vermicompost (Parthasarathi and Ranganathan, 1999; 2000); mucus contribution from the gut of earthworm and incorporation of dead earthworm biomass into the compost.

Vermicomposting is due to the roles played together by the earthworm and the microorganisms in the gut of earthworms. There is a great diversity in the microbial population with reference to the different regions of the gut, nature of feed, type of habitat (soil types) and age of earthworms (Cooke and Luxton, 1980; Flack and Hartenstein, 1984; Dash *et al.*, 1986; Ghosh *et al.*, 1989; Parthasarathi, 1997; Parthasarathi and Ranganathan, 1998; Wolter and Scheu, 1999). The microbivorous nature of earthworms is well known (Flack and Hartenstein, 1984; Edwards and Bohlen, 1996; Ranganathan and Parthasarathi, 1999; Wolter and Scheu, 1999; Pizl and Novakova, 2003). Bacteria, fungi, actinomycetes and protozoa play a major role in the composting process; and nematodes, earthworms, mites and various other organisms may also be involved (Macdonald Dow and Guffin Shay, 1981). But, Singh (1987) found the heterotrophic microorganism to be the sole agents promoting the decomposition of carbanaceous material. It is seen from the table -7 that some specific types of bacteria are propagated and some are digested by the earthworms during the passage of pressmud through the gut. Most of the fungi are not digested. They probably contribute enzymes for decomposition.

Actinomycetes are not digested probably because of secretion of antibiotics. The yeasts are completely digested indicating their digestibility and as source of nutrients (Ranganathan and Parthasarathi, 1999). It was observed that these microbes play significant role in decomposition, humification, nitrogen fixation, phosphate mobilization and secretion of plant growth promoting substances (Parthasarathi and Ranganathan, 1999)

The diversity of microbial population (fungi, bacteria and actinomycetes), enzymatic activities (cellulase, amylase, invertase, protease, phosphatases and dehydrogenase) and humic acid contents in pressmud and pressmud vermicomposts of *P. excavatus* and *L. mauritii* are summarised in the table 6. It is seen that total microbial population, enzymatic activities and humic acid content are significantly more in the pressmud vermicomposts of both worms than those of worm unworked pressmud. Many studies have demonstrated increased microbial populatin during passage of food through the gut in earthworms (Parle, 1963a; Parthasarathi and Ranganathan, 1998) and higher number of fungi, bacteria and actinomycetes in the vermicomposts, especially fresh ones, compared to those of the surrounding soils (Scheu, 1987; Lavelle and Martin, 1992; Edwards and Bohlen, 1996; Parthasarathi and Ranganathan, 1999). The presence of enhanced microbial population and activity (dehydrogenase) in the pressmud vermicomposts of both species of worms are due to rich nutrients, multiplication of microbes, optimal moisture level and large surface area in the particles of vermicomposts ideally suited for better feeding and multiplication of microbes (Parthasarathi and Ranganathan, 1999). Earlier studies of Parthasarathi and Ranganathan (1998; 1999; 2000) and Vinotha *et al.*, (2000) demonstrated the presence of increased cellulolytic, hemicellulolytic, amylolytic, proteolytic, phosphate solubilizing and nitrifying microbes in the pressmud vermicasts than those of worm unworked pressmud. Also the enhancement of enzyme activities in the pressmud vermicompost are due to the gut and cast associated processes and the presence of increased amount of organic substances such as sugars, cullulose, protein, P, OC, microorganisms and ideal moisture level. The increased microbial activity in pressmud vermicompost is reflected by increased dehydrogenase activity–an intracellular enzyme related to oxidative phosphorylation (Parthasarathi and Ranganathan, 1999).

Microbial decomposition of organic matter forms humus. Humus consists of humic acid, fulvic acid and humin. Humic substances are very stable (Riffaldi *et al.*, 1992). Humus contributes nutrients to the soil, improves the physical characteristics of the soil, particularly the water-holding capacity, aeration and tilth. Recent studies have shown that the humic acid content had been increased due to vermicomposting a mixture of plant residues and cattle manure (Canellas et al., 2002). Our recent studies in the pressmud vermicasts (Ranganathan and Parthasarathi, 2005) fall in line with these observations.

Conclusion

In the light of these evidences it becomes clear that vermitechnology in India - a predominantly agrarian country with largest cattle population and more than 350 different species of earthworms — has to be more vigorously pursued, if the ecology, particularly that of the soil, has to be conserved. Intensive agriculture in our tropical Indian soil could be sustained only when soil is periodically amended with organic manures like vermicompost.

References

Amoji, S.D., Shagoti, V.M. and V.A.Biradav, 1998. Selective preferences for agricultural organic wastes under multiple choice by epigenic earthworms. J. Environ. Biol. 19: 375-380.

Bano, K. and R.D. Kale, 1986. Conversion of poultry resource into protein. In: Proc. Nat. Sem. Org. Waste Utiliz. Vermicomp. Part B: Verms and Vermicomposting (Dash, M.C., B.K.Senapati and P.C.Mishra, eds) Burla, Orissa, p. 145-150.

Bansal, S. and K.K. Kapoor, 2000. Vermicomposting of crop residues and cattle dung with *Eisenia fetida*. Bioresource Technology 73: 95-98.

Benitez, E., Sainz, H., Melgen, R. and R. Nogales, 2002. Vermicomposting of a lignocellulosic waste from olive oil industry - A pilot scale study. Waste Management and Research, 20: 134-142.

Buckerfield, J.C., C.T. Flavel, K.E. Lee and K.A. Webster, 1999. Vermicompost in solid and liquid form as a plant-growth promoter. Pedobiologia, 43: 753- 759.

Canellas, L.P., Olivares, F.L., A.L.Okorokova -Fucanha and A.R. Facanha, 2002. Humic acids isolated from earthworm compost enhance root elongation, lateral root emergence and plasma membrane H+ -ATP are activity in maize root, Plant Physiology, 130: 1-7.

Cegarra, J. E.H. Orozeo., A. Roig and L.M.Trujillo, 1996. Vermicomposting of coffee pulp using the earthworm, *Eisenia fetida* - Effects on C and N contents and the availability of nutrients. Biol. Fertil. Soils, 22: 162-166.

Chaudhuri, P.S., Pal, T.K., Bhattacharjee, G. and S.K. Dey. 2001. Nutrient changes during vermicomposting by *Perionyx excavatus* of the aquatic weed, *Trapa bispinosa*. Phillipine J. Sci. 130(2): 127-133.

Chaudhuri, P.S., Pal, T.K. Bhattacharjee, G. and S.K. Dey. 2003. Rubber leaf litters (*Hevea brasiliensis*, Var RRIM 600) as vermiculture substrate for epigeic earthworms, *Perionyx excavatus, Eudrilus eugeniae, Eisenia fetida*. Pedobiologia, 47: 796-800.

Chaoui, H.I. Zibilske, L.M. and T.Ohno. 2003. Effects of earthworm casts and compost on soil microbial activity and plant nutrient availability, Soil BioI. Biochem., 35: 295-302.

Cooke, A and Luxton, M. 1980. Effects of microbes on food selection by *Lumbricus terrestris*. Rev. Ecol. BioI. Soil. 17: 365-370.

Daniel, O. and Anderson, J.M. 1992. Microbial biomass and activity in contrasting soil materials after passing through the gut of the earthworm, *Lumbricus rubellus*, Soil BioI. Biochem., 24: 465-470.

Daniel, T. and N. Karmegam. 1999. Bio-conversion of selected leaf litters using an African epigeic earthworm, *Eudrilus eugeniae*. Ecol. Env. Cons. 5(3): 271-275.

Dash, H.K., Beura, B.N. and Dash, M.C. 1986. Gut load, transit time, gut microflora and turnover of soil, plant and fungal material by some tropical earthworms. Pedobiologia, 29: 13-20.

Dominguez, J., Edwards, C.A. and J.Ashby. 2001. The biology and population dynamics of *Eudrilus eugeniae* (Kinberg) (Oligochaeta) in cattle waste solids. Pedobiologia, 45: 341-353.

Edwards, C.A and Fletcher, K.E. 1988. Interaction between earthworms and microorganisms in organic matter breakdown. Agricultural Ecosystem and Environment, 24: 235-247.

Edwards, C.A. and P.J. Bohlen. 1996. Biology and Ecology of Earthworms. 3rd Edition, Chapman and Hall, London.

Edwards, C.A., Dominguez, J. and E.F.Neuhauser. 1998. Growth and reproduction of *Perionyx excavatus* (Perr.) (Megascolecidae) as factors in organic waste management. BioI. Fertil. Soils, 27: 155-161.

Elvira, C., Goiwechea, M., Sampedro, L, Mato, S. and R Nogales 1996. Bioconversion of solid paper-pulp mill sludges by earthworms. Bioresource Technology, 57: 173-177.

Elvira, C., Sampedro, L., Benitez, E. and R.Nogales, 1998. Vermicomposting of sludges from paper mill and dairy industries with *Eisenia andrei*: A pilot-scale study. Bioresource Technology, 63: 205-211.

Flack, F.M. and Hartenstein, R. 1984. Growth of the earthworm *Eisenia fetida* on microorganisms and cellulose. Soil BioI. Biochem,16: 491-495.

Gajalakshmi, S. and S.A.Abbasi, 2004. Vermiconversion of paper waste by earthworm born and grown in the waste fed reactors compared to the pioneer's raised to adulthood on cowdung feed. Bioresource Technology, 94: 53-56.

Gajalakshmi, S., Ramasamy, E.V. and Abbasi, S.A. 2002. Vermicomposting of different forms of water hyacinth by the earthworm, *Eudrilus eugeniae*, Kinberg. Bioresource Technology, 82: 165-169.

Garg, K. and N. Bhardwaj. 2000. Effect of vermicomposts of Lantana on two cultivars of wheat, Indian J. Environ & Ecoplan, 3: 539-348.

Ganihar, S.R. 2003. Nutrient mineralization and leaf litter preference by the earthworm, *Pontoscolex corethrurus* on iron ore mine wastes. Restoration Ecology , 11: 475-482.

Ghosh, N., Basu, S. and Behera, N. 1989. Microfungi in the gut and cast of *Perionyx millardi*, a tropical earthworm. *J. Soil Biol. and Ecol.* 9(1): 46-50.

Jain, A.J. 1994. Affordable water supply and sanitation – solid waste management in India. 20th WEDC Conference, Colombo, Sri Lanka.

Jayanthi, L., K.Parthasarathi and. L.S.Ranganathan, 2005. Influence of moisture on growth and reproduction of earthworm, *Perionyx excavatus* (Perrier) and total microbial population and activity in the pressmud vermicompost. In: National Seminar on Biovision. Organized by Department of Zoology, 21-22 January, Annamalai University, India.

Kale, R.D. 1988. Annelids (Terrestrial oligochaetes) In: Applied Soil Biology and Ecology (Veeresh, G.K and D.Rajagopal, eds). Oxford and IBH Publ. Co. Pvt. Ltd., p.90-110.

Kale, R.D. and N.S. Sunitha, 1993. Utilization of earthworms in recycling of household refuse - a case study. In: Biogas Slurry Utilization Conservation on Rural Technology (CORT), New Delhi, p.75-79.

Kale, R.D., B.G. Mallesh, K. Bano and D.J. Bagyaraj. 1992. Influence of vermicompost application on the available macronutrients and selected microbial populations in a paddy field. Soil BioI. Biochem., 24(12): 1317-1320.

Kaushik, P. and V.K.Garg. 2003. Vermicomposting of mixed solid textile mill sludge and cowdung with the epigeic earthworm, *Eisenia fetida*, Bioresource Technology, 90: 311-316.

Kaviraj and S.Sharma. 2003. Municipal solid waste management through vermicomposting employing exotic and local species of earthworms. Bioresource Technology, 90: 169-173.

Lavelle, P. and A. Martin. 1992. Small scale and large scale effects of endogeic earthworms on soil organic matter dynamics in soils of the humid tropics. Soil BioI. Biochem, 24: 1491-1498.

Lavelle, P., Lattand, C., Trigo, D. and I. Barois, 1995. Mutualism and biodiversity in soil. In: The significance and Regulation of Soil Biodiversity, (H.P.Collins, G.P.Robertson and M.J.Kling eds.) p.23- 33. Kluwer Academic Publisher, The Netherlands.

Loehr, R.C., Martin, J.H., Neuhauser, E.F. and Malecki, M.R. 1984. Waste

Management using earthworms engineering and scientific relationships, Final report, project ISP-8016764. National Science Foundation.

Loh, T.C., Lee, Y.C., Liang, J.B. and D.Tan. 2005. Vermicomposting of cattle and goat manures by *Eisenia fetida* and their growth and reproduction performance, Bioresource Technology, 96: 111-114.

Maboeta, M.S. and L.V. Rensburg. 2003. Vermicomposting of industrially produced woodchips and sewage sludge utilizing *Eisenia fetida*. Ecotoxicology and environmental safety, 56: 265-270.

Macdonald Dow, M.G.C. and Guffin Shay, E. 1981. Returning waste to the land. In: Food, Fuel and Fertilizer from Organic Wastes. Report of Adhoc panel of the Advisory Committee on Technology for International Development Commission on International Relations. National Research Council. National Academy Press, Washington. DC.

Manivannan, S., 2005. Standardization and nutrient analysis of vermicomposting sugar cane wastes, pressmud, trash-bagase by *Lampito mauritii* (Kinberg) and *Perionyx excavatus* (Perrier) and the effect of vermicomposts on soil fertility and crop productivity, Ph.D Thesis, Annamalai University, India.

Manna, M.C., S. Jha., P.K. Ghosh and C.L. Acharya. 2003. Comparative efficacy of three epigeic earthworms under different deciduous forest litters' decomposition. Bioresources Technology, 88: 197-206.

Mishra, L., S. Subler, S. Mishra and M. Marini. 2005. Suitability of aquaculture effluent solids mixed with cardboard as a feedstock for vermicomposting. Bioresource Technology, 96: 413-418.

Mitchell, M.J. 1978. Role of invertebrates and microorganisms in sludge decomposition. In: Utilization of Soil Organism in Sludge Management, (eds. R.Hartenstein), Natl. Tech. Inf. Services, PB286932, Springfield, Virginia, p.35-50.

Nogales, R. Melgar, A. Guerrero, G. Lozada, E. Benitez, R. Thompson and M. Gomez. 1999. Growth and reproduction of *Eisenia andrei* in dry olive cake mixed with other organic wastes, Pedobiologia, 43: 744-752.

Orozco, F.H., J. Cegarra., L.M.Trujillo and A. Roig. 1995. Vermicomposting of coffee pulp using the earthworm, *Eisenia fetida:* Effects on C and N contents and the availability of nutrients. Biol. Fertil. Soils, 20: 1-5.

Palaniappan, 2002. Efficient management of organic residues / wastes for sustainable crop production. In: National Seminar on Recent Trends on the Use of Humic Substances for Sustainable Agriculture. Organized by Department of Soil Science and Chemistry, Annamalai University, Tamilnadu.

Parle, J.N.1963a. Microorganisms in the intestine of the earthworm.J. Gen. Microbiol. 31 :1-11.

Parthasarathi, K. 1997. Influence of pressmud-sawdust mixture on the microbes of the gut, vermicasts, enzyme profiles and neurosecretory cells of brain-ovary axis in *Lampito mauritii* (Kinberg) and *Eudrilus eugeniae* (Kinberg) reared on different substrates. Ph.D Thesis, Annamalai University, India.

Parthasarathi, K. and L.S.Ranganathan, 1998. Pressmud vermicasts are the 'hot spots' of fungi and bacteria. Ecol. Environ. Cons., 4: 81- 86.

Parthasarathi, K.and L.S.Ranganathan. 1999. Longevity of microbial and enzyme activity and their influence on NPK content in pressmud vermicasts. Europ. J. Soil Biol. 35 (3):107-113

Parthasarathi, K. and L.S. Ranganathan, 2000. Aging effect on enzyme activities in pressmud vermicasts of *Lampito mauritii* (Kinberg) and *Eudrilus eugeniae* (Kinberg). Biol. Fertil. Soil, 347-350.

Parthasarathi, K. and L.S. Ranganathan, 2002. Supplementation of pressmud vermicasts with NPK enhances growth and yield of leguminous crops black gram (*Vigno mungo*) and groundnut. (*Arachis hypogea*) .J. Curr. Sci. 2: 35-41.

Pizl, V. and A. Novakova, 2003. Interaction between microfungi and *Eisenia andrei* (Oligochaeta) during cattle manure vermicomposting. Pedobiologia, 47: 895-899.

Ramalingam R. 1997. Studies. on the life cycle, growth and population dynamics of *Lampito mauritii* (Kinberg) and Eudrilus eugeniae (Kinberg) cultred in different organic wastes and analysis of nutrients and microbes of vermicompost (Annelida: Oligochaeta), Ph.D. Thesis, Annamalai University, Annamalainagar, Tamilnadu, India.

Ramamoorthy, P. 2005. Standardization and nutrient analysis of vermicomposting sugarcane wastes, pressmud-trash-bagasse by *Eudrilus eugeniae* (Kinberg) and *Eisenia fetida* (Savigny) and the effect of vermicompost on soil fertility and crop productivity, Ph.D. Thesis, Annamalai University, India.

Ranganathan, L.S. and K.Parthasarathi. 1999. Precocious development of *Lampito mauritii* and *Eudrilus eugeniae* reared in pressmud. Pedobiologia, 43: 904-908.

Ranganathan, L.S. and K. Parthasarathi. 2005. Humification of cane sugar mill wastes by *Eudrilus eugeniae* (Kinberg). J. Ann. Univ. 41: 1-8.

Reinecke, A.J., S.A. Viljeon and R.J. Saayman. 1992. The suitability of *Eudrilus eugeniae*, *Perionyx excavatus* and *Eisenia fetida* (Oligochaeta) for vermicomposting in southern Africa, in terms of their temperature requirements, Soil Biol. Biochem, 24: 1295-1307.

Riffaldi, R., Levi-Minzi, R., Sanozzi, A. and H. Capurro, 1992. Evaluating garbage composts. Biocycle, 33: 66-69.

Scheu, S. 1987. Microbial activity and nutrient dynamics in earthworm casts (Lumbricidae). Biol. Fertil. Soils, 5: 230-234.

Singhal S. and Pandey, S. 2001. .Solid waste management in India: Status and Future directions. TERI Information Monitor on Environmental Science 6(1): 1-4.

Singh, C.P. 1987. Preparation of high grade compost by an enrichment on organic matter decomposition. Biol. Agria. Hort. 5: 41-49.

Singh, N.B., Khare, A.K., Bhargava, D.S. and S. Agrawal. 2003. Vermicomposting of tomato skin and seed waste, IE (I) Journal- EN, 84: 30-34.

Taiwo, L.B. and B.A. Oso. 2004. Influence of composting techniques on microbial succession, temperature and pH in a composting municipal solid waste, African J. Biotechnology, 3(4): 239- 343.

Tripathi, G. and P .Bhardwaj 2004a. Comparative studies on biomass production, life cycles and composting efficiency of *Eisenia fetida* (Savigny) and *Lampito mauritii* (Kinberg). Bioresource Technology , 92: 275-283.

Tripathi, G. and P. Bhardwaj. 2004b. Decomposition of kitchen waste amended with low manure using an epigeic species (*Eisenia fetida*) and a anecic species (*Lampito mauritii*) .Bioresource Technology, 92: 215-218.

Viljoen, S.A. and A.J. Reinecke, 1994. The life-cycle and reproduction of *Eudrilus eugeniae* under controlled environmental conditions. Mitt. Hamb. Zool. Mus. Inst. 89 (2): 149-157.

Vinotha, S.P., K. Parthasarathi and L.S. Ranganathan, 2000. Enhanced phosphatase activity in earthworm casts is more of microbial origin. Curr. Sci., 79 (9): 1158-1159.

Wolter, C. and Scheu, S. 1999. Changes in bacterial numbers hyphal lengths during the gut passage through *Lumbricus terrestris* (Lumbricidae: Oligochaeta). Pedobiologia, 43: 891-900.

Yadav, D.V. 1995. Recycling of sugar factory pressmud in agriculture. In: Recycling of Crop, Animal, Human and Industrial wastes in Agriculture (ed. Tandon, H.L.S). Fertilizer Development and Consultation Organization, New Delhi.

Chapter **10**

Vermicomposting of Biodegradable Institutional Solid Wastes

A.K. Sannigrahi

Proof and Experimental Establishment, Ministry of Defence, DRDO, Chandipur, Balasore, Orissa-756 025

e-mail: sannigrahi_ak@rediffmail.com

The widespread energy crisis due to quick declination of fossil fuels and the problems arising from environmental degradation, rise in population and price hike of fertilizers have forced people to develop the appropriate technology in using waste materials for beneficial purposes. More than 90 percent Institutional solid wastes are of biodegradable nature, which can easily be converted to good quality vermicompost. Segregation of these wastes at source is easier with little cooperation of employees in comparison to segregation after collection. At Proof and Experimental Establishment, Chandipur, it is found that eight types of solid wastes are generated regularly; major four are biodegradable type (paper wastes, canteen wastes, garden wastes and sweeping wastes); while others are minor and of non-biodegradable nature (metal scraps, plastic wastes, broken glasses and thermo-cool packaging materials). The vermicomposting of biodegradable solid wastes helps to maintain the pollution-free and healthy environment in the Institute and also creates employment opportunity by generating revenue from solid wastes. ISO 14001 also gives emphasis on environmental protection by conserving the resources and their optimal use with little or no harmful impact on living being and environment. Scientific disposal of solid wastes at Institute level will, no doubt, reduce the load of urban wastes in the city. Application of vermicompost in soil helps to preserve the good health and productivity of Mother Earth by returning valuable plant nutrients and arresting the carbon sequestration.

Institutional solid wastes are the wastes produced regularly during working in the government or private offices, educational institutes, research laboratories, hospitals and nursing homes, etc. The wastes generated in the hospitals and nursing homes are also known as bio-medical wastes which include biodegradable cotton bandages, clothes, blood, body fluid, unused drugs, human tissues, organs etc. and non-biodegradable injection syringes, needles, scalpel blades, saline and chemical bottles, etc. These are unsafe to handle due to their health hazardous or infectious character. The used chemicals of research laboratories and acid materials of used batteries are also known as hazardous wastes. All these wastes need special care for disposal through standard Incineration or Plasma Pyrolysis (Moses *et al.*, 2002). Paper wastes such as used paper, old newspaper, books, magazines, computer papers, carbon papers, cartoon boxes, etc.; garden wastes like weeds, grasses, uprooted matured flower plants, etc; wastes collected during sweeping such as dust particles and dry leaves of avenue trees grown in Institute premises; wet canteen wastes like vegetable peels and cuttings, rotten vegetables, left over foods, used tea leaves, crushed bones, broken egg shells, etc. are known as biodegradable Institutional solid wastes. Certain packing materials like polythene sheets or packets, thermocool materials, etc. used plastic items and electronic wastes, broken glass materials, metal scraps and vehicle wastes such as condemned tires, tubes, vehicle parts, batteries etc. are also generated as non-biodegradable wastes. All these institutional solid wastes are generally disposed off either by burning in the open field or dumping in the low-lying outskirts or in the Municipality dustbin.

Open burning of solid wastes like newspaper, books, magazines, junk mail, cardboard, milk cartons, food wastes, various types of plastic, assorted cans, bottles, and jars, etc. is potentially a large source of poisonous gases like dioxins and furans besides production of smoke, carbon monoxide and dioxide gases (Anon., 2000). Exposure to certain dioxins has been clearly shown to cause adverse effects in laboratory animals, such as immune dysfunction, cancer, hormonal changes and development of abnormalities. The people sometimes face difficulty in breathing, dry throats and burning eyes due to smoke produced by burning these solid wastes. Open dumping of solid wastes containing food wastes on the outskirts spread unhygienic situation in the surroundings as the materials stinks with decomposition. It also helps in multiplication of harmful microorganisms, flies and mosquitoes, attracts pigs, rats, snakes, dogs and other animals (Kamalamma and Rajarajeshwari, 1996). Micorooganisms growing in such piles pollute the air, soil and water and spread diseases like tuberculosis, cholera,dysentery liver disease, etc. The ground water and soils are also contaminated with heavy metals and poisonous chemicals present in dumped wastes. Stray dogs and cats which feed and breed in the dumping area without human touch, become feral (half wild) and bite children and passers by spreading rabies and causing road accidents. The possibility of snake bite also increases. Rats living in garbage are the primary carriers of plague. Mosquitoes breed in garbage cause malaria and brain fever, fatal for human life.

Scientific management of solid wastes is an important part of Environmental Management System (EMS) of every organization generally concerned for providing a pollution-free and healthy environment to its employees. In the era of widespread energy crisis and quick declination of natural resources, efforts should be taken to reuse the wastes for beneficial purposes instead of burning or throwing away. Keeping this in view a project entitled "Development of eco-friendly model for combating Institutional solid wastes" was carried out during November 2003 to November 2004 at Proof and Experimental Establishment (PXE), a prestigious century old Defence Research and Development Organization at Chandipur, Orissa, where about 1200 employees are busy in carrying out proofs of guns and ammunitions either manufactured in India or imported from other countries. The present article deals with scientific disposal of biodegradable portion of institutional solid wastes. Sannigrahi and Chakrabortty (2000) showed that vermicomposting was the quicker method in comparison to other conventional methods for composting biodegradable wastes.

Collection of solid wastes at PXE

It is found that eight types of wastes are generated in considerable quantity regularly at the office premises out of which four are biodegradable type such as canteen wastes (10 to 38 kg/day), garden wastes (01 to 19 kg/day), sweeping wastes (10 to 250 kg/day) and waste papers and cartons (02 to 53 kg/day); while the other four are non-biodegradable in nature e.g. plastic wastes (0 to 2 kg/day), glass materials (0 to 3 kg/day), iron scraps (0 to 5 kg/day) and thermo cool packing materials (0 to 3 kg/day). On an average every month about 1169 kg dry leaves of avenue trees as sweeping waste, 142 kg paper waste, 101 kg garden waste, 466 kg waste foods and vegetable peels as canteen waste were collected from Establishment premises during December 2003 to November 2004 (Table 1). About 237 kg waste plastics, 27 kg thermocool packing materials, 49 kg metal scraps and 89 kg glass materials were also collected as non biodegradable wastes through segregation during this period. Waste paper though recyclable for making new paper and can be sold to scrap dealer but in Defence institute these waste papers are burnt to avoid any possibility of leaking out of any valuable and confidential information. It is interesting to note that about 98% solid wastes of PXE are organic in nature and 59% of non-biodegradable wastes are plastic wastes. Since the condemned vehicles, tires, tubes and old batteries of this Establishment are sent regularly to Vehicle Depot, Panagarh for further disposal, these are not wastes for PXE.

Table 1. Collection of biodegradable solid wastes (kg) from PXE

Month	Sweeping wastes	Paper wastes	Garden wastes	Canteen wastes
December, 03	1865	272	490	435
January, 04	1205	226	82	374
February, 04	1731	149	35	417
March, 04	2755	94	34	561
April, 04	2252	54	32	376
May, 04	697	72	55	494
June, 04	801	130	132	575
July, 04	612	56	109	557
August, 04	524	93	39	463
September, 04	541	257	113	448
October, 04	496	240	49	376
November, 04	550	60	42	510
Total	14029	1703	1212	5586
Average	**1169**	**142**	**101**	**466**

Materials required for Vermicomposting

Wastes are segregated after collection in to biodegradable wastes, metal, scraps, glass materials, plastic wastes and thermo-cool packing materials. Non-biodegradable wastes are stored separately for time-to-time selling to scrap dwellers. (Photo-1).

Paper wastes are shredded into small pieces either in shredding machine or through hand shredding. Waste papers, carton boxes, garden wastes, sweeping wastes and vegetable peels from canteen are mixed together and used as biodegradable wastes for vermicomposting.

A shade with cemented floor or unused room is required for carrying out composting work since direct sunlight and rain affects vermicomposting. Plastic sheet can also be used in the floor in absence of cemented floor.

Photo 1. Segregation of Institutional solid

Arrangement of cow dung in the Institute is either problematic or costly affair since the cost of 1 tractor load is approximately 200 rupees at Orissa whereas transportation charges to bring cow dung to the Institute is about 600 rupees. Hence trails were conducted to find out the replacement of cow dung. It was observed that though initially cow dung was required for starting the composting work but afterwards by mixing the partially decomposed waste materials (obtained as unsived materials during sieving of prepared vermicompost) in lieu of cow dung with fresh wastes during preparation of aerobic composting beds, similar or slightly better performance was achieved. Different cellulose decomposing microorganisms can also be mixed with waste materials for getting better decomposition at the initial stage.

Process adopted in PXE

- Aerobic/heap compost beds (length–as convenient, width 1 m and height more than 1 m) are prepared in the open field over plastic sheet by mixing biodegradable wastes and partially decomposed waste materials or cow dung as slurry in 4:1 ratio (weight wise). Beds are moistened properly and covered with black polythene sheets to enhance decomposition and to prevent fly breeding. (Photo-2).
- Materials are mixed four times at 15 days interval for well mixing, for increasing microbial decomposition, proper watering and airing in the beds, which are then covered again with same polythene sheets.

Photo 2. Preparationof aerobic compostig beds using biodegradable solid wastes in open ground (1st stage)

- Vermicompost beds (length 5 m or as convenient, width 1 m and height 0.50 to 0.60 m) are prepared using these partially decomposed materials of aerobic compost beds after two months following windrows method under the shade or inside the room to prevent beds from sunshine and rain water. Five thousands epigeic earthworms (*Eisenia fetida* species) are then added in the top of each bed and beds are covered with moist Hessian cloth or gunny bags. Watering was done on each bed periodically using sprayer to keep bed moist only. Addition of excess of less water to beds hampers vermicomposting. (Photo-3).

Photo 3. Preparation of vermicomposting beds using partially decomposed solid wastes under a shade (2nd stage)

- Earthworms deposited their excreta, known as vermicompost on the top of beds. These were collected from top layer at fortnightly interval from 30 or 45 days onwards. Watering is stopped for three days before harvesting of vermicomposts.
- Vermicompost is then, partially air dried under shade after separating earthworms by hand screening, sieved through 2 mm wire mesh and is stored in Plastic bucket or Plastic/Nylon bags for selling. (Photo-4).

Vermicompost is sold regularly at the rate of Rs. 4 /-per kg.

Waste foods are collected everyday separately, mixed with cow dung or partially decomposed wastes in 1:4 ratios and heap-like beds

Photo 4. Packaging of sieved vermicompost for storing and selling

are prepared weekly for decomposition. Water should not be added during mixing as water comes out from the wastes during decomposition. The top should be covered with black polythene sheet to avoid animal interference and spreading of foul smell. Mixed materials are taken out for vermicomposting after three months following the above-mentioned procedure when materials become partially decomposed and foul smell subsides.

To study the quality, Vermicomposts were prepared separately from 100 kg each of waste papers, garden wastes, dry leaves of avenue trees and also from the mixture of waste papers (50 kg) and dry leaves (50 kg) after mixing with slurry of 25 kg cow dung respectively and following the above-mentioned two stage (aerobic-vermi) composting procedure. Vermicompost was also prepared from 25 kg waste food materials after mixing with 100 kg cow dung. Vermicomposts were harvested on 45th day after vermicomposting procedure started, air dried partially, sieved (2 mm) and analyzed in the chemical laboratory for pH, potassium dichromate oxidized organic carbon, total nitrogen, phosphorus, potassium, calcium, magnesium, iron, zinc, copper and manganese following standard procedure (Tandon,1993).

Experimental findings

It was found that all biodegradable wastes of the institute could be converted to good quality compost by following heap/aerobic composting technique initially for two months and then vermicomposting technique using *Eisenia fetida* earthworms. The rate of vermicomposting was found in the order: Garden waste> paper waste> canteen waste> sweeping wastes. Mixing different wastes together helped in rapid decomposition. The author in his earlier work with biodegradable house refuses using *Perionyx excavatus* earthworms at Tezpur, Assam also recorded similar pattern of vermicomposting from vegetable wastes, waste newspaper and kitchen wastes (Sannigrahi, 2002).

The analytical data as given in Table 2 and 3 showed that about 1.10 to 1.23 percent Nitrogen, 0.15 to 0.31 percent Phosphorus, 0.43 to 0.58 percent Potassium, 2556 to 3805 ppm Calcium, 1400 to 2700 ppm Magnesium, 3820 to 7620 ppm Iron, 81.8 to 109.4 ppm Zinc, 12.6 to 16.5 ppm Copper and 192 to 304 ppm Manganese were present in these vermicomposts prepared from different biodegradable Institutional solid wastes. The employees, who used these vermicompost in their kitchen gardens or flower plants, have reported that it boosted the growth of both flower and vegetable plants. This is obvious as vermicompost, being balanced organic fertilizer, provides all essential nutrients to plants and improves the status of soil organic carbon which again acts as store house of plant nutrients in soil.

Table 2 : Major nutrient analysis of vermicompost samples

Solid wastes	pH	Org. C (%)	N(%)	P (%)	K (%)
Garden wastes	6.9	10.28	1.22	0.22	0.53
Waste papers	7.1	10.38	1.11	0.22	0.45
Dry leaves	6.9	09.65	1.10	0.15	0.43
Paper + leaves	6.8	11.60	1.12	0.20	0.58
Food wastes	7.0	11.60	1.23	0.31	0.48

Table 3 : Secondary and micronutrient contents of vermicompost samples

Solid wastes	Ca (ppm)	Mg (ppm)	Fe (ppm)	Zn (ppm)	Cu (ppm)	Mn (ppm)
Garden wastes	3611	1400	7620	85.2	14.8	192
Waste papers	3504	2700	3820	82.4	16.5	204
Dry leaves	3804	2120	7530	81.8	12.6	304
Paper + leaves	3612	1600	5060	109.4	15.6	248
Food wastes	2556	1990	7520	96.4	15.4	296

As a part of awareness program of the project work, employees of this Establishment were intimated about the menace of managed solid wastes to the environment as well as to the people working in the Institute and also about their eco-friendly as well as economical recycling tehnicques by organizing two workshops in the Establishment and also through practical demonstration of project activities. It has been pointed out that cooperation from employees is of utmost importance for successful management of Institutional solid wastes.

Successful completion of this project has brought the following changes in the Establishment.

1. Throwing of solid wastes here and there has been stopped.
2. Burning or dumping of wastes has been prevented.
3. Efforts are continuing to reduce the generation of wastes as less as possible through mass awareness program.
4. Every month about 500 kg vermicompost is harvested and sold to interested nursery people at the rate of Rs. 4/-per kg.
5. Vermicomposting technology developed in the Establishment is a low cost technology and easy to follow even by less qualified or unemployed youths. No extra micorbial culture is added with the mixture in this technique since sometimes those are not available in the local market or may be expensive to procure.
6. Non-biodegradable wastes are segregated regularly and stored for time-to-time selling to scrap dealers.

Conclusion

Management of solid wastes in the Institute automatically reduces the load of urban solid wastes. It is a round-the-year program. It keeps the environment of the premises clean and pollution-free, which is the basic objective of ISO 14001. Without employee's wholehearted support and cooperation this work cannot be successful. Since proper management of solid waste offers a scope of revenue generation, it increases the employment opportunity for the less qualified youths. However, training on vermicomposting technique and minimum infrastructure (shade and composting place) facility in the Institute are necessary. This Establishment is organizing training courses for interested people.

References

Anonymous. 2000. Backyard burning. The Hindu, January 20. p. 21.

Kamalamma, N. and Rajarajeswari, M. 1996. Improved pit method of composting. Invention Intelligence. 31 (1): 38-40.

Moses, A., Ranjani, R., Sangeetha, P. and Maheshwari, U. 2002. Biomedical waste management – a case study in Tiruchirapalli, Tamilnadu. In: Solid Waste Management-Current status of strategies for the future (ed. R.K. Somashekar and M.A.R. Iyengar). Allied Publishers Pvt. Ltd. New Delhi. p. 71-85.

Sannigrahi, A. K. 2002. Vermicomposting of biodegradable house refuse for reducing municipality solid waste load. In: Solid Waste Management-Current status and strategies for the future (ed. R.K. Somashekar and M.A. R. Iyengar). Allied Publishers Pvt. Ltd. New Delhi. p. 107-111.

Sannigrahi, A.K. and Chakrabortty, S. 2000. Impact of composting techniques on the availability of NPK and microbial population in composts. Environment & Ecology. 18 (4): 888-890.

Tandon, H.L.S. 1993. Method of Analysis of soils, plants, water and fertilizers. Fertilizers Development and Consultation Organization. New Delhi.

Chapter **11**

Vermicomposting of Sericultural Wastes and its Impact on Mulberry Production

P.K. Das; K. Bhogesha; L. Rajanna and S.B. Dandin

Central Sericultural Research and Training Institute, Central Silk Board, Government of India, Manandavadi Road, Srirampuram, Mysore-570 008.

Mulberry plant is exploited mainly for commercial production of silk. Nearly 60 % of the cost of cocoon production accounts for mulberry leaf production. The quality of mulberry leaf alone contributes to the tune of 38.2 per cent for the success of the silkworm crops. Therefore, the production of good quality mulberry leaf with reduced cost is a pre requisite for the sustained growth of sericulture industry. Mulberry being a perennial crop, consistently optimum yeild of good quality leaf can be obtained continuously for a period of 10-15 years from establishment of plantation, provided proper soil fertility is maintained through continuous replenishment of nutrients by addition of fertilizers and manures. The quantity of manure and chemical fertilizers recommended for mulberry cultivation is quite high as compared to other agricultural crops. It is estimated that under tropical conditions, mulberry requires 20 metric tones of farm yard manure, besides, 300 kg nitrogen, 120 kg phosphorus and 120 kg potash per hectare per year for its optimum growth and yield.

In the present days of shortage of fuel 60 per cent of cow dung in India is utilized for fuel purpose and very less quantity of cow dung is left for production of FYM. Besides, the quality of FYM produced by the farming communities is very poor in nutrient contents (0.5, 0.3 and 0.4% nitrogen, phosphorus and potash, respectively) due to improper production system existing in the field.

Under such circumstances, recycling of sericultural farm wastes can help farmers in a big way and can substantially bring down the dependency and expenditure on farm yard manure and chemical fertilizers. A sericulture farm of one hectare size can generate approximately 12-15 metric tons of wastes per hectare per year including silkworm litter, left over mulberry leaves, soft twigs and farm weeds, which has tremendous manurial value of nitrogen (280-300 kg), phosphorus (90 -100kg) and potash (150-200 kg) as well as micro nutrients like iron, zinc, copper etc. At present most of the sericulturists in south India dispose of these valuable sericultural farm wastes directly to the mulberry field for crop nutrition without proper care.

Application of sericultural wastes directly to the mulberry field is not advisable as the heat liberated during decomposition of the wastes may affect the roots of mulberry adversely and do not meet the actual nutrient demand of crops immediately. Further, direct application may lead to unhygienic condition and harbour a lot of infectious diseases including pebrine from the infected silkworm larvae, which may lead to frequent failure of cocoon crops. The mulberry cultivation can be made sustainable and economical by recycling all the organic wastes of sericultural origin as vermicompost. Vermicomposting technique in waste recycling for production of quality manure has often been unsuccessful due to ignorance and unrealistic belief that these are natural processes and need little management. Successful vermicomposting requires adequate care and management for deriving full potential from the technology. The importance of biological process like vermicomposting in plant nutrient management needs no emphasis. In fact, farmyard manure and compost have been used to increase the soil fertility and productivity, all along the history of farming. Major role of organic wastes in primitive agriculture was to restore the soil health through balanced nutrition. The organic manure is a balanced manure, which is bulky in nature. In addition to organic matter, it also supplies macro and micro nutrients. The importance of organic manuring in enriching the fertility status of arable soils of tropics and sub tropics which are poor in organic matter has been well recognized.

The ceaseless efforts of many dedicated practitioners of alternative agriculture like organic, natural and bio dynamic farming have now shown that it is possible to achieve good soil fertility with reduced or even without chemical fertilizers.These systems are based on the use of organic manure produced by natural biological processes in which earthworms, bacteria and other micro-organisms including saprophytic organisms play an important role. Such a system would also reduce the cost of farming while maintaining the soil productivity, improving ecosystem, ultimately resulting in improved soil plant and animal health. To maintain high productivity of both soil and crop, balanced use of chemical fertilizers and organic manures is indispensable. The similar principle can also be followed in mulberry cultivation for better economic returns. Thus, application of plant nutrients through recycling of sericulture farm wastes as compost, vermicompost and judicious use of chemical fertilizers in mulberry cultivation can facilitate quality leaf production for a better and sustainable silkworm cocoon production. Hence, it is necessary that a suitable system be developed in sericultural farms for better and efficient management of the farm wastes through recycling technique to make sericulture more remunerative.

Vermicomposting is a technology of using earthworms as versatile bioreactor for rapid conversion of any organic wastes into value added manure. Thus it can be profitably used in sericulture industry for rapid conversion of wastes in nutrient rich manure. In this process, earthworms act as versatile bioreactor converting organic materials into fine granules called vermicast. The pioneering work of J.V. Bhat, a microbiologist, on the earthworm microbe association in early 1950 was the major contribution towards the applied biology of earthworms. In the Indian sub-continent earthworm research picked up momentum only in the latter 20th century. Voracious feeding habit of selected species of earthworms on rich sources of organic matter and their high reproductive potential were exploited both in tropical and temperate countries. Several studies on the effect of different levels of nutrient value of food material on earthworms cocoon production revealed that with nitrogen rich diet the earthworms grow faster and produce more cocoons than those feeding on mineralized soil. Even litter feeding worms show an order of preference for certain leafy matter.

Use of earthworms for processing waste materials including compost, sewage sludge, cattle and horse manure have been well documented. Voracious agricultural wastes like post harvest stubbles, sugarcane trash coir waste, paper pulp and faecal matter of cow, sheep, horse, pig, biogas sludge of poultry droppings and organic wastes of areca nut and cocoa have been tried as food source for earthworms and were observed that the breakdown of these materials was enhanced considerably in the presence of earthworms. Research reports from India and abroad during the late eighties revealed that organic waste could be efficiently converted into vermicompost with a recovery of 75-85 per cent in a composting period of 2 to 3 months in addition to increase in macro and micro nutrients concentration. Many reports revealed that the earthworms biomass could be doubled in a period of 2 months. They effectively harness the beneficial soil microflora and destroy the soil pathogens in addition to conversion of organic wastes into valuable products such as bio-fertilizer, bio-pesticides, vitamins, enzymes and growth hormones and also protein rich worm biomass. The vermicast is also a suitable base for free living beneficial microbes whose activites are essential for releasing nutrients to crop plants. Vermicomposting of paddy straw and plant twigs showed a significant narrowing down of C:N ratio and an appreciable increase in total nitrogen and phosphorus. Several reports have been published on the potential of *Eudrilus euginiae, Eisenia fetida* and *Perionyx excavatus* for the vermicomposting under Indian situation and suggested that vermicomposting is an important component of organic farming.

Technique of Vermicomposting using Sericultural Wastes:

A thatched shed of approximately 7.5 m x 6.0 m is to be constructed for a mulberry farm of 1 hectare area. The shed should be constructed on a slightly elevated ground level, with soil and stone bunds all around to prevent predators. Eight trenches measuring 2.4 m x 0.6 m 0.45 m each should be prepared parallel to each other in two rows of 4 each inside the shed and lined with polythene sheet or stone lines at the bottom and side walls to avoid migration of earthworms (**Plate-1**). Concrete trenches can also be made at ground level or vertically raised concrete tanks of the said dimension can also be made.

Plate 1. Vermicomposting of seri-wastes under progress in trenches lined with polythene sheet.

The depth of the trench should not be more than 0.45m. For making feed for earthworms, the wastes including weeds should be mixed with cow dung/biogas spent slurry (5 kg mixed with 100 liters of water) solution and should be left in a open pit for 10-15 days for semi decomposition as the earthworms cannot feed on fresh wastes **(Plate-2).**

Plate 2. Preparation of earthworm feed by semi decomposition using seri-wastes in a open pit.

While decomposing, material should contain minimum of 30-40% moisture. During this process, the temperature of the semi decomposing material will rise up to 50-60°C. Hence once or twice the material should be turned upside down. Doing this, the temperature will come to a normal state. Later, each trench should be filled up with 200-300 kg semi-decomposed seri cultural wastes having 30-40% moisture. A mixed culture of earthworms, *Eudrilus euginiae*, *Eisenia fetida* and *Perionyx excavatus* in juvenile stage **(Plate-3)** can be introduced in the feed @ 1.5 kg per ton of wastes in each trench and left for earthworm activity for 7-8 weeks.

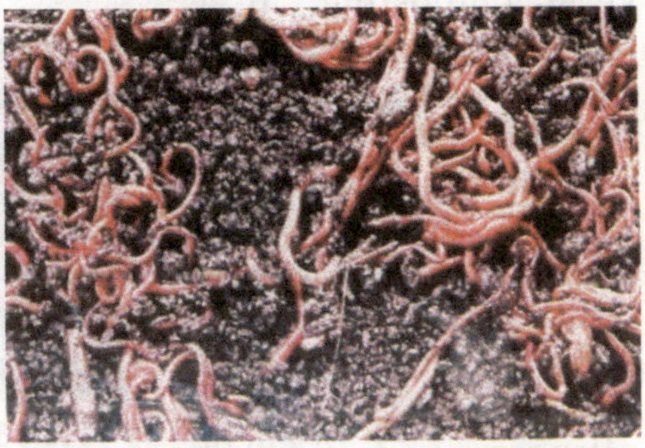

Plate 3. Mixed culture of earthworm used for vermicomposting.

While releasing earthworms, care should be taken to ensure sufficient moisture (30-40%) in the feed. In every 2-3 days, water should be sprinkled from the top to keep the feed moist and covered with coconut fronds or any green leaves to check evaporation. After 3-4 weeks, feed should be carefully observed, for presence of vermicasts on top of the feed. Dark brown to black, granular vermicasts can be found deposited on the top of the feed which appears like tea powder **(Plate-4)**.

Watering should be stopped for 2-3 days for drying the upper layer and gently vermicasts can be scrapped from top layers or to a depth it is present. Removal of vermicasts from time to time is very important as the earthworms cannot survive on its excreta. The same process of collection can be followed after every 1-2 weeks till all the feed is converted to vermicast except a small quantity of unconverted feed with earthworms which can be reused with new feed. One can also collect vermicast by using a sieve (2 mm mesh galvanized) and reuse earthworms and cocoons for next cycle of vermicomposting. It is highly necessary to keep the shed almost dark, moist and cool while vermicomposting is under progress to get good result, since earthworms do not prefer light. The final product vermicompost **(Plate-5)** contains 1.875-2.0% nitrogen, 0.6-0.9% phosphorus and 1.0-1.5% potash besides, 84.6 ppm zinc, 1247 ppm iron, 509.7 manganese and 61.5 ppm copper.

Plate 4. Presence of granular vermicasts on the top layer of feed.

Plate 5. A heap of vermicompost prepared out of seri-wastes ready for use.

Precautions

Earthworms should not be released in the hot fermenting sericultural wastes and should be protected from direct sun light and rain by covering the trenches with thatched shed. The feed should be free from any insecticides or pesticides. The moisture content of the feed should be maintained at 30-40%. The prepared vermicompost should be used in fresh condition before desiccation of useful microflora to get good results.

Merits

It is an ecofriendly technology and needs only 70-75 days for sericultural wastes to get nutrient rich vermicompost.The manure becomes free from pathogens. Research conducted at CSR & TI,

Mysore revealed that quality-wise 6 metric tons of vermicompost is as good as 20 metric tons of farmyard manure (FYM).

Impact of vermicompost in mulberry production

A field study was conducted with graded doses of vermicompost on mulberry leaf yield and quality. The experiment was conducted with S-36 mulberry variety having six treatments with three replications in a randomized block design to study the effect of vermicompost @ 10 MT and 20 MT/ha/year with and without chemical fertilizers keeping a control using full dose of FYM (20 Mt/ha/yr) and chemical fertilizers (300:120:120 NPK kg/ha/yr).

A total of five crops were harvested for one year. The data on plant growth and yield parameters were recorded. Chemical analysis of leaf and silkworm rearing trials were also conducted. The pooled data of one year (five crops) indicated that application of 10 MT of

Table 1: Effect of graded doses of vermicompost on various growth and yield parameters of S_{36} mulberry (Pooled of 5 crops)

Treat ments	Av. Height of plants (cm)	Total leaf area/plant (cm^2)	Total leaf yield/ha /yr (MT)	Total stem yield/ha/yr (MT)	Total above ground fresh biomass/ ha/yr (MT)	Total above ground dry biomass/ha/ yr (MT)
T0	174.04	43270	57.035	34.115	91.145	2.925
T1	148.33	33187	54.195	29.670	83.865	2.155
T2	175.73	54227	56.740	34.155	90.895	3.335
T3	153.06	44125	53.205	30.655	83.760	2.235
T4	172.83	49771	59.340	34.770	96.710	2.720
T5	144.46	25933	33.515	18.905	52.425	1.245
CD at 5%	23.87	17961.02	0.500	3.037	1.284	0.319

Legends:

T0-20 MT of FYM + 300: 120:120 NPK kg/ha/yr (Control)
T1-10 MT Vermicompost/ha/yr alone
T2-10 MT Vermicompost + 150:60:60 NPK kg/ha/yr
T3-20 MT Vermicompost/ha/yr alone
T4-20 MT Vermicompost + 150:60:60 NPK kg/ha/yr
T5-No Vermicompost and no NPK

Table -2: Effect of graded doses of vermicompost on various leaf quality parameters of S_{36} mulberry assessed by chemical analysis and silkworm rearing (CSR2 x CSR5)

Treatments	Leaf N (%)	Leaf P (%)	Leaf K (%)	Weight of 10 matured larvae (g)	Actual yield of cocoons by number	Actual yield of cocoons by weight (kg)	ERR/10000 larave brushed by numbers	ERR/10000 larvae brushed by weight (kg)	Single cocoon weight (g)	Single shell weight (g)	Shell Ratio (%)
T0	3.17	0.37	1.70	49.2	198.3	0.403	9918	20.18	1.994	0.455	22.80
T1	3.37	0.37	1.66	48.3	197.6	0.384	9883	19.25	1.879	0.415	22.00
T2	4.10	0.34	1.70	50.0	196.6	0.389	9833	19.60	1.974	0.462	23.40
T3	3.00	0.43	2.00	49.0	197.0	0.385	9850	19.49	1.992	0.464	23.20
T4	3.10	0.36	2.00	49.4	198.0	0.389	9900	19.48	1.990	0.455	22.80
T5	2.30	0.34	1.50	48.6	194.3	0.379	9716	18.96	1.917	0.428	22.20
CD at 5%	0.44	0.03	0.19	N.S.	N.S.	0.014	N.S.	0.68	0.074	0.024	0.52

Table 3: Economic analysis of vermicomposting technology using sericultural wastes (for one hectare unit)

PARTICULARS	UNITS	YEARS									
		1	2	3	4	5	6	7	8	9	10
1. CONSTRUCTION OF VERMI SHED	7.5 M X 6.0 M	4000					4000				
2. CONSTRUCTION OF VERMI TRENCHES (8 Nos)	2.4 M X 0.6 M X 0.45 M	350									
3. COST OF EARTHWORMS	4 Kg @ Rs. 2000 = 00 /kg	8000									
A. TOTAL FIXED COST		12350					4000				
4. COST OF SERICULTURAL WASTE	15 MT @ Rs. 50 = 00 /MT	750	750	750	750	750	750	750	750	750	750
5. LABOUR CHARGES FOR 1 YEAR	208 MD @ Rs. 85 = 00 / MD	17680	17680	17680	17680	17680	17680	17680	17680	17680	17680
6. LABOUR FOR MAINTENANCE OF STOCK	25 MD @ Rs. 85 = 00 /MD	2125	2125	2125	2125	2125	2125	2125	2125	2125	2125
B.. TOTAL VARIABLE COST	-	20555	20555	20555	20555	20555	20555	20555	20555	20555	20555
TOTAL COST OF PRODUCTION (A+B)	-	32905	20555	20555	20555	20555	24555	20555	20555	20555	20555
C. RETURNS THROUGH SALE OF. V.C.	13 MT @ Rs. 2000 = 00 /MT	26000	26000	26000	26000	26000	26000	26000	26000	26000	26000
D. RETURNS THROUGH SALE OF E.W.	3 Kg. @ Rs. 2000 = 00 /Kg	6000	6000	6000	6000	6000	6000	6000	6000	6000	6000
E. GROSS RETURN (C+D)	-	32000	32000	32000	32000	32000	32000	32000	32000	32000	32000
F. NET RETURNS	-	-905	11445	11445	11445	11445	7445	11445	11445	11445	11445

C:B RATIO = 1 : 1.40 I.R.R : Above 40% AVERAGE COST OF V.C/MT = Rs. 1700 AVERAGE COST OF V.C./ Kg = Rs. 1.70

vermicompost in addition to 50% of recommended dose of chemical fertilizers (T2) could maintain the same growth (175.73 cm as plant height) and leaf yield (56.7 MT/ha/yr) as against the control (T0) which recorded 174.04 cm plant height and 57.0 MT of leaf yield/ha/yr (Table-1). Chemical analysis of leaf in the same treatment indicated 4.10% N, 0.34% P and 1.70%K as against control which showed 3.17% N, 0.37% P and 1.70%K (Table-2). The silkworm rearing trial also indicated that all the economic characters of cocoons were at par with the control. However, the application of vermicompost alone @ 10 to 20 metric tons per hectare per year could not maintain the same plant growth or leaf yield when compared with control or combined application of vermicompost with 50% chemical fertlizers (Table-2).

Economics of Vermicomposting

The economics of vermicomposting using sericultural wastes was also calculated and cost benefit ratio was worked out to be 1:1.40 (Table-3) which was found to be highly profitable.

Conclusion

Thus vermiculture holds out a good prospect for transforming the colossal sericultural wastes into nutrient rich organic manure. Besides being economical, this organic manure is richer in nitrogen, phosphorus, potash and micronutrients and enzymes, thus, can promote luxurious growth of mulberry leading to better quality and overall sericultural productivity. The study also indicated that vermicompost prepared from sericultural farm wastes can be a better alternative to the traditionally prepared FYM, besides cutting down the costly chemical inputs. This can also become an essential component to the integrated plant nutrient management (IPNM) in mulberry cultivation. It can be used for all mulberry varieties.

References

Biocycle International Journal of composting and organic recycling. 419 State Avenue Emmaus, PA 18049. 610-967-4135.

Compost Science and Utilization: A Biocycle publication 419 State Avenue Emmaus, PA 18049. 610-967-4135.

Organic farming for sustainable agriculture, A.K. Dhama (1999 ed.) Published by Agro Botanica, 4E-176 J.N. Vyas Nagar, Bikaner (Rajasthan).

Ecotechnology for pollution control and environmental management. R.K. Trivedy and Arvind Kumar. Enviro media, Karad (Maharashtra).

Organics in sustaining soil fertility and productivity. First edition (1998). Edited by G.D. Raddar, C.J. Itnal, V.S. Gidnavar, B.N. Patil, B.M. Chittapur, H.B. Babalad, U.A.S., Dharwad-580 005, Karnataka.

Handbook of Sericulture Technologies (2000). Edited by S.B. Dandin, Jayant Jayaswal and K. Giridhar, Published by Central Silk Board, Ministry of Textiles, Govt. of India, Bangalore.

Chapter 12

Vermicomposting of three Organic Wastes and its Impact on *Phaseolus aureus*

Satyendra M. Singh*

Vermiculture and Environmental Research Laboratory, Department of Animal Science, M.J.P. Rohilkhand University, Bareilly-243 006 (U.P.)

e-mail-satyendramsingh@rediffmail.com

Continuous generation of huge amount of organic wastes due to fast pace of industrialization and urbanization all over the country and its improper dumping has created alarming situations to the environment. Several Non Government Organizations, research institutions and universities are trying to find out effective measures to solve the problem around the world. Vermicomposting–one of the biological techniques in balancing the disbalances of nature and making the environment eco-biologically fit to live has been accepted world-wide, but the vermicompost transformed from a particular organic waste is useful up to what extent-is a question to be answered. The aim of the present study was to investigate the usefulness of the vermicompost transformed from three kinds of organic wastes using the worm, ***Eudrilus eugeniae,*** on the rate of germination of seeds of ***Raphanus sativus*** and ***Phaseolus aureus.*** Further investigations were also taken to observe the establishment of the seedlings in these vermicomposts to assess the possibility of using such biofertilizers in agricultural lands.

EXPERIMENTAL WASTES

Vermicomposts were derived from the waste of a biotechnology unit (BIOCON), effluent of processing unit of a dairy and waste from a pharmaceutical unit.

* INSA Visiting Fellow at the University of Agricultural Sciences, GKVK Campus, Bangalore-5560 065

Biocon

It is a plant material, usually wheat bran after extracting enzymes from it, produced from a biotechnology unit in Karnataka state. Proper disposal of this waste is a big problem. Although Karnataka Compost Development Corporation (KCDC) – a government body, established in 1975, is working for the disposal of wastes but mainly for municipal waste. In the state, approximately 6000 tons garbage is generated/ day and 2000 tons/day from the city of Bangalore alone.

Dairy

In a dairy industry, nearly 80000 to 100000-litre milk is processed/ day. Out of this, 5 to 10% is fat, which is segregated as processing waste. If it is not utilized or transformed, causes many health hazards to the entire living community including man.

Pharmaceutical

A pharmaceutical drug unit produces some antipyretics and antibiotics and releases two types of sludge, namely chemical and biological. These wastes are produced in the industry either at drug synthesis stage or formulation stage or accumulated due to improper dumping of expired drugs etc. In India, around 10,000 registered pharmaceutical industries, nearly 65 R & D industries, 20 registered research centers are working at present. Apart from these recognized industries, a large number of unregistered industries including 2000 cosmetics industries, research and chemical laboratories are generating pharmaceutical wastes in enormous amount (Indian Pharmaceutical Guide, 2001).

PROCESS ADOPTED

Preparation of vermicompost

Vermicompost of three wastes (i.e., Biocon, dairy and pharmaceutical) was prepared separately. Vermicompost from Biocon waste was prepared by using it with cattle dung in the ratio of 1:3, 1:1 and 3:1. From dairy waste, it was obtained in three forms. First by taking dairy waste (DW) and coir pith (CP) in the the ratio of 3:00 litre: 2.5 kg : second as DW: CP: Water = 1.5 litre: 2.5 kg: 1.5 litre and third as DW: CP: Water = 0.75 litre: 2.5 kg: 2.25 litre. Vermicompost from pharmaceutical waste (in the form of chemical and biological sludges) prepared by mixing biological and chemical sludges with cattle dung separately in the ratio of 1:1, and both the wastes in equal amounts with cattle dung in the ratio of 1:1. Normal vermicompost (NVC) was prepared by using cattle dung and plant biomass in the ratio of 1:1.

In each medium of 4 kg, 20 mature earthworms, *Eudrilus eugeniae* were introduced to work in the waste mix for 45 days. Moisture content was maintained by adding appropriate amount of water as and when required. After that, earthworms and cocoons were segregated from the prepared vermicompost. Farmyard manure (FYM) was collected from a nearby village.

Seed germination experiment

10% aqueous extract of each of the prepared vermicompost from all the three wastes, NVC and FYM were prepared separately. A wet filter paper with the extract of vermicompost of 1:3 ratio of Biocon waste was kept in a petridisc (size 6" diameter) and 20 healthy seeds of *Phaseolus aureus* and *Raphanus sativus,* 10 in each, were put on it. Another wet filter paper with the same extract was put over the seeds. Moisture was maintained by wetting the filter papers with the respective extract as and when required. Rate of germination of plumules and radicles was recorded after 96 hrs. Such observations were also noted for the seeds kept in the vermicompost extracts of other two ratios (1:1 and 3:1) of Biocon waste as well as for other vermicomposts and FYM.

Shoot length experiment

Influence of different concentrations of vermicompost on the shoot length of *P. aureus* was assessed by using two sets of media (2:1:3 and 1:1:1 as sand: vc: soil) in circular plastic containers, in triplicate. Three healthy seeds of *P. aureus* were sown in each container at the depth of 1 cm from the surface. Moisture was maintained by adding suitable amount of water everyday. Measurement of length of shoot of *P. aureus* plants was taken at weekly intervals for three weeks and the results were compared with that of FYM and NVC.

EXPERIMENTAL FINDINGS

Germination rate of seeds of *Phaseolus aureus* and *Raphanus sativus* in 10% extract of different vermicomposts prepared from three wastes has been shown in Table-1. Performance of germination of both species of seeds was the best in the vermicompost prepared by using one part of "Biocon" waste and three parts of cattle dung. Increasing

Table-1 Rate of germination of seeds of *Phaseolus aureus* and *Raphanus sativus* in 10% extract of vermicomposts derived from different organic wastes after 96 hrs. of sowing (SEM±5)

Vermi-compost transformed from	**Conc. of Media**	***P. aureus* Average shoot length (in cm)**		***R. sativus* Average shoot length (in cm)**	
		Plumule	Radicle	Plumule	Radicle
Biocon waste	BW + CD(1:3)	4.8±0.68	4.5±0.63	4.7±0.40	5.1±0.23
	BW + CD (1:1)	2.0 ±0.22	2.1±0.26	4.0±0.26	4.7±0.40
	BW + CD (3:1)	1.4±0.17	1.9±0.28	3.7±0.45	4.3±0.43
Diary waste	DW + CP (3L + 2.5 kg)	*P. aureus*		*R. sativus*	
		Plumule	Radicle	Plumule	Radicle
		3.5 ± 0.32	3.9 ± 0.33	3.5 ± 0.63	3.8 ± 0.20
	DW + C P + water (1.5 L+2.5 kg + 1.50L)	5.7±1.55	6.4±1.70	3.7±0.37	4.0±0.54
	DW+CP + water (0.75 L + 2.5 kg + 2.25 L)	2.6±0.24	3.3±0.80	4.3±0.45	6.5±0.57
Pharmaceutical waste	Biol. w +CD (1:1)	4.3±0.37	4.2±0.66	4.4±0.45	6.3±0.66
	Chem. w +CD (1:1)	4.9±0.38	5.3±0.43	4.5±0.34	5.0±0.44
	Mixed +CD (1:1)	3.3±0.20	2.2±0.31	4.1±0.60	3.8±0.48
N.V.C.	CD + Pl. Biom (1:1)	4.2±0.55	5.2±0.58	4.4±0.69	5.8±0.58
F.Y.M.	FYM (100%)	2.0±0.38	3.3±0.71	2.6±0.59	2.4±0.18

*BW = Biocon Waste, CD = Cattle Dung, DW= Diary Waste, CP = Coir Pith, Bio. w = Biological waste, Chem. w= Chemical waste, Pl. Biom = Plant Biomass, N.V.C. = Normal Vermicompost, F.Y.M. = Farm Yard Manure.

concentration of 'Biocon' waste in the preparation of vermicompost resulted in deterioration in the performance of the seeds.

The germination of the seeds of *P. aureus* in 10% extract of vermicompost prepared by using different levels of diluted dairy effluent (1:1 and 1:3, dairy effluent: water) and decomposed coir pith was found to be better in vermicompost prepared from higher concentration of dairy effluent. In case of *R. sativus,* the performance was better in the vermicompost extract prepared by using low concentration of dairy effluent.

The chemical and the biological sludge of a pharmaceutical unit were subjected to vermicomposting by mixing them with equal proportions of cattle dung independently and also by mixing both the sludges and cattle dung in equal proportions. Surprisingly, the germination of the tested seeds was better in 10% extract of vermicomposted chemical sludge than that of the biological sludge.

When the data were analyzed to see the influence of waste derived vermicompost on the growth of shoot of *P. aureus* (Table-2), it may be noticed that 2:1:3 mixture medium was better than 1: 1:1 in most of the cases including FYM except the vermicompost derived from a mixture of chemical and biological sludges in equal proportions.

Vermicompost of 'Biocon' waste with cattle dung (1:1) has a better potential on plant growth when used in 2:1:3 ratio than either of the ratios (1:3 or 3:1). It was recorded that vermicompost from dairy effluent waste has great impact on the plant growth when derived in the ratio of 1:3 (dairy waste: water) and coir pith as a base substrate than other media.

Growth of *P. aureus* was significantly ($P<0.05$) better in the vermicompost derived from chemical sludge than that of the biological. Interestingly, influence of both these vermicomposts was recorded more than the vermicompost prepared from a mixture of biological and chemical sludges in equal amounts but inferior to NVC. If the data were compared with FYM, it may be concluded that FYM is least useful for plant growth than that of the vermicompost derived from different wastes. Improvement in plant growth could be partially due to large increase in soil microbial biomass after mixing vermicompost leading to the production of hormones or humates in the vermicompost acting as plant growth regulators independent of nutrient supply.

DISCUSSION

Ang Lopez *et al.,* (2002), while working on the quality and maturation of vermicompost affecting germination and growth of selected plants, noted that seed germination was inhibited by pure vermicompost. However, 10% vermicompost with soil enhanced germination of radish and marigold; while vermicompost water extract provided the best germination medium. Arancon *et al.,* (2003) have also reported about the effect of vermicomposts produced

Table 2: Showing impact of different vermicomposts on the shoot length of *Phaseolus aureus*

Vermicompost transformed from	Conc. of media	Average shoot length (in cm) in mixture medium (2:1:3 sand:vc:soil)			Average shoot length (in cm) mixture medium (1:1:1 sand:vc:soil)		
		After 7 days	After 14 days	After 21 days	After 7 days	After 14 days	After 21 days
Biocon waste	BW+CD (1:3)	13.83±0.66	16.17±0.68	17.50±0.72	11.97±0.22	14.73±0.73	16.17±0.64
	BW+CD (1:1)	14.10±0.57	19.17±0.52	19.73±0.32	11.60±0.09	15.17±0.40	16.33±0.62
	BW+CD (3:1)	13.43±0.58	17.20±0.48	17.76±0.46	13.43±0.68	16.03±0.03	18.33±0.29
Dairy waste	DW+CP (3L+2.5 kg)	17.16 ± 0.88	19.33±0.79	20.16±0.76	15.76±0.84	18.23±0. 84	18.76±0.63
	DW+CP + Water (1.5 L + 2.5kg + 1.50 L)	17.13±0.97	19.06 ±0.86	19.40±0.88	14.76±0.42	17.53±0.78	18.40±0.22
	DW + CP + Water (0.75 L + 2.5 kg + 2.25 L)	18.93 ±0.80	21.10±0.66	22.06±0.75	16.10±0.86	18.37±0.62	19.30±0.89
Pharmaceutical waste	Biol. w + CD (1:1)	14.0±0.09	16.00±0.62	15.50±0.28	10.00±0.64	11.60±0.60	13.50±0.78
	Chem. w + CD (1:1)	13.8±0.05	16.60±0.12	16.00±0.12	14.30±0.88	16.30±0.26	16.80±0.56
	Mixed + CD (1:1)	12.8 ±0.27	16.60±0.18	17.50±0.24	12.50±0.45	14.80±0.64	17.70±0.29
N.V.C	CD + Plant Biom.	15.2 ±0.22	16.80±0.54	18.13±0.42	13.40±0.08	16.13±0.27	17.30±0.62
F.Y.M	FYM (100%)	12.9±0.37	15.76±0.62	17.63±0.86	11.0±0.46	14.96±0.70	16.83±0.68

*BW = Bicon Waste, CD = Cattle Dung, DW = Dairy Waste, CP = Coir Pith, Biol. w = Biological Waste, Chem. w = Chemical Waste, Pl. Biom = Plant Biomass, N.V.C. = Normal Vermicompost, F.Y.M. = Farm Yard Manure.

commercially from cattle manure, market food waste and recycled paper waste. They have mentioned that marketable tomato yields in all vermicompost-treated plots were consistently greater than yields from the inorganic fertilizer-treated plots. There were significant increase in shoot weights, leaf areas and total and marketable fruit yields of pepper plants from plots treated with vermicomposts compared to those that received inorganic fertilizers only.

The results of above workers are parallel to the present findings, reflecting the idea about the organic wastes, produced in huge amounts from various resources, which may be processed into vermicompost by using suitable species of earthworms and used as organic manures in the crops.

Eudrilus eugeniae can be adapted to feed on different types of agricultural and agro-industrial waste materials. This will certainly help to bring down the pollution levels. But how much of these materials can be used along with cattle dung or other biomass finally depends on bio assays conducted by using these vermicomposts to test their stimulatory or inhibitory effects on the plants. The present study is an indication to highlight the possibilities of some of these materials when used in large quantities for production of vermicompost.

Conclusion

Vermicompost transformed from different organic wastes showed better response on the germination of seeds than that of normal vermicompost and NVC was better than FYM; while 2:1:3 (sand:vc:soil) mixture medium was the most suitable medium for the shoot length of experimental plants than that of 1:1:1 medium. Vermicompostinfluenced the shoot length of the plants, which suggest the linkage between biolgoical effects of it and microbial metabolites that influence the plant growth and development (Tomati *et al.* 1987). However, the quality of vermicompost and its effect on plant growth may depend upon a variety of factors, which needs further investigations.

References

Ang Lopez, M.J., Warman, P., Hoyle, J. and Asiedu, S.K. 2002. Quality and maturation of vermicompost affecting germination and growth of selected plants. In the proceedings of ISEE VII at Cardiff University, Wales (U.K.) from September 1-6. p. 257-58.

Aranon, N.Q., Edwards, C.A., Bierman, P., Metzger, J., Lee, S. and Welch. 2003. Effect of vermicomposts on growth and marketable fruits of field-grown tomatoes, peppers and strawberries, Pedobiolgoia 47. p. 731-35.

Edwards, C.A. 1988. Breakdown of animal, vegetable and industrial organic wastes by earthworms: Agriculture, Ecosystems and Environment, 24:21-23.

Edwards, C.A., and Bohlen, P.J. 1996. Biology of Earthworms. Chapman and Hall, London p. 426.

Graff, O. 1974. Gewinnung von Biomasse ans Abfallsto feen durch Kultur des Kompostreqenwurms *E. fetida*, Landbanforsch volkenrode. 2: 137-42.

Kaplan, D.L., Hartenstein, R., Neuhauser, E.F., and Malecki, M.R. 1980. Physicochemical requirements in the environment of earthworm, *Eisenia fetida*, Soil Biol. Biochem., 12: 347-52.

Tomati, U., Grapelli, A. and Galli, E. 1987. The hormone-like effect of earthworm casts on plant growth. Biol. Fert. Soil. 5: 288-294.

Vail, V.A. 1974. Contributions on North American earthworms. I. Natural history and reproduction in *Diplocardia mississippiensis*. Bull. Tall Timbers, Res. Stn. 16: 1-8.

Chapter **13**

Vermicompost–An Organic Supplement for Improving Soil Fertility and Productivity

Manjushri Tadvalkar

Institute of Natural Organic Agriculture, 11-b, Kulkarni Bungalow, Shikshak Nagar, Paud Road, Kothrud, Pune-411 038.

Real soil

Real soil consists of more than mineral particles. It is a furiously busy community of living things in stupendous variety. They range from viruses to slime molds, bacteria algae, protozoa, worms, rotifers, nematodes and multi-cellular fungi on up to earthworms.

These organisms require moisture, fuel and food. Organic matter and their use of it supply these needs. Their excretions, secretions, their growth and physiological activity, their bodies and breakdown products of the organic matter all add valuable traits to the soil making it crumbly, well drained, dark and spongy.

Today, the organic matter in our soils is half mineral and the other half is mostly air and water, with only 1% or so of it as organic matter. In the last hundreds of years, the 10% or more of humus has been depleted by bad treatment, it took thousands of years to make it, but only a comparatively short time to destroy it.

Soil Organic Matter (SOM) is the link for sustained bio-physical-chemical fertilizers of soil.

Importance of earthworms in agro-ecology

Earthworms in Agriculture

The value of earthworms in agriculture lies in their ability to change the physical, chemical and biological properties of the soils. Their importance in agriculture is studied from two aspects:

I) Influence of earthworms on soil organic matter dynamics, nutrient dynamics and microbiological ecology.

- Earthworms are known to select the organic and mineral components that they ingest. As a result their casts often have much higher contents of SOM and nutrients than the surrounding soil. This is due to preferential ingestion of plant residues and clay materials (Table - 1).

Table 1. Mineral elements in soil and worm casts (Edwards & Bohlen, 1996)

Mineral elements	Casts	Soil
C	8550	3925
N	536	350
C:N ratio	16	11
P (aqua regia)	102	68
P (lactate-soluble)	13.7	2.2
K (lactate-soluble)	44.6	7.0
pH (H_2O)	5.8	5.0
pH (KCl)	5.4	4.0

1. Influence on Organic Carbon

- Endogeic earthworms may deposit 20 to 200 tons surface casts per hectare that contains a significant amount of organic matter, these casts influence organic matter and nutrient cycles on four scales-

(a) Transformation of organic matter through the earthworm gut

(b) In freshly deposited casts

(c) In aging casts

(d) In interaction with constituents of soil profile.

The types and amounts of carbon in earthworm casts differ from those of the surrounding soil. There is an increase in the polysaccharides content, which promotes this stabilization of soil carbon through binding with clays.

The body secretions i.e., mucus is mainly responsible for addition of organic carbon to the soil.

2. Influence on Nitrogen

Significant amount of nitrogen can pass directly through the earthworm biomass in soil ecosystems. This is in the form of dead tissues of earthworms, urine and mucus deposited by these earthworms. Earthworms consume large amounts of plant organic matter that contains considerable quantities of nitrogen which is recycled back to the soil system.

The concentrations of inorganic nitrogen in fresh cast and around the lining of burrows are usually much greater than in bulk soil, with ammonium usually being the dominant form of inorganic nitrogen in the cast. This increase in inorganic nitrogen in casts is due to excretory products and mucus from the earthworm and through increased rates of mineralization of organic nitrogen by microorganisms in the cast.

Nitrogen fixation is mediated by microorganisms when passing through earthworm gut, the activity of nitrogen fixing enzyme, nitrogenase, increases 10 fold in earthworm cast than in the un-ingested soil. (Edwards & Bohlen, 1996)

3. Influence on C:N ratio

Earthworms are known to decrease the C:N ratio in soil because they increase combustion of carbon by enhancing total soil respiration. They also influence the C:N ratio of soil organic matter by feeding selectively on organic matter with a high nitrogen content.

4. Influence of Phosphorus

It is evident that the available phosphorus is more in casts than the surrounding soils. This is attributed to enhanced phosphatase activity in the casts. This increased enzyme activity may also be due to microbial associations.

5. Influence on other Micro and Macro nutrients

The concentrations of exchangeable Ca, Mg, K, are usually greater in earthworm casts than in un-ingested soil. The increase in available cations in earthworm casts are related to the greater amounts of plant tissues in earthworm cast than in soils. In case of Ca, the earthworms are known to possess calciferous glands that are involved in the production of calcium carbonate which is also egested in casts thereby increasing the availability of Ca for the uptake by roots (Table-2).

Table 2. Available minerals in earthworm casts and soil (Edwards & Bohlen, 1996)

Mineral level	Earthworms Excreta	Depth of soil layer	
		(0.15 cm)	(20-40 cm)
Loss by ignition (%)	13.1	9.8	4.9
Carbon/nitrogen ratio	14.7	13.8	13.8
Nitrate nitrogen (ppm)	21.9	4.7	1.7
Calcium: Total (%)	1.19	0.88	0.91
Exchangeable (ppm)	2793	1993	481
Exchangeable Ca/Total Ca (%)	25.6	24.4	6.1
Magnesium: Total (%)	0.545	0.511	0.548
Exchangeable (ppm)	492	162	69
Exchangeable Magnesium/total Magnesium	9.19	3.24	1.29
Phosphorus available (ppm)	150	20.8	8.3
Potassium available (ppm)	358	32.0	27.0
pH	7.00	6.36	6.05

6. Effect of earthworms on the number, biomass and activity of microorganisms

The microorganisms occurring in the gut of earthworms are usually the same as in the milieu exterior where the worms live. The increase in number of microorganisms in the gut is partially due to large amount of water and mucus that earthworms secrete into the gut. Their intestinal mucus contains large amount of water-soluble organic compounds, which are easily assimilated by microbes, and thus their community enhances in the gut. Research states that particular groupsof microorganisms are stimulatedselectively during passage through earthworm gut, these include actinomcycetes and bacteria. Although many microorganismscan survive passage through the earthworm gut not all emerge in a viable form. This is probably due to selective digestion of those microbes. Antibiotic substances produced by actinomycetes in the intestine of earthworms can inhibit the growth of fungi and gram-positive bacteria.

7. Earthworm casts, burrows and microorganisms

Chemical transport through the burrows is significant. Burrow lining is rich in organic matter, microorganisms and available plant nutrients providing a channel ideal for root growth.

Mucus secreted through the earthworm cuticle is often noted on burrow walls, neutralizes the pH of drilosphere by raising or lowering pH when the surrounding conditions are too acidic or alkaline. The burrows is the main channel for disposal of microorganisms. Earthworms have significant influence on the dispersal of vesicular-arbuscular mycorrhizae (VAM) fungi which form an important mutual association with plant roots. This was especially observed in the grape cultivations in Nashik area where vermicompost was used in root zones, which were mulched and provided with drip irrigation.

8. Influence of earthworms on soil structure

I) The activities of earthworms influence soil structure by-

a) Ingestion of soil, partial breakdown of organic matter, intimate mixing of organic matter, humus, intimate mixing of these fractions and egestion of materials as surface or sub-surface casts.

b) Burrowing through the soil and bringing sub-soil to the surface.

c) Formation of soil aggregates.

d) Aeration, porosity and infiltration improvement.

II) Earthworm, vermicompost and its use for improving soil fertility and productivity-

a) In Indian conditions high temperature and moisture condition limits us from using or increasing earthworm populations directly in soil cultures. This is mainly because 70% of our agricultural area is rain fed and high temperature makes it difficult to retain organic matter level in the soil.

b) To circumvent the above situation, the epigeic varieties of earthworms are applied for production of vermicompost as they are secondary decomposers and have an extensive role in the break down of organic matter and release of nutrients.

Vermicomposting

The application of earthworms for conversion of organic refuse into compost is called vermicomposting. This organic refuse can include bio solids, manures of pigs, cattle, goats, horses, horticultural residues and biodegradable wastes generated in urban areas. The process requires conditions for acclimatizing worms in composting windrows where worms feed on biosolids and egest castings (Table-3). The process is maintained in such a way that worm population is very high so that the converted compost has high proportion of castings than other aerobically digested organic matter. The physico-chemical and biological parameters of vermicompost have been presented in Table-4, 5 and 6, respectively.

Table 3. Optimal conditions for vermicompost production

Condition	Requirements
Temperature	15-20°C (limits 4-30°C)
Moisture content	80-90% (limits 60-90%)
Oxygen requirements	Aerobicity (maintained by low windrow profile)
Ammonia content of waste	Low: < 0.5 mg/g
Salt content of waste	Low: < 0.5%
pH	> 5 and < 9

Table 4. Physical composition of vermicompost: Vermicompost analyzed, produced from different organic wastes as raw material, with 25% dung as a necessary ingredient, Source: INORA, Pune

1.	Bulk Density	0.5 to 0.6 g/cc
2.	Water-holding capacity	150 to 200%
3.	Pore space	40 to 60%
4.	Moisture	20 to 25%
5.	Colour	Black/Brown
6.	Texture	Non sticky granular

Table 5. **Chemical composition of vermicompost :** Vermicompost analyzed, produced from different organic wastes as raw material, with 25% dung as a necessary ingredient. Source: NORA, Pune

1.	Organic Carbon	8.00 to 22%
2.	Total Nitrogen	0.5% to 1.5%
3.	Available Phosphorus	0.3% to 0.5%
4.	Available Potassium	0.25% to 0.6%
5.	Available Sodium	500 to 600 ppm
6.	Calcium and Magnesium	20 to 75 Meq/100 g
7.	Copper	2.0 to 23.0 ppm
8.	Iron	2.0 to 10.0 ppm
9.	Zinc	5.0 to 15.0 ppm
10.	Available Sulphur	100 to 66 ppm

Table 6. **Biological composition of vermicompost:** Vermicompost analyzed, produced from different organic wastes as Raw Material, with 25%, dung as a necessary ingredient, Source: Inora, Pune

1.	Total Bacterial Count	2×10^6 /g
2.	Total Nitrogen Fixing bacteria	3×10^4/g
3.	Phosphorus solubilising bacteria	5×10^4/g
4.	Live earthworms and cocoons	Present

Vermicompost as organic supplement for soil fertility

1. Vermicompost is formed from dead tissues of plants and animals and thus is natural source of macro and micronutrients in limited quantities.
2. The organic carbon of vermicompost helps in replenishing the carbon pools of impoverished soils.
3. Vermicompost organic carbon is highly oxidisable and helps in slow release of nutrients from the manure thus curbing the leaching losses.
4. The beneficial microbes present in vermicompost and soil increase their activity due to presence of readily assimilable organic compounds.
5. The stable organic component of vermicompost i.e, humus, is in good percentage which acts as a natural chelator in the soils.
6. The secretions of worms mixed in vermicompost and the

associated microbes act as growth promoters along with other nutrients.

7. Vermicastings, the major component of vermicompost have immobilized enzymes like protease, lipase, cellulase, lichenase, and chitinase which keep on their function of biodegradation of polymers of agricultural residues so that further attack is speeded up.
8. Vermicompost is rich in vitamins, antibiotics and growth hormones.
9. Vermicompost has immobilized micro flora which functions in the soil to produce useful products.
10. Vermicompost has live stages of cocoons or young ones and these can be used as further population growing media. For this effect, vermicompost once applied to soil must be covered with a layer of mulch and provided with proper moisture requirements.
11. Vermicompost encourages while root, mycorrhizae associations in the rhizosphere.
12. Vermicompost is a fine granular organic matter which when added to the clay soil looses the soil and provides aeration.
13. Mucus associated with the vermi-cast is hygroscopic which absorb water and improves water-holding capacity as well as soil infiltration rate.
14. Vermicompost added in root zones has shown encouraging results in increasing the local earthworm activity. For this, covering the soil with mulch and retaining appropriate moisture levels is important. The probable recommended doses of vermicompost for some of the tested crops have been shown in Table-7.

Table 7. Probable recommendation of vermicompost (VC) for some experimentally-tested crops for optimum yield.

Crop	**Vermicompost with chemicals/acre**	**Vermicompost without chemicals/acre**	**Green manure [GM] /FYM and Vermicompost combination**
Tomato [Vaishali]	0.5 tons and 50% recommended dose (15:15:15: per plant)	5 tons	GM FYM 3 tons, VC 2 tons
Chilli (var. Pusa jwala)	0.5 tons/acre & 50% recommended dose (17:17:17)	5 tons	GM FYM 3 tons VC 2 tons

Crop	Vermicompost with chemicals/acre	Vermicompost without chemicals/acre	Green manure [GM] /FYM and Vermicompost combination
Brinjal (var Manjri gota)	0.5 tons & 50% recommended dose [25 kg N, 20 kg P, 10 kg K]	5 tons	GM FYM 3 tons VC 2 tons
Radish	1.0 tons & 50% recommended dose [15 kg N, 7.5 kg each of P & K.]	8 tons	GM FYM 3 tons VC 2 tons
Carrot	1.0 tons & 50% recommended dose [7.5 kg N, 6.25 kg P & 5 kg K]	8 tons	GM FYM 3 tons VC 3 tons
Bhendi [Phule kirti]	1.0 tons & 50% recommended dose [10 kg N, 4 kg P, & 5 kg K]	5 tons	GM FYM 3 tons VC 2 tons
Sugarcane	2.0 tons and 50% of recommended dose	5 tons + Incorporation of Sugarcane trash and mixed green biomass.	GM FYM 3 tons VC 2 tons
Fruiting orchards: Mango, Chikoo, Coconut, Cashew, Orange, Lime, Pomegranate.	25 kg per plant and 50% of recommended dose.	100 kg per plant mulching green manure	-
Floriculture	Roses-15 kg per plant + recommended fertigation	-	-
	Gladiola-500 g per bulb + recommended dose of chemical fertilizers	-	-
	Carnation-500 g per plant + recommended dose of Chemical fertilizers.	-	-

Crop	Vermicompost with chemicals/acre	Vermicompost without chemicals/acre	Green manure [GM] /FYM and Vermicompost combination
	Gerbera-500 g per plant + Spray of liquid Vermicompost	-	
	Anthuriums - Spray of liquid Vermicompost	-	
	Orchids-Spray of liquid Vermicompost and 20 kg per vine + recommended dose of chemical fertilizers	-	-
Cotton	1 ton Vermicompost + 300 kg per acre oil cake 50% recommended dose of chemical fertilizers	8 tons	-
Nursery	Vermicompost and sand vermicompost and coco-peat 1:3 or 1:4 portions		
Banana	2.5 tons Vermicompost + 50% recommended dose of chemical fertilizers	5 tons + 300 kg + neem cake	
Ginger	5 tons of Vermicompost + 50% recommended dose of chemical fertilizers	8 tons + 500 kg neem cake	
Tumeric	5 tons Vermicompost + 50% recommended dose of chemical fertilizers	8 tons + 500 kg neem cake	
Paddy	1 ton + 50 % recommended dose of chemical fertilizers	3 tons + 200 kg bone meal	
Wheat	1.5 tons + 50% recommended dose of chemical fertilizers	3 tons + 200 kg bone meal	

Source: Field trials conducted by INORA on farmers' land.

Economic feasibility of use of Vermicompost

Vermicompost if produced on the farm by the farmer himself proves to be ecomomically a viable solution than depending on purchased compost. Production cost of vermicompost on farm including raw material and labor costs is below Rs. 1000.00; while commercial vermicompost is available between Rs. 3000 to 6000 per ton.

Starting a vermicompost facility is a low cost venture, wherein major cost is involved in erection of shed and initial purchase of vermiculture.

Conclusion

For overall development of soil amelioration and sustaining fertility, vermicompost acts as a major link. It enriches the top soil as an organic component and promotes local soil dwelling earthworm fauna which has beneficial effects on pedogenesis, and therefore, it may be said that earthworm are bio-indicators of the relative health of soil ecosystems.

Reference

Edwards, C.A. & Bohlen, P.J. 1996 : Biology and ecology of earthworms, Chapman and Hall, London. 3rd edi, p. 426.

Chapter **14**

Vermicomposting for Soil Fertility Improvement and Solid Waste Management in Plantations

George V. Thomas, Murali Gopal & Alka Gupta

Division of Crop Production, Central Plantation Crops Research Institute, Kasaragod-671 124, Kerala

Sustainable agriculture (including forestry) involves the successful management of agricultural resources to satisfy human needs, while maintaining or enhancing environmental quality and conserving natural resources for future generations. Improvement in agricultural sustainability requires, alongside effective water and crop management, the optimal use and management of soil fertility and soil physical properties. Both rely on soil biological processes and soil biodiversity. This calls for the widespread adoption of management practices that enhance soil biological activity and thereby build up long-term soil productivity and health.

The goal of efficient agriculture is, therefore, to develop agro-ecosystems with minimal dependence on agrochemicals and energy inputs in which agroecological interactions and synergy among biological components provide the mechanisms for the system to sponsor their own soil fertility and crop production functions. The array of organisms in the soil also partially determines soil resilience, the desirable ability of a given soil to recover its functions after a disturbance such as fire, compaction and tillage.

I. Soil biodiversity and sustainable agriculture

Soil is a dynamic, living matrix that is an essential part of the terrestrial ecosystems. Soil contains enormous number of diverse living organisms assembled in complex and varied communities. Soil biodiversity includes invisible microorganisms like bacteria, fungi and actinomycetes to the more familiar macro-fauna such as earthworms and termites. Plant roots can also be considered as soil organisms in view of their symbiotic relationships and interactions with soil components. Each of these organisms has a specific role in the complex web of life under the soil.

- The activities of certain organisms affect soil structure–especially the so-called "soil engineers," such as earthworms and termites-through mixing soil horizons, organic matter and augmenting porosity. This directly determines vulnerability to soil erosion and availability of soil profit to plants;
- The functions of soil biota are central to decomposition processes and nutrient cycling. They, therefore, affect plant growth and productivity as well as release of pollutants in the environment, leaching of nitrates in water resources, methane emission;
- Certain soil organisms can be detrimental to plant growth, for example, nematodes under certain cropping practices. However, they can also protect crops from pest and disease outbreaks through biological control and reduced susceptibility.
- The activities of certain organisms determine the carbon cycle, the rates of carbon sequestration and gaseous emissions and soil organic matter transformation;
- Plant roots, through their interactions with other soil components and symbiotic relationships, especially *Rhizobium* bacteria, P-solubilizers, PGPRs and mycorrhizae, play a key role in the uptake of nutrients and water and contribute to the maintenance of soil porosity and organic matter content through their growth and biomass.
- Soil organisms can also be used to reduce or eliminate environmental hazards resulting from accumulations of toxic chemicals or other hazardous water.

II. Role of earthworms in improving soil fertility

Earthworms are so called because they are almost always terrestrial and burrow into moist-rich soil, emerging at night to forage. Charles Darwin (1981) had written that earthworms are great benefactors of soil and agriculture and the earthworm casts are good fertilizer. These worms continuously till and aerate the soil, supply it with organic matter, and help moisture reaching it via the burrows they make. The earthworm activity in soil is known to reduce plant pathogens (Szczeck, 1999) and releases enzymes and hormones in their excreta which are beneficial for plant growth (Tomati *et al.*, 1987,

Spain *et al.*, 1992, Chaoui *et al.*, 2003). Thus earthworms that constitute highest biomass among tropical macrofauna and have been indicated as potential indicators of sustainability of agroecosystems (Christenson, 1991) play a vital role in restoring the degraded soil fertility (Joshi and Kelker, 1951; Lavelle, 1988).

III. Distribution and classification of earthworms

There are more than, 1800 known species of earthworms (Minnich, 1977) which are found in most parts of the world with exception of deserts, areas under snow and ice mountain ranges, areas bereft of soil and vegetation. Species of earthworms which are widely distributed are described as peregrine earthworms,and species which occur in specific areas have been termed endemic (Michaelson, 1910).

a) Classification based on habitat

Earthworms have been classified into 3 broad categories based on the ecological habitat (Bouche, 1977), These forms are (i) *epigeics*, (ii) *anecics* and (iii) *endogeics*. The different characteristics used for distinguishing the 3 ecological types are given below in Table-1

Table 1. Characteristics used for distinguishing different ecological types of earthworms (Bouche, 1977)

Character	Ecological type		
	Epigeics	Anecics	Endogeics
Body	small	moderate	large
Burrowing	reduced	strongly developed	developed
Longitudinal contraction	absent	present	least developed
Hooked chetae	absent	present	absent
Sensitivity to light	feeble	moderate	strong
Mobility	rapid	moderate	feeble
Skin moistening	developed	developed	feeble
Pigmentation	homochronic	dorsal and anterior	absent
Fecundity	high	moderate	limited
Maturation	rapid	moderate	slow
Respiration	high	moderate	feeble
Survival in adverse condition	as cocoons	true diapause	by quiescence

(i) *Epigeics*: Epigeic earthworms live above the mineral soil surface (Lee, 1985). They are phytophagous and generally have no effect on the soil structure, as they cannot dig into the soil. They are small in size with uniform coloration.

(ii) *Anecics*: These worms live in burrows in mineral soil layer, but come to surface to feed on dead debris/litters, which they drag into their burrows. They are geophytophagous as they ingest both soil as well as plant litter. Presence of vertical tunnel in soil indicates the activity of anecic earthworms.

(iii) *Endogeics*: These species inhabit the mineral soil zones feeding on soil which is enriched with organic matter (Lee, 1985), They are geophagous and construct horizontal branching burrows in soil. They are not pigmented.

The endogeics were further categorised into mesohumic endogeics, polyhumic endogeics and oligohumic endogeics based on their preference of soil with organic matter content (Lavelle, 1981). However, such demarcation could not be made with respect to earthworms in Indian tropics where majority of the worms are endogeic and only few are epigeics or anecics (Kale and Krishnamoorthy, 1978).

b) Classification based on diet

Earthworms are generally known to consume food every day equivalent to their body weight (Minnich, 1977). The bulk of their diet consists of decaying organic waste of almost any origin. Living organisms like fungi and bacteria are also ingested (along with decaying organic matter) and this forms an important part of their diet (Lee, 1985). Lee (1985) described earthworms, which feed on plant debris that is only slightly decomposed as *humus formers* and those which feed on plant debris that is already much decomposed as humus feeders. Besides these, Lee also classified worms that feed on a high proportion of raw humus as *detrivorous* and those that feed on amorphous humus and mineral material as *geophagous*.

IV. Environmental requirements for earthworms

Earthworms like all life forms require particular environmental parameters within which they flourish. Most important among these are soil moisture, pH and temperature. Food requirements, limiting light and soil composition are also important.

Soil moisture: Earthworms have very few mechanisms to preserve their body moisture. Their moist body surface requires moist environment without which they perish in short time. Optimum cocoon production occurs between 28 and 42 per cent soil moisture (Evans and Guild, 1982) and population densities are usually the highest between 12 and 30 per cent soil moisture (Minnich, 1977). In practice this means keeping the earthworm medium moist but not wet. These are the reasons why earthworms do not thrive well in dry soils or during drought season and heavy flooding. Moisture also governs the growth, maturation and cocoon production of worms (Veljoen and Reinecke, 1989).

Soil pH: Earthworms are very sensitive to pH. They prefer a soil with a neutral pH, or slightly alkaline (Lee, 1985). Acidic soils do not harbour earthworms in large numbers.

Temperature: It has been reported that the structure of earthworm community is mainly determined by temperature (Lavelle, 1983) and tropical countries harbour more species. In temperate countries, the most favourable temperature for most of the earthworms is between 13 to 18°C (Minnich, 1977). However, in tropical country like India, the earthworms particularly *Eudrillus euginiae*, have been reported to perform well between 25.9 and 27.7°C (Amoji et al., 1999). However, there is very less information available on the life cycle of the earthworm under tropical and subtropical climatic conditions (Kale *et al.*, 1982).

Light: Light can injure or kill earthworms, especially ultra-violet light. The only concern this will pose is keeping the earthworm 'farm' away from intense crop light.

Earthworm population: Earthworms are capable of growing at very high population densities. The best natural ecosystem (Nile Valley) has roughly a million earthworms per area which works to 5000/m^2 (Hopp and Slater, 1948). Commercial growers can support densities of 100,000 earthworms/m^3 (Minnich, 1977).

V. Earthworm activity: Earthworms perform three main activities viz. burrowing, feeding and casting which are responsible for improving the soil health and fertility.

i) **Burrowing**: Earthworms create horizontal and vertical tunnels in soil as they move. Burrows range from 3-12 mm in diameter. These are cemented internally by secretion of worms cutaneous glands. Soil porosity, aeration and friability are significantly improved due to burrowing activity.

ii) **Feeding**: Earthworms mainly feed on the decaying organic matter found in the soil. The food is moistened by alkaline enzymatic secretion, which digests starch, making it easier to shred.

iii) **Castings**: The organic matter consumed by the earthworms is degraded by microorganisms and enzymes present inside the gut of the worm. After getting digested in the gut, the food emerges as a compact concentrated mass termed as 'casting' or 'vermicast'. These casts are rich in microorganisms, inorganic minerals and organic matter in a form available to plants. These are also rich in enzymes such as protease, amylase, lipase, cellulase and chitinase, which continue to disintegrate organic matter even after they have been excreted. Table-2 gives the details of earthworm casts and soil from a cultivated field.

Table 2. Properties of earthworm casts and soil from a cultivated field (Lunt and Jacobson, 1944)

Compound	Casts	Cultivated soil	
		0-6'	8-16' depth
Total N	0.035	0.24	0.08
Organic carbon (%)	5.17	3.35	1.11
C:N ratio	14:7	13:8	13:8
NO_3 Nitrogen (ppm)	21.9	4.7	1.7
Available P (ppm)	150.0	20.8	8.3
Exchangeable calcium (ppm)	2,793.0	1993.0	418.0
Exchangeable magnesium (ppm)	492.0	162.0	69.0
Exchangeable potassium (ppm)	358.0	32.0	27.0
Total calcium (%)	1.19	0.88	0.91
Total magnesium (%)	0.54	0.511	0.54
Percent saturation	92.9	71.1	55.5
pH	7.0	6.36	6.05
Moisture equivalent	31.4	27.4	21.1

VI. Vermicomposting for solid agricultural waste management

Vermicomposting (Vermes, a Latin word = worm) is a kindered process to composting, featuring the addition of certain species of earthworms used to enhance the process of waste conversion and produce a quality end product. It differs from composting in several ways. Chiefly, vermicomposting is a mesophilic process, utilizing micro-organisms and earthworms that are active in temperature range of 50-90° F (not the ambient temperature but temperature within the pile of moist organic material). Common composting on other hand is produced entirely by the activity of micro-organisms on organic matter. Vermicomposting process is considered faster than composting as the material passes through the earthworm's gut where transformation takes place, whereby the resulting earthworm castings (vermicast, worm manure), abundant in microbial activity and plant growth regulators and fortified with pathogen suppressing attributes. In recent years, earthworms have been increasingly employed in vermicomposting of agricultural wastes (Edward *et al.*, 1985; Amoji et al., 1998). A wide variety of agricultural wastes beginning with straw (Curry and Byrne, 1992), vegetable wastes, fruit rinds, leaf-litter, grass clippings, weeds (Rao, 2005) and neem leaves (Gajalakshmi and Abbesi, 2004) have been successfully converted to vermicompost by earthworms which are being used for improving soil fertility and increasing plant productivity in an ecologically safe and sustainable way.

VII. Systems of vermicomposting

Vermicomposting can be carried out in indoor systems and outdoor systems based on the availability of facilities.

1. Indoor systems

This method is used for commercial exploitation of earthworms for vermicompost production. Vermicomposting can be carried out inside permanent or temporary structures such as sheds. The indoor systems have the advantages in providing the optimal conditions for vermicomposting and proper protection for the worms from predators like rodents, wild boars and birds. Small scale vermicomposting at individual house level can also be carried out in plastic buckets, wooden boxes or cement tubs. Medium to large scale composting can be done in cement rings or tanks built of bricks or cement. Large scale vermicomposting is carried out by heaping the soil wastes in the shape of a cone under roof. This has been found to favour fast composting by ensuring proper aeration, allowing the worms to feed from all sides.

2. Outdoor systems

In this, composting is done at the source of organic wastes such as orchards and plantations with grown up trees and proper shade.

These systems have the advantages that the wastes as well as compost require very little transport, thus saving a lot of labour. The free space available in the garden may also be utilized for composting by heaping method. Vermicomposting in irrigated gardens and indoor composting systems have been exploited to achieve three benefits.

1. Management of organic wastes and abatement of pollution by rapid reduction in bulk density and elimination of foul odour.
2. Production of vermicompost containing easily available nutrients and plant growth promoting microbes and biochemicals.
3. Production of vermiprotein as feed for poultry and fishes.

VIII. Plantation waste management by vermicomposting

Plantation crops are high value commercial crops which are valued for their contribution to the national exchequer by way of export earnings. It covers a variety of crops like coconut, arecanut, cocoa, cashew, oil palm, spices, besides well known conventional crops like coffee, tea and rubber. These crops are cultivated in diverse farming systems and are known for their high socio-economic relevance. The major area under these crops belong to small holder sector with notable exception of tea. Plantation crops, being perennial in nature, provide vegetative cover and prevent soil erosion and foster the ecological balance. Apart from the economic product, the plantation crops produce large quantities of lignocellulosic biomass, which are often wasted in plantations without proper use. Considerable success has been achieved in bioconversion of the lignocellulosic biomass from the plantation crops to acceptable organic manure using different species of epigeic earthworms. Successful technologies have been developed to vermicompost wastes from plantations such as coconut leaves (Prabhu *et al.*, 1998), coconut coir waste (Ramesh and Gunathilegeraj, 1996), arecanut and cocoa wastes (Chowdappa *et al*, 1999) and coffee pulp (Orozco *et al.*, 1996). The vermicomposting technology and characteristics of vermicompost obtained from waste biomass of plantation crops such as coconut, arecanut, cocoa and coffee are described below:

VIII. 1. Vermicomposting of coconut palm wastes

The coconut palm is an important oil yielding plantation crop grown in an area of 18.92 lakh hectares in coastal regions of the country. It is a small holders plantation crop mostly grown in homestead gardens. Studies conducted at Central Plantation Crops

Research Institute, Kasaragod have revealed that one hectare of coconut plantation produces about 8000 kg dry organic biomass per year in the form of leaves. As the use of this biomass as fuel and thatching material has declined over the years, its disposal in a meaningful way has become a problem in many coconut gardens. If we can recycle all the organic wastes available from a plantation, it can supply the major portion of nitrogen and apart of other nutrients required by the palms. This waste is rich in ligno-cellulosic complexes and polyphenols which have the potential to produce humus, nitrification and urease inhibitors respectively. These biochemicals can influence soil health and long-term soil fertility. But, because of high proportion of lignin, these wastes undergo decomposition rather slowly. The possibility of using earthworms to enhance the decomposition rate was examined, as it is known that the action of earthworms is more important and pronounced on recalcitrant wastes than easily decomposable ones.

a) Earthworm species suitable for coconut palm wastes

Among the local earthworms tested for their ability to multiply and produce vermicompost from coconut palm wastes, a strain of *Eudrilus* was the best and hence more studies were conducted. *Eudrilus* sp. was located from a heap of coconut palm wastes, which were seen fully converted into vermicasts, leaving behind only mid-ribs of the leaves. Methods for maintenance and large-scale mutliplication have been standardized. It can be multiplied fast in 1-1 mixture of cow dung and decayed leaves mulched properly with grasses.

Studies conducted have revealed that this strain of *Eudrilus* is different from *Eudrilus eugeniae,* the African night crawler, which has its origin in tropical and subtropical Africa. The strain of *Eudrilus* located at Kasaragod differs from the African strain in its colour, vigour, behaviour, cocoon colour and reproductive rate on coconut wastes. It is also capable of active feeding on soil and digested soil in the form of pellets which are deposited around burrow holes.

(b) Vermicomposting technology for coconut leaves: A low cost technology has been standardized for vermicomposting, the biomass from coconut palms left exposed to the action of weather in the field for about 3 months. (Prabhu *et al.*, 1998). The weathered wastes obtained during rainy seasons is preferred. This waste can be used without chopping thus saving a lot of a labour. The coconut wastes used for oyster mushroom cultivation were also found suitable for vermicomposting. These organic wastes are treated with cow dung at the rate of 10% by weight, in the form of slurry to undergo a preliminary decomposition for about 2-3 weeks. The earthworms at the rate of 1000 worms per ton of coconut leaves are introduced. The compost bed should be mulched properly using any locally available plant material or gunny bags and has to be protected from direct sunlight. Watering is done periodically to maintain enough moisture. As full leaves are used for composting, compact mass is not formed thus allowing free movement of air of the bed. In about 60-75 days, compost will be ready, leaving behind only mid ribs of the leaves. This method was tested in cement tanks and under the root of a shed by heaping. Composting was after in heaps and earthworms were seen feeding and castings from all the sides, may be due to better aeration and exposure. On an average, 70% recovery of vermicompost was obtained. Similar technology for vermicomposting was also tested in large pits taken in the inter spaces of four coconut palms ine sandy loam and coastal sandy soils and was found to work well. As composting is done in the itself, lot of labour required for transportation of the biomass and compost can be saved. This technology can be tried even in plantations with very limited irrigation facilities, as only limited number of pits or trenches need to be watered. The coconut palm waste was also vermicomposted in the basins and inter spaces and these methods are suited for irrigated garden. If all the available biomass from a plantation is recycled through vermicomposting, itcan meet a part of nutrient requirements and especially in coastal regions it could improve soil organic matter content.

c) Characteristics of vermicompost from coconut leaves

The average nutrient composition of the vermicompost recovered was: N% (1.8), P% (0.216), K% (0.16), Organic carbon % (17.84), and C/N ratio (9.96). Total microbial counts and beneficial microbial population were also more in the compost compared to the base material. Two types of active nitrogen fixing bacteria not commonly isolated from soils have also been found regularly associated with vermicast.

d) Vermicomposting of coconut waste (coir pith)

Coir pith accumulates as a waste material near coir processing factories after extraction of coir fibre from coconut husk. Application of coir pith as manure in crop production has not been recommended due to its high C:N ratio and high lignin and polyphenol contents. Vermicomposting of coir pith using a local strain of *Eudrilus sp.* has been found to be effective for bioconversion of these waste materials to useful organic manure (Prabhu *et al.*, 2001; Thomas *et al.*, 2001). Pre treatment with lime and rock phosphate makes the coir pith amenable for earthworm activity. Layering with uncut coconut leaves was also found to be necessary to facilitate aeration. A granular vermicompost with 1.2% nitrogen and a C:N ratio of 16.7:1 could be obtained in two months. Other epigeic or compost worms such as *Perionyx excavatus* (Ramesh and Gunathilagaraj, 1996) and *Eudrilus eugeniae* (Patil *et al.*, 1999) have also been utilized for vermicomposting of coir pith.

VIII. 2. Vermicomposting of areca and cocoa wastes

Arecanut (*Areca catechu L*) is an important commercial plantation crop grown in humid tropics of India. Cocoa (*Theobroma cacao L.*), a shade-loving crop is an ideal mixed crop in arecanut garden (Bhat and Leela, 1968; Bhat, 1978). The area under arecanut cultivation in India is 2.54 lakh hectares (1995-96); while cocoa is cultivated in 14100 ha. Arecanut is generally grown in laterite soils with acidic nature and low nutrient retention capacity.

Successful conversion of available organic wastes of arecanut (*Areca catechu L.*) and cocoa (*Theobroma cacao L.*) gardens into quality vermicompost, using African night crawler (*Eudrilus eugeniae*) was reported by Chowdappa *et al.*, (1999). The level of various nutrients in dry leaves and corresponding vermicompostare presented in Table 3. The recovery of vermicompost was 74.65 to 87.75% in a composting period of 3 months. Earthworm biomass doubled irrespective of organic waste used in a period of two months. Macro nutrients (NPK) and micronutrients (Cu, Zn, Fe and Mn) were slightly higher in all the vermicompost samples than that of normal compost. Vermicompost had lower C: N ratio and pH than normal compost irrespective of the source of organic waste. The population of beneficial micro-organisms was considerably higher in vermicompost than in normal compost. Vermicompostwas found to be a profitable venture to enhance income from their holdings. Economics of vermicompost production revealed that the profit of Rs.1.51 to 1.69 could be realized from 1 kg of the compost. Estimated cost of commercial vermicompost production showed that a profit of Rs.11,114/- could be obtained from the vermicompost production from organic wastes available in 1 hectare of arecanut plantation.

Table 3. Nutrient composition in two organic wastes and vermicompost produced from them.

	Cocoa leaves		Areca leaves	
Nutrients	**Dried leaves**	**Vermicompost**	**Dried leaves**	**Vermicompost**
Organic carbon (%)	47.10	24.4	44.20	33.1
N %	1.27	1.65	0.71	1.38
P %	0.17	0.19	0.08	0.35
K %	0.27	0.32	0.94	0.98
C:N ratio	37.00	14.78	62.25	23.18
Cu (ppm)	32.66	83.60	100.59	120.18
Fe (ppm)	1157.41	2593.0	1745.61	2561.00
Zn (ppm)	228.39	367.7	307.08	395.68
Mn (ppm)	363.1	679.84	81.73	241.68
Moisture		29.94		31.82
pH		7.5		7.3

VIII. 3. Vermicomposting of coffee pulp.

Coffee pulp, comprising the outer hull of the fruit and some of the juices after extraction of the seed, is produced in large quantities as waste material. The transformation of these wastes into a useful organic fertilizer utilizing the earthworm. *Eisenia fetida* has been reported (Orozco *et al.,*1996). A study on the influence of bed depth and time indicated that the C and N contents of the compost were not affected by the depth of the bed whereas time affected both. An increase in the fractionation ratio and low values of humic-like substances were recorded during vermicomposting. The ingestion of the pulp by the earthworms resulted in an increase in available P, Ca and Mg but a decrease in K. The mean increase in available P in the vermicompost compared with the original pulp was about 54%.

IX. Conclusion

Vermicomposting has gained importance as an alternative method for a conversion of degradable organic wastes generated in agriculture and agro industries into manure by the activity of selected species of earthworms. The findings from a number of research institutions and many non-governmental organizations have promoted vermicompost production in rural areas in a manner that is suitable to the local conditions with respect to the availability of waste. Efficient technologies have also been developed for bioconversion of plantation wastes to acceptable organic manure with the utilization of particular species of earthworms suitable for the type of waste material. The vermicompost produced from different agrò wastes proved to be a promising soil amendment with respect to nutrient content, growth promoting properties and occurrence of beneficial microbial communities. There is enormous potential for the management of solid wastes generated from agriculture and agro-waste industries in an eco-friendly and cost effective way by vermicomposting.

References

Amoji, S D., Shagoti, U.M. and Biradar V.A. 1998. Selective preference for agri-culture organic wastes under multiple choices by epigeic earthworms. *J. Environ. Biol.* **19(4)**: 375-380.

Amoji, S.D., Shagoti, U.M., Biradar, V. A. and Biradar, P. M. 1999. Growth and reproduction of the epigeic earthworm, *Eudrilus eugeniae* as influenced by the seasonal factors in semi-arid climatic regions. *J. Soil Biol. Ecol.* **19:** 122-126.

Bouche, M. B. 1977. Strategies lombricicnnes in soil organisms as components of ecosystems. (eds.) U. Lohm and Persson). *Biol. Bull* (Stockholm) **25:** 122-132.

Bhat., K. S. 1978. Performance of cocoa as mixed crop with arecanut. *Proc. PLOCROSYM* (Plantation Crops Symposium) -I, Rubber Research Institute of India, Kottayam, p 377 -382.

Bhat, K.S. and Leela, M.1968. Cocoa and arecanut are good companions for more cash. *Indian Fmg.* **18(4)**: 19-20.

Chaoui, H.I., Ziblske, L.M. and Chino, T. 2003. Effect of earthworm casts and compost on soil microba1 activity and plant nutrient availability. *Soil Biol. Biochem.* **36:** 295-302.

Chowdappa,-R., Biddappa, C.C. and Sujatha, S. 1999. Effective recycling of organic wastes in arecanut (*Areca catechu L*) and cocoa (Theobromea cacao, L.) plantation through vermicomposting. *Indian J. Agric. Sci.* **69:** 563-566.

Christenson, O. 1991. Lumbricid earthworms as bio-indicators relative to soil factors in different organoecosystems. In: Advances in management and conservation of soil fauna (Veeresh, G. K., Rajagopal, D. and Vivaktameth, C.A. eds.) Oxford & IBH Pub. Co., New Delhi p. 839-840.

Curry J.P. and Byrne, D. 1992. The role of earthworms in straw decomposition and nitrogen turnover in arable land in Greenland Soil Biol. Biochem.,

24: 1409-1412.

Darwin, Charles, 1881. The formation of vegetable mould through the action of worms with observation on their habits. Murray, London, p 326.

Edwards, C.A., Burrows, I., Fletcher, K. E. and Jones, B.A. 1985. The use of earthworms for composting farm wastes. In: *Composting of agricultural and other wastes* (ed.) *JKR Grasser, Elesevier* Appl. Science, Oxford p. 229-241.

Evans, A.C. and Guild. W.J. 1982. Studies on the relationships between earthworms and soil fertility. IV. On the life cycle of some British Lumbricids *Ann. Appl. Biol.* **35(4)**: 471-484.

Gajalakshmi, S. and Abbesi, S.A. 2004. Neem leaves as a source of fertilizer-cum-pesticide vermicompost. *Bioresource Tech.* **92:** 291-296.

Hopp. H. and Slater, C. S. 1948. Influence of earthworms on soil productivity. Soil Science 66: 421-428.

Joshi, N.V. and Kelkar, B. 1951. The role of earthworms in soil fertility. *Indian J. Agric. Sci.* **22:** 189-196.

Kale, R. D. and Krishnamoorthy, R. V. 1978. Distribution and abundance of earthworms in Bangalore. *Proc. Indian Acad. Sci.* **878**: 23-25.

Kale, R. D., Bano, K. and Krishnamoorthy, R. V. 1982. Potential of. *Perionyx ecavatus* for utilizing organic wastes. *Pedobiologia* **23:** 419-425.

Lavelle, P. 1981. Strageties de reproduction chez less vers de terrc. *Acta Oewl* **2:** 117- 133.

Lavelle, P. 1983. The structure of earthworm communities. In: Earthworm ecology from Darwin to vermiculture (Satchell, J.E. ed.) Chapman and Hall, U.K. p. 449-465.

Lavelle, P .1988. Earthworm activities and soil system. *Biol. Fert. Soil.* **6:** 237 -251.

Lee, K.E. 1985. Earthworms: The ecology and relationships with soils and land use. Academic Press, New York p. 420.

Lunt, H.A. and Jacobson, G.M. 1944. The chemical composition of earthworm casts. *Soil Science*, **58:** 5.

Michaelson, W. 1910. Dic oligochatefayba der virderubduscgctkibuscgeb reguip. *Abh Natural Hab.* **19.**

Minnich, J. 1977. The earthworm book. Rodale Press, Emmaus, Philadelphia.

Orozco, F. H., Cagarra, J.,Trujillo, L.M. and .Roig. A. 1996. Vermicomposting of coffee pulp using the earthworm, *Eisenia fetida*. Effect on C and N contents and the availability of nutrients. *Biol. Fert. Soils* **22:** 162-166.

Patil, C. R., Radhakrishna D., Mailesh, B. C. and Kale, R.D. 1999. Use of mushroom spent material and earthworms to recycle coir waste. *Coir News* **28(4):** 27-32.

Prabhu, S. R., Subramanian, P., Biddappa, C .C. and Bopaiah, B. M. 1998. Prospects of improving coconut productivity through vermiculture Technology, *Indian Coconut J.* **29 (4):** 79-84.

Ramesh P. T. and Gunathilagaraj., K. 1996. Degradation of coir waste and tropioca peel by earthworms. *Madras Agric. J.* **83(1)** : 26-28

Rao, B.R.C. 2005. Vermicomposting, IEC Cell kudcemp, State Resource Centre, Mysore, p. 39

Spain, A., Lavelle, P and Mariotti, A., 1992. Stimulation of plant growth by tropical earthworms. *Soil Biol. Biochem.* **16(2):** 185-189.

Szczeck, M.M. 1999. Suppressiveness of vermicompost against Fusarium wilt of tomato. *J. Phytopathol.* (Ber.) **147:** 155-189.

Thomas G. V. Prabhu, S.R., Subramanian, P., and Iyer R. 2001. Organic farming technologies in coconut. ATIC series Publication No.4, CPCRI, Kasaragod.

Tomati, U. Grapelli, A., Galli, E. 1987. The hormone-like effect of earthworm casts on plant growth. *Biol. Soils* **5:** 288-294.

Viljoen, S.A. and Reinecke, A.J. 1989. Moisture and growth maturation and cocoon production of *Eudrilus engeniae* (Oligochaeta) *South African J. Zool.* **24:** 27 -32.

Index